Basics of Programming: A Comprehensive Guide for Beginners

Essential Coputer Skills, Volume 1

DG. Junior

Published by DG Junior, 2023.

BASICS OF PROGRAMMING: A COMPREHENSIVE GUIDE FOR BEGINNERS

First edition. August 8, 2023.

ISBN: 979-8223229988

Written by DG. Junior.

Table of Contents

Basics of Programming: A Comprehensive Guide for Beginners

PART I: INTRODUCTION TO PROGRAMMING

Chapter 1: Introduction to Programming Concepts

1.1 What is Programming?

Programming is the art and science of instructing computers to perform specific tasks. It is a process of creating sets of instructions, known as code, that tell a computer how to solve problems and accomplish various operations. By writing code in programming languages, programmers can develop software applications, design websites, analyze data, automate processes, and much more.

1.2 Evolution and History of Programming

Programming has come a long way since the early days of computing. Initially, programming involved writing machine code, which consisted of binary instructions that directly communicated with the computer's hardware. As technology advanced, higher-level programming languages were developed to simplify the coding process. These languages, such as Fortran, COBOL, C, and Java, allowed programmers to write code using more human-readable syntax and abstract away complex machine-level details.

Over time, programming languages continued to evolve, offering new features, libraries, and frameworks to support a wide range of applications. Today, there is a vast ecosystem of programming languages and tools available, catering to different programming paradigms and application domains. Each programming language has its own strengths, syntax, and community support, making it suitable for specific types of projects.

1.3 Importance of Learning Programming

In the digital age, programming skills have become increasingly important. Programming enables individuals to harness the power of technology and create innovative solutions to real-world problems. It enhances critical thinking, logical reasoning, and problem-solving abilities, allowing programmers to break down complex tasks into manageable steps and develop efficient algorithms.

Moreover, programming is a sought-after skill in various industries. Companies and organizations across sectors rely on software applications and systems to streamline operations, analyze data, and provide digital services. Proficiency in programming opens up numerous career opportunities, ranging from software development and web development to data science and artificial intelligence.

1.4 Programming in Various Industries

Programming plays a vital role in transforming industries and driving innovation. In software development, programmers create applications that run on desktops, mobile devices, and the web. Web development involves designing and building websites using programming languages such as HTML, CSS, and JavaScript. Data analysis and machine learning rely on programming to extract insights from large datasets and build predictive models.

Beyond traditional domains, programming finds applications in fields like finance, healthcare, transportation, entertainment, and many more. From developing trading algorithms in finance to creating medical software for healthcare professionals, programming has become an integral part of modern workflows and processes.

1.5 Programming Paradigms

Programming paradigms are different approaches to structuring and organizing code. They provide a conceptual framework for solving problems and designing software. Some commonly used programming paradigms include procedural programming, object-oriented programming (OOP), and functional programming.

Procedural programming focuses on organizing code into reusable procedures or functions, emphasizing the sequence of steps to execute a program. OOP, on the other hand, revolves around the concept of objects that encapsulate data and behavior, promoting modularity, code reusability, and scalability. Functional programming treats computation as the evaluation of mathematical functions, emphasizing immutability and avoiding side effects.

Choosing the appropriate programming paradigm depends on the nature of the project, its requirements, and the desired programming style.

1.6 Programming Languages and Tools

Programming languages serve as the foundation for writing code. There are numerous programming languages available, each with its own syntax, features, and areas of specialization. Popular programming languages include Python, Java, C++, JavaScript, Ruby, and many more. The choice of language depends on factors such as project requirements, performance needs, community support, and available libraries or frameworks.

Integrated Development Environments (IDEs) and code editors provide a comprehensive environment for writing, testing, and debugging code. IDEs like Visual Studio, PyCharm, Eclipse, and Xcode offer features such as code autocompletion, debugging tools, and project management capabilities. Code editors like Sublime

Text, Atom, and Visual Studio Code provide lightweight environments with customizable features and extensions.

In addition to programming languages and development environments, programmers utilize various tools, such as compilers, interpreters, and runtime environments, to translate and execute their code efficiently.

1.7 Ethical Considerations in Programming

With the increasing reliance on technology, programming carries ethical implications that programmers should consider. Privacy, security, data integrity, and responsible data handling are important ethical considerations in software development. Programmers have a responsibility to develop systems that protect user data, respect privacy, and prevent potential misuse.

Adhering to ethical guidelines and best practices, such as writing secure code, following industry standards, and staying updated on security vulnerabilities, is crucial for maintaining trust and integrity in the digital world. Programmers should also consider the broader societal impact of their creations, ensuring that their work aligns with ethical and moral standards.

1.8 Trends and Future of Programming

Programming is an ever-evolving field, constantly adapting to emerging technologies and trends. New programming languages, frameworks, and tools continue to emerge, catering to evolving needs and demands. Machine learning, blockchain, Internet of Things (IoT), and augmented reality are some of the technologies shaping the future of programming.

As the world becomes more interconnected and technology-driven, the demand for skilled programmers is expected to rise. Continuous learning, staying updated with industry developments, and exploring new technologies will be essential for programmers to remain competitive and meet the evolving demands of the digital landscape.

By providing an in-depth overview of programming, this section of the book equips readers with a solid understanding of the field. They gain insights into the definition and history of programming, recognize its importance in various industries, explore different programming paradigms and languages, and understand the ethical considerations associated with programming. Furthermore, readers get a glimpse into the emerging trends and future directions of programming, enabling them to embark on their programming journey with a strong foundation.

Chapter 2: Setting up the Development Environment

2.1 Choosing a Programming Language

Selecting the right programming language is an essential step when setting up your development environment. Different programming languages have distinct features, syntax, and areas of application. Here are the key factors to consider when choosing a programming language:

1. **Project Requirements:**
    - **Consider the specific requirements of your project. Does it involve web development, mobile app development, data analysis, or artificial intelligence? Different languages excel in different domains, so aligning the language with your project requirements is crucial.**
2. **Learning Curve:**
    - **Evaluate the learning curve associated with each programming language. If you are a beginner, it may be advantageous to choose a language with a gentle learning curve and comprehensive documentation to support your learning journey.**
3. **Community and Support:**
    - **Assess the size and vibrancy of the programming language's community. A large and active community means more resources, libraries, frameworks, and community support available to help you overcome challenges and find solutions to problems.**

4. Performance:
    - Consider the performance requirements of your project. Some programming languages are known for their speed and efficiency, making them suitable for tasks that demand high performance, such as game development or complex calculations. Others prioritize ease of development and may sacrifice some performance.
5. Scalability:
    - Evaluate the scalability of the programming language. Will the language and its associated tools support the growth of your project in the long run? Consider factors like modularity, extensibility, and the availability of frameworks that facilitate scalability.
6. Ecosystem and Libraries:
    - Investigate the ecosystem surrounding each programming language. Check the availability of libraries, frameworks, and development tools that can expedite your development process and provide ready-made solutions for common tasks.
7. Integration:
    - If your project requires integration with existing systems or technologies, consider the compatibility and interoperability of the programming language with those systems. Ensure that the language has the necessary tools and libraries to facilitate seamless integration.

Popular Programming Languages and Their Applications:

1. **Python:**
    - Python is a versatile language known for its simplicity and readability. It is widely used in web development, scientific computing, data analysis, machine learning, and automation tasks.
2. **JavaScript:**
    - JavaScript is primarily used for web development, both on the client-side (frontend) and server-side (backend). It enables interactive web elements, dynamic content, and is the backbone of many popular frameworks like React and Node.js.
3. **Java:**
    - Java is a general-purpose language renowned for its platform independence and robustness. It is widely used for building enterprise-level applications, Android app development, and large-scale systems.
4. **C++:**
    - C++ is a powerful language known for its high performance and low-level control. It is commonly used in game development, system programming, embedded systems, and performance-critical applications.
5. **Swift:**
    - Swift is specifically designed for developing iOS, macOS, watchOS, and tvOS applications. It provides a modern syntax, safety features, and efficient memory management.

6. **Ruby:**
    - **Ruby is a dynamic and expressive language, favored for its simplicity and productivity. It is commonly used in web development, particularly with the Ruby on Rails framework.**

Matching the Language to the Project Requirements and Goals:

Consider the unique requirements and goals of your project and match them to the strengths and characteristics of each programming language. Ensure that the language you choose aligns with the nature of the project, its scalability needs, performance expectations, and the availability of relevant libraries and frameworks. By making an informed decision, you set yourself up for success and optimize your development process from the start.

2.2 Installing the Necessary Tools and Software

To set up your development environment, you need to install the necessary tools and software, including an Integrated Development Environment (IDE). Here's what you need to know:

Introduction to Integrated Development Environments (IDEs):

An Integrated Development Environment (IDE) is a software application that provides a comprehensive environment for writing, testing, and debugging code. IDEs offer features that streamline the development process, such as code editing, syntax highlighting, code completion, debugging tools, and project management capabilities. They enhance productivity by providing an all-in-one solution for writing and managing code.

Selecting an IDE suitable for the chosen programming language:

Different programming languages have their own preferred IDEs. When selecting an IDE, consider the following factors:

1. Language Support:
    - Ensure that the IDE supports the programming language you have chosen. IDEs often provide language-specific features and integrations that enhance productivity and code quality.
2. Features and Tools:
    - Evaluate the features and tools offered by the IDE. Look for code editing capabilities, debugging tools, version control integration, project management features, and code refactoring options. Consider the features that align with your development workflow and project requirements.
3. Community Support and Documentation:
    - Check the availability of community support and documentation for the IDE. A strong community ensures access to tutorials, forums, and resources that can help you troubleshoot issues and learn more about the IDE's capabilities.

Step-by-step installation guide for the chosen IDE:

Once you have selected an IDE, follow these general steps to install it:

1. Download the IDE:
    - Visit the official website of the chosen IDE and navigate to the download page. Select the appropriate version for your operating system (Windows, macOS, or Linux).
2. Run the Installer:
    - Locate the downloaded installation file and run it. Follow the on-screen instructions to begin the installation process.

3. Configure Installation Settings:
   - During the installation, you may be prompted to choose installation options such as the installation location and additional components. Customize the settings according to your preferences.
4. Complete the Installation:
   - After configuring the installation settings, wait for the installation process to finish. Once completed, you should see a confirmation message indicating a successful installation.

Configuring the IDE settings for optimal development experience:

After installing the IDE, it's important to configure the settings for an optimal development experience. Some configuration steps you may need to perform include:

1. Theme and Appearance:
   - Customize the theme, font size, and appearance of the IDE to suit your preferences and improve readability.
2. Code Formatting and Style:
   - Set up code formatting rules to ensure consistent code style throughout your projects. Configure indentation, spacing, and other code formatting preferences.
3. Plugins and Extensions:
   - Explore the available plugins and extensions for your IDE. These can add additional features, integrate with other tools, and enhance your productivity.
4. Debugging and Testing:
   - Configure the debugging and testing settings,

including breakpoints, watch variables, and testing frameworks, to facilitate efficient debugging and testing processes.

5. Version Control Integration:
   - Connect your IDE to a version control system, such as Git, and configure the integration settings. This allows you to track changes, collaborate with others, and manage your code repository seamlessly.

By following these steps to install and configure the IDE, you create a comfortable and productive development environment tailored to your programming language of choice. Customizing the settings and taking advantage of the IDE's features will help streamline your coding process and improve your overall programming experience.

2.3 Setting Up a Text Editor

In addition to Integrated Development Environments (IDEs), another option for programming is using a lightweight text editor. Here's what you need to know to set up a text editor for programming:

Overview of Lightweight Text Editors for Programming:

Lightweight text editors are simple yet powerful tools that provide a minimalistic and customizable environment for writing code. They often have a smaller footprint compared to IDEs and are favored by programmers who prefer a more streamlined and flexible development experience. Some popular lightweight text editors for programming include:

1. Sublime Text:
   - Sublime Text is a cross-platform text editor

known for its speed and responsiveness. It offers a wide range of features, including multiple selections, powerful search and replace functionality, and a highly customizable interface.

2. Atom:
    - Atom is an open-source text editor developed by GitHub. It is built with web technologies and offers extensive customization options through its vast library of community-created packages and themes.
3. Visual Studio Code:
    - Visual Studio Code (VS Code) is a free and highly extensible text editor created by Microsoft. It provides a rich ecosystem of extensions, enabling developers to customize and enhance their coding experience.
4. Notepad++:
    - Notepad++ is a Windows-based text editor that supports a wide range of programming languages. It offers features like syntax highlighting, code folding, and macro recording.

Choosing a Text Editor Based on Personal Preferences and Project Needs:

When selecting a text editor, consider the following factors:

1. Simplicity vs. Features:
    - Determine whether you prefer a simple and lightweight editor or if you need advanced features like code linting, built-in terminal, or language-specific tooling.
2. Customization:
    - Assess the level of customization options available

in the text editor. Some editors offer extensive customization through themes, plugins, and configuration files.

3. Language Support:
   - Ensure that the text editor supports the programming languages you commonly work with. Look for syntax highlighting, code completion, and other language-specific features.
4. Community and Support:
   - Check the availability of a vibrant community around the text editor. A strong community ensures access to support, documentation, and a wide range of user-contributed packages and extensions.

Installing and Configuring the Selected Text Editor:

To install and configure your chosen text editor, follow these general steps:

1. Download the Text Editor:
   - Visit the official website of the text editor and navigate to the download page. Choose the appropriate version for your operating system.
2. Run the Installer:
   - Locate the downloaded installation file and run it. Follow the on-screen instructions to begin the installation process.
3. Configure Installation Settings:
   - During the installation, you may have the option to customize settings such as the installation location and additional components. Adjust these settings according to your preferences.
4. Explore and Install Plugins:

    - After installing the text editor, explore the available plugins or packages specific to your editor. These plugins can add features and functionality, such as additional language support or code formatting.
5. Customize the Editor:
    - Configure the text editor to your liking. This may involve setting preferences for indentation, tab width, font, and color schemes. Explore the editor's settings to tailor it to your needs.

By following these steps, you can set up and configure a lightweight text editor for programming. Choose the one that best aligns with your personal preferences, project needs, and the features you require. A well-configured text editor can provide a focused and efficient coding environment for your programming tasks.

2.4 Managing Dependencies and Package Managers

Managing dependencies is a crucial aspect of programming, especially when working on projects that require external libraries or modules. Package managers are tools that help handle dependencies efficiently. Here's what you need to know:

Understanding the Concept of Dependencies in Programming:

Dependencies in programming refer to external libraries, modules, or packages that your project relies on to function correctly. These dependencies provide pre-written code and functionality, allowing you to leverage existing solutions instead of reinventing the wheel. Managing dependencies involves ensuring that the required libraries or modules are available and properly integrated into your project.

Introduction to Package Managers:

Package managers are software tools designed to automate the process of installing, updating, and managing dependencies. They simplify the management of external libraries by providing a centralized repository of packages that you can easily install and configure for your projects. Some popular package managers include:

1. npm (Node Package Manager):
    - npm is the default package manager for Node.js, a JavaScript runtime environment. It allows you to install and manage packages specific to JavaScript and Node.js development.
2. pip (Python Package Installer):
    - pip is the package manager for Python. It enables you to install, upgrade, and uninstall Python packages from the Python Package Index (PyPI).
3. Maven:
    - Maven is a package manager and build automation tool primarily used for Java projects. It manages dependencies and provides a consistent build process.
4. RubyGems:
    - RubyGems is the package manager for Ruby programming language. It allows you to install, manage, and distribute Ruby libraries and applications.

Installing and Configuring the Appropriate Package Manager for the Selected Programming Language:

To install and configure the package manager for your chosen programming language, follow these general steps:

1. Check if the Package Manager is Included:
    - Some programming languages, such as Node.js (with npm) and Python (with pip), come with their default package managers pre-installed. Verify if your chosen programming language already includes a package manager.
2. Install the Package Manager:
    - If the package manager is not included, visit the official website of the package manager and follow the installation instructions specific to your operating system.
3. Verify the Installation:
    - After the installation, verify that the package manager is properly installed by running a version check command in the command line interface.
4. Explore Package Manager Commands:
    - Familiarize yourself with the package manager's commands and syntax. Learn how to search for packages, install specific versions, and manage dependencies for your projects.
5. Configure Package Manager Settings (if applicable):
    - Some package managers allow you to configure settings, such as package installation locations or repository sources. Review the documentation to understand the available configuration options and adjust them according to your needs.

By installing and configuring the appropriate package manager for your chosen programming language, you gain the ability to easily install and manage dependencies for your projects. Package managers provide a streamlined process for handling dependencies, ensuring that your projects have the required external libraries or modules integrated correctly.

2.5 Version Control and Collaboration Tools

Version control systems and collaboration tools are essential for efficient project management and collaboration among developers. Let's explore the key concepts and steps involved:

Introduction to Version Control Systems (e.g., Git):

Version control systems (VCS) are tools that track and manage changes to files and directories over time. They enable you to store and manage different versions of your code, facilitating collaboration, bug tracking, and code review. One popular version control system is Git, known for its speed, flexibility, and distributed nature.

Setting up a Git Repository for Version Control:

To set up a Git repository for version control, follow these steps:

1. Install Git:
    - Download and install Git from the official website (https://git-scm.com/) based on your operating system. Follow the installation instructions provided.
2. Initialize a Repository:
    - Create a new directory for your project, or navigate to an existing project folder using the command line interface. Run the command **git init** to initialize a new Git repository in that directory.
3. Add and Commit Files:
    - Add files to the Git repository using the command **git add <file>** or **git add .** (to add all files in the current directory). Then, commit the changes using **git commit -m "Commit message"**.
4. Branching and Merging:

- Git allows you to create branches to work on different features or bug fixes independently. Use the commands **git branch <branch-name>** to create a new branch and **git checkout <branch-name>** to switch between branches. Merge changes from one branch to another using **git merge <branch-name>**.

Collaborating with Others using Git and Platforms like GitHub or Bitbucket:

Git provides powerful collaboration capabilities when combined with platforms like GitHub or Bitbucket. Here's how to collaborate effectively:

1. Create a Remote Repository:
   - Sign up for a Git hosting platform like GitHub (https://github.com[1]) or Bitbucket (https://bitbucket.org[2]). Create a new repository on the platform.
2. Connect Local and Remote Repositories:
   - Link your local Git repository to the remote repository using the command **git remote add origin <repository-url>**. Replace **<repository-url>** with the URL of the remote repository.
3. Push and Pull Changes:
   - To share your changes with collaborators, use **git push origin <branch-name>** to push your local changes to the remote repository. Collaborators can then fetch and merge your changes using **git pull origin <branch-name>**.
4. Branching and Pull Requests:
   - Collaborators can create their branches, make

1. https://github.com/

2. https://bitbucket.org/

changes, and push them to the remote repository. They can then create a pull request, suggesting their changes for review and integration. Reviewers can provide feedback and approve the changes before merging them.

5. Issue Tracking and Code Reviews:
    - Git platforms like GitHub and Bitbucket provide features for issue tracking, allowing you to create and track tasks, bugs, and feature requests. They also offer code review functionalities, enabling collaborative code reviews and discussions.

By utilizing Git and collaborating through platforms like GitHub or Bitbucket, you can effectively manage version control, track changes, and collaborate with other developers. These tools enhance productivity, facilitate code review processes, and ensure efficient collaboration throughout the development lifecycle.

2.6 Configuring Development Environment Preferences

Configuring your development environment to align with your personal preferences and coding standards is crucial for a productive and comfortable programming experience. Here are some key aspects to consider when customizing your development environment:

Customizing the Development Environment for Personal Preferences:

1. Editor/IDE Themes:
    - Choose a theme or color scheme that is visually appealing and comfortable for long coding sessions. Most text editors and IDEs provide a

variety of themes to choose from.

2. Keybindings and Shortcuts:
    - Customize keybindings and shortcuts to match your preferred workflow. Assign shortcuts for commonly used actions or create custom keybindings for specific commands.
3. Font and Font Size:
    - Select a font that is easy to read and adjust the font size to your preference. Finding the right font can improve readability and reduce eye strain.

Setting Up Code Formatting and Style Guidelines:

1. Coding Style Guides:
    - Familiarize yourself with the coding style guidelines recommended for the programming language you're working with. These guidelines define conventions for indentation, naming conventions, line length, and more.
2. Code Formatting Tools:
    - Configure code formatting tools such as Prettier, Black, or ESLint to automatically format your code according to the defined coding style guidelines. These tools help maintain a consistent and readable codebase.

Configuring Code Linting and Static Analysis Tools for Code Quality:

1. Code Linting:
    - Set up code linting tools like ESLint, PyLint, or RuboCop to identify and report common code errors, style violations, and potential bugs.

Customize linting rules to match your coding standards and project requirements.

2. Static Analysis Tools:
   - Integrate static analysis tools such as SonarQube or FindBugs to perform deeper analysis of your codebase. These tools can identify complex code issues, security vulnerabilities, and performance bottlenecks.
3. Editor/IDE Integration:
   - Install and configure plugins or extensions in your editor/IDE to leverage the power of code linting and static analysis. These integrations provide real-time feedback, highlighting issues directly in the code editor.

By customizing your development environment preferences, setting up code formatting and style guidelines, and configuring code linting and static analysis tools, you create a coding environment that suits your preferences and promotes code quality. A well-tailored development environment can enhance your productivity, help you maintain consistent code standards, and catch potential issues early in the development process.

2.7 Testing and Debugging Tools

Testing and debugging are essential processes in software development to ensure the reliability and quality of your code. Let's explore the key aspects of testing frameworks, setting up a testing framework, and debugging tools and techniques:

Overview of Testing Frameworks and Libraries:

1. Unit Testing:
   - Unit testing frameworks, such as JUnit for Java,

pytest for Python, or Jasmine for JavaScript, provide a structure for writing and executing tests for individual units of code, typically functions or methods.

2. Integration Testing:
   - Integration testing frameworks, like NUnit for .NET, behave as a bridge between individual units of code and the system as a whole. They help verify that components work correctly when integrated.
3. Functional Testing:
   - Functional testing frameworks, such as Selenium or Cypress, enable the automation of tests that simulate user interactions with the software, validating the system's behavior.

Setting Up a Testing Framework Suitable for the Chosen Programming Language:

1. Research Available Testing Frameworks:
   - Identify the testing frameworks commonly used with the programming language you're working with. Explore their features, documentation, and community support to determine the most suitable one for your project.
2. Install the Testing Framework:
   - Follow the installation instructions specific to the chosen testing framework. Typically, you will need to use a package manager like npm, pip, or Maven to install the necessary dependencies.
3. Write Tests:
   - Familiarize yourself with the syntax and structure of the testing framework. Write tests that cover

different aspects of your code, including boundary cases, edge cases, and expected behaviors.

4. Execute Tests:
    - Run the tests using the testing framework's command-line interface or integration with your development environment. Analyze the test results to identify any failures or errors.

Introduction to Debugging Tools and Techniques for Identifying and Fixing Issues in Code:

1. Debugging Tools:
    - Integrated Development Environments (IDEs) often provide built-in debugging tools. These tools allow you to set breakpoints, inspect variables, and step through code execution to identify and fix issues.
2. Logging and Error Handling:
    - Incorporate logging statements throughout your code to track program flow and capture error messages. Use appropriate error handling techniques, such as try-catch blocks, to gracefully handle exceptions.
3. Interactive Debugging:
    - Utilize interactive debugging techniques to pinpoint issues. This may involve printing debug statements, using the interactive shell, or employing debugging tools specific to your programming language.
4. Analyzing Stack Traces:
    - When errors occur, examine the stack traces to identify the sequence of function calls leading to the error. Understand the error messages and use

them as clues to find and resolve the issue.

5. Debugging Techniques:
   - Familiarize yourself with techniques like stepping through code, inspecting variable values, and using watches or conditional breakpoints to troubleshoot and fix problems effectively.

By setting up a suitable testing framework and leveraging debugging tools and techniques, you can ensure the quality and reliability of your code. Testing frameworks help automate testing processes, while debugging tools assist in identifying and fixing issues, ultimately leading to more robust and stable software solutions.

2.8 Working with Documentation and References

Working with documentation and references is vital for programmers to enhance their knowledge, learn new concepts, and troubleshoot issues effectively. Here are some key aspects to consider:

Accessing Official Documentation for the Chosen Programming Language:

1. Official Documentation:
   - Identify the official documentation for the programming language you're working with. It is typically available on the language's official website. The documentation provides detailed explanations of language features, libraries, and APIs.
2. Language Guides and Tutorials:
   - Explore language-specific guides and tutorials

within the official documentation. These resources often provide step-by-step instructions and examples to help you understand and implement specific concepts.

3. API References:
    - Utilize API references to understand the functionality and proper usage of libraries and frameworks. API references provide details on classes, methods, and parameters, along with code examples.

Exploring Online Resources, Tutorials, and Forums:

1. Online Tutorials and Blogs:
    - Browse online tutorials and blogs related to your programming language. These resources offer practical examples, tips, and insights into various programming topics.
2. Video Tutorials and Online Courses:
    - Consider video tutorials and online courses available on platforms like YouTube, Udemy, or Coursera. These resources provide visual demonstrations and interactive learning experiences.
3. Developer Forums and Q&A Websites:
    - Participate in developer forums such as Stack Overflow, Reddit communities, or language-specific forums. Ask questions, seek guidance, and contribute to discussions. These platforms are excellent for troubleshooting and gaining insights from experienced developers.

Leveraging Code Repositories and Open-Source Projects:

1. GitHub and Bitbucket:
    - Explore code repositories on platforms like GitHub and Bitbucket. These platforms host numerous open-source projects where you can review code, learn from experienced developers, and gain inspiration for your own projects.
2. Open-Source Projects:
    - Contribute to open-source projects to enhance your skills and collaborate with other developers. Open-source projects provide an opportunity to work on real-world codebases and learn from the community.
3. Readme Files and Project Documentation:
    - When exploring code repositories, pay attention to the Readme files and project documentation. These resources provide information about the project's purpose, usage instructions, and often include additional references and resources.

By accessing official documentation, exploring online resources, tutorials, and forums, and leveraging code repositories and open-source projects, you can continuously expand your knowledge, learn from others, and find solutions to challenges you encounter during programming. Documentation and references serve as valuable sources of information, guidance, and inspiration throughout your programming journey.

2.9 Building a Sample Project

Building a sample project is an excellent way to apply the concepts you've learned and gain hands-on experience. Here's a step-by-step guide on how to build a basic project and run a "Hello, World!" program:

Creating a Basic Project Structure:

1. Choose a Project Directory:
   - Select a directory on your computer where you want to create the project. This directory will serve as the root folder for your project.
2. Create Project Subdirectories:
   - Depending on the programming language and project type, create the necessary subdirectories within the project directory. Common directories include "src" (source code), "tests" (test files), and "docs" (documentation).
3. Initialize Project Configuration (if applicable):
   - If your programming language or framework requires a project configuration file (e.g., package.json, setup.py, pom.xml), initialize it in the project directory. Follow the documentation or conventions specific to your chosen technology.

Writing and Running a "Hello, World!" Program:

1. Create a Source Code File:
   - In the "src" directory, create a new file with an appropriate name and the required file extension for your programming language (e.g., "main.py" for Python, "Main.java" for Java). This file will contain the "Hello, World!" program.
2. Write the "Hello, World!" Program:
   - Inside the source code file, write the necessary code to display the "Hello, World!" message. The code may vary depending on the programming language. For example, in Python, you can write: **print("Hello, World!")**.

3. Save the Source Code File:
    - Save the source code file in the appropriate location within the project's "src" directory.

Verifying the Setup by Executing Sample Code and Ensuring Expected Output:

1. Open a Terminal or Command Prompt:
    - Navigate to the project directory using a terminal or command prompt. Ensure you are in the root directory of the project.
2. Compile (if required) and Run the Program:
    - Depending on the programming language, you may need to compile the source code before running it. Refer to the documentation or language-specific instructions if compilation is necessary.
    - Execute the program by running the appropriate command for your programming language. For example, in Python, you can use the command **python main.py**. This will execute the "Hello, World!" program.
3. Verify the Output:
    - Check the output displayed in the terminal or command prompt. It should show the "Hello, World!" message if the program executed successfully.

By following these steps, you can build a basic project, write a "Hello, World!" program, and verify that the setup is working as expected. This initial project structure and program execution serve as a foundation for further development and exploration of your chosen programming language.

Chapter 3: Basics of Programming

Chapter 3 focuses on the fundamental building blocks of programming. By covering variables, data types, operators, expressions, and input/output operations in Chapter 3, readers will gain a solid understanding of the foundational concepts necessary to write basic programs. This knowledge sets the stage for more advanced programming topics covered in subsequent chapters.

3.1 Variables and Data Types:

3.1.1 Introduction to Variables:

Variables are essential elements in programming that enable the storage and manipulation of data. In this section, we will explore the concept of variables, their significance in programming, and how to declare and initialize them in different programming languages.

What are Variables and Why are They Important in Programming?

Variables are named containers that hold values, such as numbers, text, or objects, which can change during program execution. They serve as placeholders for data that the program needs to remember and manipulate. Variables allow programmers to store, retrieve, and modify values, making them fundamental to the functioning of programs.

The importance of variables in programming stems from their ability to:

1. Store and Retrieve Data: Variables provide a means to store values temporarily or permanently in computer memory, allowing programs to access and manipulate data when needed.

2. Enable Data Manipulation: Variables can be used in calculations, comparisons, and other operations, allowing programs to perform complex tasks by manipulating data.
3. Facilitate Code Readability and Reusability: By assigning meaningful names to variables, code becomes more readable and self-explanatory. Variables also promote code reusability as they can hold different values throughout program execution.

Declaring and Initializing Variables in Different Programming Languages:

The process of declaring and initializing variables may vary slightly across programming languages. Here's an overview of the general steps involved:

1. Variable Declaration:
    - Declare a variable by specifying its name and optionally indicating its data type. For example:
        - In JavaScript: **let age;**
        - In Python: **age = None**
        - In Java: **int age;**
2. Variable Initialization:
    - Assign an initial value to the declared variable. The initialization can be done at the time of declaration or later in the program. For example:
        - In JavaScript: **let age = 25;**
        - In Python: **age = 25**
        - In Java: **int age = 25;**
3. Data Types and Syntax:
    - Pay attention to the syntax and rules specific to the programming language you're using. Some languages require explicit data type declarations, while others support type inference.

4. Variable Naming Conventions:
    - Follow the naming conventions specified by the programming language or community guidelines. Use meaningful names that reflect the purpose or content of the variable.

Understanding how to declare and initialize variables in different programming languages allows you to effectively utilize this foundational concept in your programs. By using variables, you can store and manipulate data dynamically, making your programs more flexible and powerful.

3.1.2 Data Types:

In programming, data types define the kind of data that variables can hold. Each data type has specific characteristics and usage, allowing programmers to work with different types of information. This section provides an overview of primitive data types commonly found in programming languages, including integers, floating-point numbers, booleans, characters, and strings.

Overview of Primitive Data Types:

1. Integers:
    - Integers represent whole numbers without any fractional part. They can be positive, negative, or zero. Examples of integer data types include **int** in languages like Java and C/C++, **Integer** in Python, and **int** in JavaScript.
2. Floating-Point Numbers:
    - Floating-point numbers, also known as real numbers, represent numbers with fractional parts. They can store decimal values and provide a higher level of precision than integers. Examples of floating-point data types include **float** and **double** in languages like Java and C/C++, **float** in

Python, and **Number** in JavaScript.

3. Booleans:
    - Booleans represent logical values that can be either true or false. They are used for logical operations, comparisons, and conditional statements. The boolean data type is represented by keywords like **boolean** (Java), **bool** (C++), **bool** (Python), and **Boolean** (JavaScript).
4. Characters:
    - Characters represent individual symbols, letters, or digits. They are typically enclosed in single quotes (') or double quotes ("). Examples include **'a'**, **'B'**, or **'7'**. Character data types are denoted by **char** (Java and C/C++), **str** (Python), and **String** (JavaScript).
5. Strings:
    - Strings are sequences of characters and are used to represent textual data. They can be enclosed in single quotes or double quotes. Examples of string data types include "**Hello**", "**world**", or "**123**". Strings are represented by **String** (Java), **str** (Python), and **String** (JavaScript).

Understanding the Characteristics and Usage of Each Data Type:

1. Integers:
    - Integers are used for counting, indexing, and performing arithmetic operations that don't require decimal precision. They have a finite range of values depending on the number of bits used to represent them.
2. Floating-Point Numbers:
    - Floating-point numbers are suitable for calculations involving fractional parts, such as scientific computations or financial calculations.

They offer a wide range of values and precision but are subject to rounding errors.

3. Booleans:
   - Booleans are primarily used for logical operations and decision-making. They determine the flow of program execution based on conditions and comparisons.
4. Characters:
   - Characters represent individual symbols or letters. They are useful for processing individual characters in text manipulation, encoding, and various string operations.
5. Strings:
   - Strings are versatile and commonly used for handling textual data. They allow concatenation, substring extraction, searching, and other string manipulation operations.

Understanding the characteristics and appropriate usage of each data type is crucial for selecting the appropriate type when declaring variables. By choosing the correct data type, you can efficiently store and manipulate different kinds of data in your programs, ensuring accuracy, efficiency, and proper memory management.

3.1.3 Type Inference and Dynamic Typing:

In some programming languages, type inference and dynamic typing are features that affect how variables are declared and handled. Let's explore these features, their implications, and the benefits and considerations associated with them.

Exploring Type Inference and Dynamic Typing:

1. Type Inference:

- Type inference is a feature in certain programming languages that allows the compiler or interpreter to automatically determine the data type of a variable based on its assigned value. This means that programmers do not need to explicitly specify the type during variable declaration.
- Programming languages like Python, TypeScript, Kotlin, and Swift support type inference. For example, in Python, you can write **age = 25** without explicitly declaring the type.

2. Dynamic Typing:
    - Dynamic typing is a feature in programming languages where variables are not bound to a specific data type during declaration. Instead, the type of a variable can change dynamically during runtime based on the value it holds.
    - Languages such as Python, JavaScript, Ruby, and PHP employ dynamic typing. For instance, in JavaScript, you can assign different data types to the same variable without explicitly specifying the type.

Understanding the Benefits and Considerations of Type Inference and Dynamic Typing:

1. Code Conciseness:
    - Type inference and dynamic typing can make code shorter and more readable by reducing the need for explicit type declarations. This can lead to cleaner and more expressive code.
2. Flexibility and Rapid Prototyping:
    - Dynamic typing allows for greater flexibility as

variables can change types during runtime. It enables rapid prototyping and iterative development, making it easier to modify and test code quickly.

3. Reduced Development Time:
    - Type inference and dynamic typing can speed up development as programmers don't have to spend time explicitly declaring and managing types. This can improve productivity, especially in scripting and dynamically-typed languages.

Considerations:

- Type inference and dynamic typing may result in potential pitfalls if not used carefully. The absence of explicit type declarations can make code less self-documenting and potentially introduce bugs.
- Dynamic typing can lead to runtime errors if variables are not properly handled, as unexpected type changes may occur.
- Lack of explicit type information can make it harder for other developers to understand and maintain the code, especially in larger projects.

It's important to strike a balance when utilizing type inference and dynamic typing. While they offer benefits such as conciseness and flexibility, careful consideration should be given to code readability, maintainability, and potential pitfalls that may arise. Understanding the strengths and limitations of these features enables programmers to make informed decisions when selecting programming languages and writing code.

3.2 Operators and Expressions:

3.2.1 Arithmetic Operators:

Arithmetic operators are fundamental operators used in programming to perform mathematical calculations. They allow you to perform operations such as addition, subtraction, multiplication, division, and modulo. This section provides an overview of common arithmetic operators and their usage in programming.

Overview of Arithmetic Operators and Their Usage:

1. Addition (+):
    - The addition operator is represented by the "+" symbol. It adds two values together.
    - Example: **5 + 3** evaluates to **8**.
2. Subtraction (-):
    - The subtraction operator is represented by the "-" symbol. It subtracts one value from another.
    - Example: 7 - **2** evaluates to **5**.
3. Multiplication (*):
    - The multiplication operator is represented by the "*" symbol. It multiplies two values.
    - Example: **4 * 6** evaluates to **24**.
4. Division (/):
    - The division operator is represented by the "/" symbol. It divides one value by another.
    - Example: **10 / 2** evaluates to **5**.
5. Modulo (%):
    - The modulo operator is represented by the "%" symbol. It returns the remainder of the division operation.
    - Example: **10 % 3** evaluates to **1** because 10 divided by 3 leaves a remainder of 1.

Performing Basic Arithmetic Calculations using Operators:

Arithmetic operators are used to perform calculations in programming. Here are a few examples:

Example 1: Addition in python

```
int a = 5;
int b = 3;
int sum = a + b; // sum is now 8
```

Example 2: Subtraction in java

```
int a = 7;
int b = 2;
int difference = a - b; // difference is now 5
```

Example 3: Multiplication in JavaScript

```
var a = 4;
var b = 6;
var product = a * b; // product is now 24
```

Example 4: Division in python

```
int a = 10;
int b = 2;
int quotient = a / b; // quotient is now 5
```

Example 5: Modulo in java

```
int a = 10;
int b = 3;
int remainder = a % b; // remainder is 1
```

Arithmetic operators can be combined and used within larger expressions to perform complex calculations. Parentheses can also be used to specify the order of operations, following the standard mathematical rules (e.g., BIDMAS/BODMAS).

By using arithmetic operators effectively, you can perform various mathematical calculations and manipulate numerical data within your programs.

3.2.2 Relational and Comparison Operators:

Relational and comparison operators are used in programming to evaluate conditions and make logical comparisons between values. These operators return a Boolean value (true or false) based on the comparison result. This section introduces common relational and comparison operators and explains their usage.

Introduction to Relational and Comparison Operators:

1. Equality (==):
    - The equality operator checks if two values are equal and returns true if they are, or false otherwise.
    - Example: **5 == 5** evaluates to **true**, while **5 == 3** evaluates to **false.**
2. Inequality (!=):
    - The inequality operator checks if two values are not equal and returns true if they are not, or false if they are equal.
    - Example: **5 != 3** evaluates to **true**, while **5 != 5** evaluates to **false.**
3. Greater Than (>):
    - The greater than operator checks if the left operand is greater than the right operand and returns true if it is, or false otherwise.
    - Example: **8 > 5** evaluates to **true**, while **3** > 7 evaluates to **false.**
4. Less Than (<):
    - The less than operator checks if the left operand is less than the right operand and returns true if it is, or false otherwise.
    - Example: **3** < 7 evaluates to **true**, while **8 < 5** evaluates to **false.**

5. Greater Than or Equal To (>=):
   - The greater than or equal to operator checks if the left operand is greater than or equal to the right operand and returns true if it is, or false otherwise.
   - Example: **8 >= 5** evaluates to **true**, while **3 >= 7** evaluates to **false.**
6. Less Than or Equal To (<=):
   - The less than or equal to operator checks if the left operand is less than or equal to the right operand and returns true if it is, or false otherwise.
   - Example: **3 <= 7** evaluates to **true**, while **8 <= 5** evaluates to **false.**

Evaluating Conditions and Making Logical Comparisons:

Relational and comparison operators are commonly used in conditional statements and loops to evaluate conditions and control the flow of a program. Here are a few examples:

Example 1: Equality in Python

```
int a = 5; int b = 3;
boolean isEqual = (a == b); // isEqual is false
```

Example 2: Inequality in Java

```
int age = 25;
boolean isTeenager = (age != 20); // isTeenager is true
```

Example 3: Greater Than in JavaScript

```
var score = 80;
var passThreshold = 70;
var isPassing = (score > passThreshold); // isPassing is true
```

Example 4: Less Than or Equal To in Python

```
int x = 10;
int y = 15;
boolean result = (x <= y); // result is true
```

Relational and comparison operators can be combined with logical operators (such as logical AND, OR, and NOT) to create more complex conditions. Understanding how to use these operators allows you to make logical comparisons, perform conditional branching, and implement decision-making logic in your programs.

3.2.3 Logical Operators:

Logical operators are an essential component of programming that allow you to manipulate boolean values and construct complex conditions. They enable you to perform logical operations on boolean expressions and make decisions based on multiple conditions. This section provides an understanding of logical operators and demonstrates how to construct complex conditions using these operators.

Understanding Logical Operators and Their Role in Boolean Expressions:

1. Logical AND (&&):
    - The logical AND operator returns true if both of its operands are true. Otherwise, it returns false.
    - Example: **(5 > 3) && (2 < 7)** evaluates to **true** because both conditions, **5 > 3** and **2 <** 7, are true.
2. Logical OR (||):
    - The logical OR operator returns true if at least one of its operands is true. If both operands are false, it returns false.
    - Example: **(5 > 3) || (2 > 7)** evaluates to **true** because at least one of the conditions, **5 > 3** or **2 >** 7, is true.
3. Logical NOT (!):
    - The logical NOT operator negates the boolean

value of its operand. If the operand is true, it returns false. If the operand is false, it returns true.
   - Example: **!(5 > 3)** evaluates to **false** because the condition **5 > 3** is true, but the logical NOT operator negates it.

Constructing Complex Conditions using Logical Operators:

Logical operators allow you to combine and manipulate boolean expressions to create more complex conditions. By using logical operators effectively, you can make decisions based on multiple conditions. Here are a few examples:

Example 1: Logical AND in Python

int age = 25;

boolean isTeenager = (age >= 13) && (age <= 19); // isTeenager is false

Example 2: Logical OR in Java

int score = 80;

boolean isPassing = (score >= 70) || (score >= 90); // isPassing is true

Example 3: Logical NOT in JavaScript

var hasPermission = false;

var canAccessResource = !hasPermission; // canAccessResource is true

By using logical operators, you can evaluate multiple conditions and determine the flow of your program accordingly. Logical operators are commonly used in if statements, while loops, and other control structures to make decisions based on the combined outcome of multiple conditions.

It's important to consider the operator precedence and use parentheses when constructing complex conditions to ensure the desired evaluation order. This helps in creating clear and unambiguous expressions.

With a solid understanding of logical operators, you can construct complex conditions and create programs that can handle different scenarios based on the evaluation of multiple conditions.

3.2.4 Assignment Operators:

Assignment operators are used in programming to assign values to variables and manipulate their values. They provide a concise way to update variables based on existing values or perform arithmetic operations along with assignment. This section introduces common assignment operators and demonstrates their usage in variable assignment and manipulation.

Exploring Assignment Operators and Their Usage:

1. Assignment (=) Operator:
    - The assignment operator (=) is used to assign a value to a variable.
    - Example: **int x = 5;** assigns the value 5 to the variable x.
2. Compound Assignment Operators:
    - Compound assignment operators combine assignment with other arithmetic operations, allowing you to update a variable's value based on its current value.
    - Common compound assignment operators include:
        - Addition assignment (+=): Adds a value to the variable's current value and assigns the result back to the variable. Example: **x += 3;** is equivalent to **x = x + 3;**
        - Subtraction assignment (-=): Subtracts a value from the variable's current value and assigns the result back to the variable. Example: **x -= 2;** is

equivalent to **x = x - 2;**

- Multiplication assignment (*=): Multiplies the variable's current value by a value and assigns the result back to the variable. Example: **x *= 4;** is equivalent to **x = x * 4;**
- Division assignment (/=): Divides the variable's current value by a value and assigns the result back to the variable. Example: **x /= 2;** is equivalent to **x = x / 2;**
- Modulo assignment (%=): Calculates the remainder of the variable's current value divided by a value and assigns the result back to the variable. Example: **x %= 3;** is equivalent to **x = x % 3;**

Performing Compound Assignment Operations:

Compound assignment operators provide a convenient way to update variables by combining assignment with arithmetic operations. Here are a few examples:

Example 1: Addition Assignment in Java

```
int count = 5;
count += 2; // count is now 7
```

Example 2: Subtraction Assignment in Python

```
x = 10;
x -= 3; // x is now 7
```

Example 3: Multiplication Assignment in JavaScript

```
var total = 5; total *= 3; // total is now 15
```

Example 4: Division Assignment in Python

```
y = 20; y /= 4; # y is now 5
```

Example 5: Modulo Assignment in Java

```
int number = 13; number %= 5; // number is now 3
```

By using assignment operators, you can assign values to variables and update their values based on arithmetic operations in a concise manner. Compound assignment operators are particularly useful when performing calculations or updating variables based on their current values.

Understanding and utilizing assignment operators effectively will allow you to manipulate variables and perform various calculations efficiently in your programs.

3.2.5 Expressions:

Expressions play a crucial role in programming as they represent computations or actions that produce a value. They consist of variables, constants, operators, and function calls, combined in a meaningful way to perform calculations, make comparisons, or manipulate data. This section provides an understanding of expressions and explores their role in programming, including evaluating expressions and understanding operator precedence.

Defining Expressions and Their Role in Programming:

An expression is a combination of one or more operands and operators that, when evaluated, produces a value. Expressions can be as simple as a single variable or constant, or they can be more complex, involving multiple operations. They are used to perform calculations, make decisions, control program flow, and manipulate data.

Examples of Expressions:

- **5 + 3** is an expression that performs addition and evaluates to the value 8.
- **x * 2** is an expression that multiplies the value of variable x by 2.
- **age >= 18** is an expression that evaluates to true or false based on the comparison of the variable age with the value

18.

Evaluating Expressions and Understanding Operator Precedence:

When evaluating an expression, the operators are applied in a specific order defined by operator precedence. Operator precedence determines which operators are evaluated first in an expression. It helps in understanding how the expression will be computed and ensures that the correct order of operations is followed.

Common Operator Precedence (from highest to lowest):

1. Parentheses: Expressions within parentheses are evaluated first.
2. Unary Operators: Unary operators (e.g., !, -, ++) are evaluated next.
3. Multiplicative and Divisive Operators: Multiplication (*), division (/), and modulo (%) operators are evaluated next.
4. Additive and Subtractive Operators: Addition (+) and subtraction (-) operators are evaluated next.
5. Relational and Equality Operators: Comparison operators (e.g., >, <, ==, !=) are evaluated next.
6. Logical Operators: Logical operators (e.g., &&, ||) are evaluated next.
7. Assignment Operators: Assignment operators (e.g., =, +=, -=) are evaluated last.

By understanding the operator precedence, you can correctly evaluate expressions and ensure that the computations are performed in the desired order.

Example: in Java

int result = 5 + 3 * 2; // The multiplication is performed first, then the addition.

// result will be 11 because 3 * 2 = 6, and then 5 + 6 = 11.

Understanding expressions and operator precedence is essential for writing correct and efficient code. It allows you to perform calculations, make comparisons, and manipulate data accurately within your programs.

3.3 Input and Output:

3.3.1 Standard Input and Output:

Standard input (stdin) and standard output (stdout) are fundamental concepts in programming that allow for interaction between the program and the user through input and output operations. This section provides an introduction to stdin and stdout, explaining their role and demonstrating how to read input from the user and display output to the console.

Introduction to Standard Input and Output:

Standard input (stdin) refers to the source from which a program reads input data. It is typically associated with user input, such as keyboard input. Standard output (stdout) refers to the destination where a program sends its output data, which is commonly displayed on the console.

Reading Input from the User:

To read input from the user through stdin, programming languages provide specific functions or methods. These functions typically allow you to read input as strings or parse it into different data types based on your program's requirements. Here's an example in Python:

Example in Python

name = input("Enter your name: ") print("Hello, " + name + "! Welcome!")

In this example, the **input()** function prompts the user to enter their name, and the entered value is assigned to the **name** variable. The **print()** function is then used to display a personalized greeting message.

Displaying Output to the Console:

To display output to the console through stdout, programming languages offer functions or methods specifically designed for output operations. These functions allow you to format and display data, messages, or results. Here's an example in Java:

Example in Java

int age = 25; System.out.println("Your age is: " + age);

In this example, the **System.out.println**() method is used to display the message "Your age is: " concatenated with the value of the **age** variable.

Both reading input from the user and displaying output to the console are essential for building interactive programs, gathering user input, and providing meaningful information to users during program execution.

By utilizing stdin and stdout, you can create programs that interact with users, prompt for input, and display output to provide a dynamic and engaging user experience.

3.3.2 Formatted Output:

Formatted output allows you to control the appearance and structure of output when displaying data or messages. It involves using placeholders or format specifiers to define the format of the output and incorporating formatting options to customize the output's appearance. This section introduces the concept of formatted output and demonstrates how to utilize placeholders and formatting options in programming.

Formatting Output using Placeholders or Format Specifiers:

Placeholders or format specifiers are special symbols or sequences that are used within a formatted string to indicate where and how values should be inserted. They serve as placeholders for the actual data that will be displayed. Common placeholders include:

%d or %i: Used for formatting integers.

%f: Used for formatting floating-point numbers.

%s: Used for formatting strings.

%c: Used for formatting characters.

%b: Used for formatting booleans.

Example in Python:

```
name = "John"
age = 25
print("Name: %s, Age: %d" % (name, age))
```

In this example, %s is a placeholder for a string, %d is a placeholder for an integer, and the values of name and age are inserted using the % operator.

Controlling the Appearance of Output using Formatting Options:

Formatting options provide additional control over the appearance of the output. They can specify the width, precision, alignment, and other aspects of the formatted output. Some common formatting options include:

Width: Specifies the minimum width of the output field.

Precision: Specifies the number of decimal places for floating-point numbers.

Alignment: Controls the alignment of the output within the field (left, right, or centered).

Zero-padding: Adds leading zeros to the output.

Example in C++:

```
#include <iostream>
#include <iomanip>
double pi = 3.14159;
std::cout << std::fixed << std::setprecision(2) << "Value of pi: "
<< std::setw(8) << std::setfill('0') << pi << std::endl;
```

In this example, std::fixed and std::setprecision(2) are formatting options to display the value of pi with two decimal places. std::setw(8) sets the field width to 8 characters, and std::setfill('0') adds leading zeros to fill the field.

By utilizing placeholders and formatting options, you can tailor the appearance of the output to meet your specific requirements, such as aligning columns, controlling decimal precision, or adding padding.

Formatted output provides a flexible way to present data or messages in a visually appealing and structured manner, enhancing the readability and usability of your programs.

3.3.3 File Input and Output:

File input/output (I/O) operations allow programs to read data from files and write data to files. Reading from files enables the program to access external data, while writing to files allows the program to store data for future use or share it with other programs. This section explores file I/O operations, including reading from and writing to files, and discusses how to handle file-related exceptions and errors.

Reading from Files:

To read data from a file, the program needs to perform the following steps:

1. Open the file: This step involves creating a connection between the program and the file using the appropriate file handling mechanisms provided by the programming language.
2. Read data: Once the file is open, the program can read the contents of the file, whether it is a single line or multiple lines.
3. Process the data: After reading the data from the file, the program can process it according to its requirements.
4. Close the file: It is important to close the file after reading to release system resources and ensure data integrity.

Example in Python:

```
try:
```

```
file = open("data.txt", "r") # Open the file in read mode
data = file.read() # Read the contents of the file
print(data) # Process the data
finally:
file.close() # Close the file
```

Writing to Files:

To write data to a file, the program follows a similar set of steps:

1. Open the file: Create a connection between the program and the file, specifying the file handling mode (e.g., write, append).
2. Write data: Write the desired data to the file, whether it is a single line or multiple lines.
3. Close the file: Close the file to release system resources and ensure data integrity.

Example in Java:

```
try {
FileWriter writer = new FileWriter("output.txt"); // Open the file for writing
writer.write("Hello, World!"); // Write data to the file
writer.close(); // Close the file
} catch (IOException e) {
e.printStackTrace(); // Handle file-related exceptions
}
```

Handling File-related Exceptions and Errors:

When working with files, it is important to handle potential exceptions and errors that may occur. File-related exceptions may include file not found, permission denied, or file corruption. Proper exception handling ensures that the program gracefully handles such situations and provides appropriate feedback to the user.

By implementing file input/output operations in your programs and handling file-related exceptions, you can effectively read from and write to files, enabling your programs to interact with external data sources and store data for future use.

Chapter 4: Control Structures

By understanding and utilizing control structures effectively, programmers can manipulate the flow of their programs, make decisions based on conditions, and execute repetitive tasks. This chapter provides a comprehensive exploration of conditional statements, looping structures, and control flow, equipping readers with the necessary knowledge and skills to implement efficient and flexible program control.

4.1 Conditional Statements

4.1.1 Introduction to Conditional Statements

Conditional statements play a crucial role in programming by allowing the execution of specific code blocks based on certain conditions. These statements enable programmers to control the flow of their programs, making decisions and executing different sets of instructions depending on whether certain conditions are met. This section provides an introduction to conditional statements, explaining their concept and highlighting their importance in controlling program flow.

Understanding the Concept of Conditional Statements:

In programming, conditional statements are used to evaluate conditions and execute different blocks of code based on the result of the evaluation. These conditions are typically expressed as logical expressions or comparisons, such as checking if a variable is equal to a specific value or if a certain condition is true.

Conditional statements provide programmers with the ability to create branching paths in their code, where the program takes different actions depending on the outcome of the condition evaluation. This allows for dynamic and adaptive program behavior, where different sets of instructions can be executed based on varying inputs or circumstances.

Overview of the Importance of Conditional Statements:

Conditional statements are fundamental to programming because they introduce decision-making capabilities into the code. By utilizing conditional statements, programmers can create programs that respond intelligently to different situations, making them more versatile and capable of handling diverse scenarios.

The ability to control program flow using conditional statements allows for the implementation of complex logic and algorithmic processes. It enables the program to handle different cases, validate input, perform error checks, and customize behavior based on user preferences or system conditions. Conditional statements also facilitate the creation of interactive programs that respond dynamically to user input, providing a more engaging and personalized user experience.

Furthermore, conditional statements contribute to code efficiency by reducing the need for repetitive code blocks. Instead of writing separate sections of code for each possible scenario, conditional statements allow programmers to consolidate and streamline their code by selectively executing relevant portions based on conditions. This promotes code reusability, maintainability, and readability.

Overall, a solid understanding of conditional statements is crucial for any programmer, as they are essential tools for controlling program behavior and enabling intelligent decision-making within software applications.

4.1.2 if-else Statements

if-else statements are one of the most commonly used conditional statements in programming. They allow programmers to perform conditional branching based on a single condition. The if-else statement evaluates a condition and executes a specific block of code if the condition is true. If the condition is false, an alternate block of code specified in the else statement is executed. This section covers the syntax and usage of if-else statements.

Syntax of if-else Statements:

The syntax of an if-else statement typically follows this structure:

Example in Visual Basic

```
if (condition) {
// Code to be executed if the condition is true
} else {
// Code to be executed if the condition is false
}
```

Usage of if-else Statements:

1. Condition Evaluation:
    - The condition within the parentheses after the **if** keyword is evaluated.
    - It can be a logical expression, a comparison, or any expression that results in a boolean value (**true** or **false**).
    - If the condition evaluates to **true**, the code block associated with the **if** statement is executed.
    - If the condition evaluates to **false**, the code block associated with the **else** statement is executed.
2. Performing Conditional Branching:
    - if-else statements allow programmers to create two distinct paths of execution based on a condition.
    - When the condition is true, the code block associated with the **if** statement is executed.
    - When the condition is false, the code block associated with the **else** statement is executed.

Example Usage of if-else Statements in Python:

```
age = 25
if age >= 18:
print("You are an adult.")
else:
print("You are not an adult.")
# Output: "You are an adult."
```

In this example, the condition **age >= 18** is evaluated. If the condition is true (in this case, when **age** is 25), the code block under the **if** statement is executed, which prints "You are an adult." If the condition is false, the code block under the **else** statement is executed, which prints "You are not an adult."

if-else statements are versatile and can be nested or combined with other conditional statements to handle more complex branching scenarios. They provide programmers with the flexibility to control the flow of their program based on specific conditions, enabling dynamic and adaptive behavior.

4.1.3 Nested if-else Statements

- Understanding nested if-else statements and their role in handling multiple conditions
- Writing nested if-else statements for complex branching scenarios

4.1.4 switch Statements

- Introduction to switch statements and their purpose in handling multiple branching options
- Syntax and usage of switch statements
- Comparing switch statements to if-else statements for specific use cases

4.2 Looping Structures

4.2.1 Introduction to Looping Structures

Nested if-else statements play a crucial role in handling multiple conditions and creating complex branching scenarios in programming. They allow programmers to evaluate multiple conditions in a hierarchical manner and execute corresponding code blocks based on the outcome of each condition. This section provides an understanding of nested if-else statements and explores their role in handling multiple conditions.

Understanding Nested if-else Statements:

Nested if-else statements involve placing one if-else statement inside another if or else block. This nesting structure allows for the evaluation of multiple conditions and the execution of specific code blocks based on the outcome of each condition.

The outer if statement serves as the primary condition, and its associated code block is executed if the condition evaluates to true. Within this code block, an inner if-else statement can be used to evaluate a secondary condition and execute a specific code block accordingly. This nesting can be continued further to handle additional conditions, creating a hierarchical structure.

Writing Nested if-else Statements for Complex Branching Scenarios:

Nested if-else statements are useful when dealing with complex branching scenarios where multiple conditions need to be checked. By nesting if-else statements, programmers can create a decision tree-like structure to handle different cases.

Example in Python:

```
num = 10
if num > 0:
print("Number is positive.")
else:
```

```
if num < 0:

  print("Number is negative.")

else:

  print("Number is zero.")

# Output: "Number is positive."
```

In this example, the outer if statement checks if the variable **num** is greater than 0. If the condition is true, the code block under the outer if statement is executed, printing "Number is positive." If the condition is false, the inner if-else statement is evaluated. If **num** is less than 0, the code block under the inner if statement is executed, printing "Number is negative." Otherwise, if **num** is neither greater nor less than 0, the code block under the inner else statement is executed, printing "Number is zero."

Nested if-else statements can be further nested to accommodate more conditions and create intricate branching scenarios. However, it is important to maintain code readability and clarity when using nested if-else statements. Proper indentation and commenting can help make the code more understandable.

By utilizing nested if-else statements, programmers can effectively handle multiple conditions and create flexible program flows that adapt to various scenarios.

4.2.2 for Loops

for loops are commonly used looping structures in programming that allow for the execution of a block of code for a predetermined number of iterations. They are particularly useful when working with collections, such as arrays or lists, or when a specific range of values needs to be iterated. This section covers the syntax and usage of for loops, performing iterative tasks, and utilizing loop control statements such as break and continue.

Syntax of for Loops:

The syntax of a for loop typically follows this structure:

```
for (initialization; condition; increment/decrement) {
// Code to be executed in each iteration
}
```

Usage of for Loops:

1. Initialization:
    - The initialization step is performed before the loop begins and typically involves initializing a loop control variable.
    - It sets the initial value of the loop control variable, which is used to control the loop's behavior.
2. Condition:
    - The condition is evaluated before each iteration.
    - If the condition evaluates to true, the code block inside the loop is executed.
    - If the condition evaluates to false, the loop terminates, and program control moves to the next statement after the loop.
3. Increment/Decrement:
    - The increment or decrement step is executed after each iteration.
    - It updates the loop control variable, bringing it closer to the termination condition.

Example Usage of for Loops in C++:

```
for (int i = 1; i <= 5; i++) {
cout << i << " ";
} // Output: 1 2 3 4 5
```

In this example, the for loop initializes the loop control variable **i** to 1. The loop continues executing as long as **i** is less than or equal to 5. In each iteration, the value of **i** is printed, and **i** is incremented by 1.

Performing Iterative Tasks with a Predetermined Number of Iterations:

for loops are ideal for situations where a specific number of iterations is known in advance. By setting the appropriate initialization, condition, and increment/decrement, programmers can control the exact number of times the loop iterates.

Utilizing Loop Control Statements such as break and continue:

- break: The **break** statement is used within a loop to exit the loop prematurely. It immediately terminates the loop, and program control moves to the next statement after the loop.
- continue: The **continue** statement is used within a loop to skip the current iteration and proceed to the next iteration. It effectively jumps to the next iteration without executing the remaining code in the loop for the current iteration.

Loop control statements like **break** and **continue** provide additional çontrol and flexibility within for loops, allowing programmers to customize the loop's behavior and handle special cases.

By utilizing for loops, programmers can efficiently perform iterative tasks with a predetermined number of iterations. The ability to control the loop's behavior using initialization, condition, and increment/decrement steps, along with loop control statements like **break** and **continue**, makes for loops powerful tools in handling repetitive tasks in programming.

4.2.3 while Loops

while loops are commonly used looping structures in programming that allow for the execution of a block of code as long as a given condition remains true. They are useful when the number of iterations is not known in advance or when the loop needs to continue until a specific condition is met. This section covers the syntax and usage of while loops, executing repetitive tasks based on a condition, and implementing loop control statements within while loops.

Syntax of while Loops:

The syntax of a while loop typically follows this structure:

```
while (condition) {
// Code to be executed as long as the condition is true
}
```

Usage of while Loops:

1. Condition:
   - The condition is evaluated before each iteration.
   - If the condition evaluates to true, the code block inside the loop is executed.
   - If the condition evaluates to false, the loop terminates, and program control moves to the next statement after the loop.
2. Code Execution:
   - The code block inside the while loop is executed as long as the condition remains true.
   - It may perform a set of tasks or calculations that need to be repeated until the condition becomes false.

Example Usage of while Loops in Python:

```
count = 0
```

```
while count < 5:
print(count)
count += 1
# Output: 0 1 2 3 4
```

In this example, the while loop executes as long as the condition **count < 5** is true. The initial value of **count** is 0, and in each iteration, **count** is printed, and its value is incremented by 1. The loop continues until **count** reaches 5, at which point the condition becomes false, and the loop terminates.

Executing Repetitive Tasks based on a Given Condition:

while loops are well-suited for situations where the number of iterations is not predetermined or where the loop needs to continue until a specific condition is met. The condition is evaluated dynamically during each iteration, allowing the loop to adapt to changing circumstances.

Implementing Loop Control Statements within while Loops:

- break: The **break** statement can be used within a while loop to exit the loop prematurely. When encountered, it immediately terminates the loop, and program control moves to the next statement after the loop.
- continue: The **continue** statement can be used within a while loop to skip the remaining code in the loop for the current iteration and proceed to the next iteration.

Loop control statements like **break** and **continue** provide additional control and flexibility within while loops, allowing programmers to customize the loop's behavior and handle special cases.

By utilizing while loops, programmers can effectively execute repetitive tasks based on a given condition. The ability to control the loop's behavior using the condition and incorporate loop control statements like **break** and **continue** makes while loops powerful tools for handling dynamic and condition-dependent iterations in programming.

4.2.4 do-while Loops

do-while loops are looping structures in programming that allow for the execution of a block of code at least once, and then continue executing the code as long as a given condition remains true. They are useful when the code block needs to be executed before the condition is evaluated and when you want to ensure that the code block executes at least once. This section covers the syntax and usage of do-while loops, performing repetitive tasks with a post-condition evaluation, and understanding the differences between do-while and while loops.

Syntax of do-while Loops:

The syntax of a do-while loop typically follows this structure:

```
do {
// Code to be executed
} while (condition);
```

Usage of do-while Loops:

1. Code Execution:
    - The code block inside the do-while loop is executed first, regardless of the condition.
    - This guarantees that the code block will be executed at least once.
2. Condition Evaluation:
    - After the code block is executed, the condition is evaluated.
    - If the condition evaluates to true, the code block is executed again.
    - If the condition evaluates to false, the loop

terminates, and program control moves to the next statement after the loop.

Example Usage of do-while Loops in Java:

```
int count = 0;
do {
System.out.println(count);
count++;
} while (count < 5);
// Output: 0 1 2 3 4
```

In this example, the code block inside the do-while loop is executed first, which prints the value of **count**. After executing the code block, the condition **count < 5** is evaluated. If the condition is true, the loop continues, and the code block is executed again. This process repeats until the condition becomes false, at which point the loop terminates.

Performing Repetitive Tasks with a Post-Condition Evaluation:

do-while loops are suitable when you want to perform repetitive tasks and ensure that the code block executes at least once, even if the condition is initially false. The post-condition evaluation allows for dynamic looping based on a condition that is evaluated after executing the code block.

Understanding the Differences between do-while and while Loops:

The primary difference between do-while and while loops is the position of the condition evaluation. In a while loop, the condition is evaluated before executing the code block. If the condition is false initially, the code block is not executed at all. In contrast, in a do-while loop, the code block is executed before evaluating the condition, guaranteeing that the code block executes at least once.

do-while loops are suitable when there is a need to perform an action first and then evaluate a condition. while loops are more appropriate when the condition needs to be evaluated before entering the loop.

By utilizing do-while loops, programmers can perform repetitive tasks with a post-condition evaluation, ensuring that the code block executes at least once. The flexibility provided by the do-while loop structure allows for more dynamic looping in certain scenarios compared to while loops.

4.3 Control Flow and Branching

4.3.1 Control Flow

Control flow refers to the order in which statements and instructions are executed in a program. It determines how the program flows from one statement to another, based on the conditions and decisions made during runtime. This section explores the concept of control flow in programming and helps in understanding the flow of program execution based on conditional statements and loops.

Exploring the Concept of Control Flow in Programming:

In programming, control flow refers to the sequence of statements and instructions that are executed in a program. It determines the path and order in which the program's code is executed, enabling the program to make decisions, perform actions, and repeat tasks based on specific conditions and loops.

Control flow is crucial for the logic and functionality of a program. It allows programmers to control the execution order of statements, respond to different conditions, and create more complex and adaptive behaviors in their software.

Example of Control Flow using Loops in python:

```
for i in range(1, 6):
if i % 2 == 0:
```

```
  print(i, "is even")
else:
  print(i, "is odd")
# Output:
# 1 is odd
# 2 is even
# 3 is odd
# 4 is even
# 5 is odd
```

In this example, a for loop is used to iterate over a range of numbers from 1 to 5. Within the loop, the program evaluates each number and prints whether it is even or odd. The control flow determines which code block to execute based on the condition **i % 2 == 0**, allowing the program to branch and provide different output depending on the value of **i**.

Understanding the Flow of Program Execution based on Conditional Statements and Loops:

Conditional statements, such as if-else statements and switch statements, play a significant role in control flow. They allow programmers to create decision points in the code, where different sets of instructions are executed based on specific conditions.

Example 1: if-else Control Flow in python

```
num = 10
if num > 0:
print("Number is positive.")
else:
print("Number is non-positive.")
# Output: "Number is positive."
```

In this example, the program evaluates the condition **num > 0**. If the condition is true, it executes the code block under the

if statement and prints "Number is positive." Otherwise, if the condition is false, it executes the code block under the **else** statement and prints "Number is non-positive." The control flow determines which code block to execute based on the value of **num**.

When a program encounters a conditional statement, it evaluates the condition. If the condition is true, the program follows the path specified in the true condition block, executing the corresponding code. If the condition is false, the program either executes the code block specified in the false condition block or moves on to the next statement after the conditional block.

Loops, such as for loops, while loops, and do-while loops, also contribute to control flow by enabling repetitive execution of code blocks. The program repeatedly executes the loop's code block until a specified condition is met or until the loop control statement indicates otherwise.

Example 2: for Loop Control Flow python:

```
sum = 0
for i in range(1, 6):
sum += i print("Sum:", sum)
# Output: "Sum: 15"
```

In this example, a for loop is used to iterate over a range of numbers from 1 to 5. The program calculates the sum of the numbers by adding each number to the variable **sum** in each iteration. After the loop completes, it prints the final sum. The control flow of the for loop ensures that the code block inside the loop is executed repeatedly until all iterations are completed.

Example 3: while Loop Control Flow in Java

```
int count = 0;
int sum = 0;
while (count < 5) {
sum += count; count++;
}
```

```
System.out.println("Sum: " + sum);
// Output: "Sum: 10"
```

In this Java example, a while loop is used to repeatedly execute a code block as long as the condition **count < 5** is true. The program calculates the sum of the numbers from 0 to 4 by adding each number to the variable **sum** in each iteration. The control flow of the while loop ensures that the code block is executed repeatedly until the condition becomes false.

The output of the program is "Sum: 10", indicating the final sum of the numbers. The control flow of the while loop allows for the iterative execution of the code block until the condition is no longer satisfied.

These examples demonstrate how control flow structures, such as if-else statements, for loops, and while loops, are used to control the flow of program execution. They allow programs to make decisions, iterate over data, and execute specific code blocks based on conditions, enabling dynamic and adaptable behavior in the program.

By combining conditional statements and loops, programmers can create complex control flows within their programs. They can control the execution order, handle different scenarios, and ensure that the program behaves as intended in various situations.

Understanding control flow is essential for writing efficient and effective programs. It allows programmers to create logic that responds dynamically to input, makes decisions based on conditions, and performs repetitive tasks when needed. By mastering control flow, programmers can create robust and adaptable software applications.

4.3.2 Branching

Branching plays a crucial role in determining the program flow by allowing different paths of execution based on specific conditions. It enables programmers to handle different scenarios, make decisions, and control the behavior of their programs. This section provides an overview of branching, explains its role in program flow, discusses handling branching scenarios using conditional statements and looping structures, and explores the impact of branching on program efficiency and logic.

Overview of Branching and its Role in Determining Program Flow:

Branching refers to the ability of a program to follow different paths of execution based on specific conditions or decisions. It allows programmers to create dynamic and adaptive behaviors in their programs, responding to varying input or circumstances. By utilizing branching, programs can take different actions, execute specific code blocks, and customize their behavior based on conditions and user interactions.

Branching provides a way to handle different scenarios and make decisions within the program flow. It enables the program to evaluate conditions, such as comparing values, checking for certain states, or validating user input, and execute different sets of instructions accordingly. This flexibility allows programmers to create software applications that respond intelligently to different situations, enhancing user experience and program functionality.

Handling Different Branching Scenarios using Conditional Statements and Looping Structures:

Conditional statements, such as if-else statements and switch statements, are essential tools for handling branching scenarios. They evaluate conditions and determine the appropriate code block to execute based on the evaluation result.

If-else statements allow programmers to perform branching based on a single condition. They execute one block of code if the condition is true and another block if the condition is false. This provides a binary branching capability.

Example of Branching using Conditional Statements in python:

```
age = 25
if age >= 18:
print("You are an adult.")
else:
print("You are not an adult.")
# Output: "You are an adult."
```

In this example, the program evaluates the condition **age >= 18**. If the condition is true, it executes the code block under the **if** statement and prints "You are an adult." Otherwise, if the condition is false, it executes the code block under the **else** statement and prints "You are not an adult." The branching occurs based on the value of **age**.

Switch statements are useful when there are multiple possible branches based on a single variable or expression. They allow programmers to specify different cases and their corresponding code blocks, executing the code block associated with the matching case.

Example of Branching using Switch Statement in java:

```
int day = 3;
String dayName;
switch (day) {
case 1:
dayName = "Monday";
break;
case 2:
dayName = "Tuesday";
break;
case 3:
dayName = "Wednesday";
break;
default:
```

```
dayName = "Unknown";
break;
}
System.out.println("Today is " + dayName);
// Output: "Today is Wednesday"
```

In this example, the program evaluates the value of the variable **day** using a switch statement. Depending on the value of **day**, it assigns the corresponding day name to the variable **dayName**. In this case, since **day** is 3, the code block under the **case 3** label is executed, assigning "Wednesday" to **dayName**.

Looping structures, such as for loops, while loops, and do-while loops, also contribute to branching scenarios. By controlling the loop condition or using loop control statements like break and continue, programmers can create branching within loops and customize the program flow based on specific conditions.

Understanding the Impact of Branching on Program Efficiency and Logic:

Branching can impact both program efficiency and logic. Excessive branching or nested branching structures can make the program more complex and harder to maintain. It is important to carefully design and optimize the branching logic to ensure efficient execution and readability of the code.

Unoptimized branching structures may introduce unnecessary computational overhead or result in redundant code execution. It is crucial to consider the complexity and frequency of branching scenarios to maintain a balance between program flexibility and efficiency.

Moreover, branching logic should be logically sound and accurately reflect the intended program behavior. Careful consideration should be given to handle all possible scenarios and edge cases, ensuring that the program behaves as expected.

By effectively handling branching scenarios using conditional statements and looping structures, programmers can create programs that make decisions, respond to conditions, and execute specific code paths. Understanding the impact of branching on program efficiency and logic enables programmers to design efficient, maintainable, and logically consistent software applications.

Part II: Problem Solving and Algorithm Design

Chapter 5: Problem-Solving Techniques

5.1 Problem Analysis and Decomposition

5.1.1 Importance of Problem Analysis in Programming

Recognizing the Importance of Problem Analysis in Programming: In the software development process, problem analysis plays a pivotal role in ensuring successful problem-solving and algorithm design. Before developers start coding, they must embark on a journey of understanding the problem space, the intricacies of the requirements, and the objectives to be achieved. This preliminary step of problem analysis is akin to laying a strong foundation for a building; without it, the entire structure is at risk of collapse.

Thoroughly Understanding the Problem Requirements, Constraints, and Objectives: Problem analysis entails delving deep into the problem's requirements and constraints. Developers need to gather information about what the problem is trying to accomplish and what limitations it has. This involves interacting with stakeholders, end-users, and domain experts to obtain a comprehensive understanding of the problem's context. It also includes analyzing any available documentation, such as specifications or project requirements, to grasp the finer details.

By leaving no stone unturned, developers can avoid ambiguous assumptions and prevent any discrepancies between what the problem truly requires and what the solution might initially propose.

With a clear understanding of the problem's scope, developers can focus their efforts on crafting an accurate and appropriate solution.

Avoiding Unnecessary Detours and Focus on the Actual Problem at Hand: When faced with a complex problem, developers might be tempted to jump into coding right away. However, this premature coding can lead to a scattered approach, wasting time and effort on implementing solutions that miss the mark. Problem analysis acts as a compass, guiding developers through the right path by identifying the core issues to address.

Through problem analysis, developers can break down the problem into its constituent components, pinpoint the essential features, and identify the critical steps required for solving it effectively. This structured approach keeps the development process on track, ensuring that developers stay focused on addressing the actual problem at hand and avoid unnecessary detours.

Incorporating problem analysis as the first step in the software development process is akin to putting on the detective's hat. Developers engage in investigation and inquiry, seeking to understand the problem's intricacies and uncovering its requirements and constraints. Armed with this valuable knowledge, developers are better equipped to design appropriate and efficient solutions that precisely meet the problem's needs. The investment in problem analysis sets the stage for a smoother development journey, resulting in higher-quality software solutions that resonate with end-users and stakeholders alike.

Understanding How Thorough Problem Analysis Leads to Better Solutions: Thorough problem analysis offers several benefits that directly contribute to the quality and effectiveness of the final solution:

1. Accurate Problem Understanding: Problem analysis helps in gaining a clear and comprehensive understanding of the

problem, its intricacies, and its context. This clarity allows developers to avoid misunderstandings and focus on delivering a solution that precisely meets the intended requirements.

2. Effective Solution Design: A well-analyzed problem guides developers in selecting the most suitable approach or algorithm for solving the problem. It enables them to identify the key components and steps required to achieve the desired outcome efficiently.
3. Identifying Potential Challenges: During problem analysis, developers can foresee potential challenges or obstacles that might arise during the solution implementation. By anticipating these issues, they can plan ahead and devise appropriate strategies to address them effectively.
4. Optimized Resource Utilization: Thorough problem analysis helps developers understand the resource requirements and constraints associated with the problem. This understanding enables them to optimize the utilization of computational resources, memory, and processing time.
5. Minimizing Errors: When developers have a clear understanding of the problem, they are less likely to make mistakes during the coding and implementation phase. This reduces the need for frequent revisions and debugging, saving valuable time and effort.
6. Improved User Experience: A well-analyzed problem ensures that the solution aligns closely with the end-users' needs and expectations. This leads to a more satisfying user experience and increases the solution's overall usefulness.

In conclusion, problem analysis is a crucial step in the problem-solving process. It provides developers with valuable insights and direction, guiding them toward designing effective and efficient solutions. By recognizing the importance of problem analysis and investing time and effort in this phase, developers can significantly enhance the quality and success of their software solutions.

5.1.2 Breaking Down Complex Problems

Breaking down complex problems into smaller, manageable components is a crucial skill that empowers developers to tackle intricate challenges effectively. Complex problems can be overwhelming, but by employing appropriate techniques, developers can simplify the problem-solving process and develop solutions with greater clarity and efficiency.

Techniques for Breaking Down Complex Problems into Smaller, Manageable Components:

Divide and Conquer:

The "Divide and Conquer" technique is a powerful problem-solving approach that has been widely used in various fields, including computer science, mathematics, and engineering. It involves breaking down a complex problem into smaller, more manageable subproblems, solving them independently, and then combining their solutions to obtain the solution to the original problem. This approach offers several advantages and is particularly useful when dealing with intricate and large-scale problems.

Breaking Down the Problem: The first step in the "Divide and Conquer" technique is to break down the complex problem into smaller, more understandable subproblems. This decomposition is often guided by identifying natural divisions or breaking points in the problem. Each subproblem should be a self-contained unit that can be solved independently.

Solving Subproblems Independently: Once the problem is divided into subproblems, developers can focus on solving each subproblem individually. This allows them to concentrate on a specific aspect of the problem without being overwhelmed by its complexity. Solving smaller subproblems is generally easier and more straightforward than tackling the entire problem at once.

Combining Subproblem Solutions: After solving the subproblems, developers combine their solutions to obtain the overall solution to the original problem. The combination process is often based on merging or integrating the solutions in a way that addresses the entire problem cohesively.

Advantages of the "Divide and Conquer" Technique:

Improved Problem Manageability: Breaking down the problem into smaller parts makes it more manageable and easier to understand. This approach allows developers to work on one subproblem at a time, which can significantly simplify the development process.

Enhanced Code Modularity: Solving subproblems independently encourages the creation of modular code. Each subproblem can be treated as a separate module, which makes the code easier to maintain, test, and reuse.

Parallel Processing: In certain cases, subproblems can be solved concurrently, enabling developers to take advantage of parallel processing and reduce the overall solution time.

Optimal Solutions for Smaller Instances: For some problems, finding the optimal solution for smaller instances may be easier and faster than finding the solution for the entire problem. By breaking down the problem, developers can apply specialized algorithms for smaller instances to improve efficiency.

Common Applications:

Sorting Algorithms: Many efficient sorting algorithms, such as Merge Sort and Quick Sort, utilize the "Divide and Conquer" technique to sort elements efficiently.

Searching Algorithms: Algorithms like Binary Search apply the "Divide and Conquer" approach to find elements in a sorted list rapidly.

Large-Scale Data Processing: When dealing with massive datasets, "Divide and Conquer" can be employed to process data in parallel, reducing computation time.

In conclusion, the "Divide and Conquer" technique is a fundamental problem-solving approach that leverages the power of decomposition to tackle complex problems effectively. By dividing a problem into smaller subproblems, solving them independently, and then combining their solutions, developers can create efficient, modular, and scalable solutions that address intricate challenges with clarity and effectiveness.

Abstraction:

Abstraction is a powerful problem-solving technique that allows developers to simplify complex problems by focusing on essential concepts and high-level ideas while ignoring irrelevant details. By abstracting away complexities, developers create a more manageable and clear representation of the problem, making it easier to reason about and develop solutions.

Identifying Core Concepts: The first step in abstraction is to identify the fundamental concepts and elements that are crucial to understanding the problem. These core concepts represent the essential aspects of the problem and are necessary for formulating a solution.

Suppressing Irrelevant Details: Abstraction involves intentionally ignoring or suppressing the irrelevant details that do not directly contribute to the problem's solution. This process helps to reduce the problem's complexity and allows developers to focus on the most critical elements.

Creating a Simplified View: By abstracting away complexities and focusing on core concepts, developers create a simplified view of the problem. This simplified representation provides a clear and high-level understanding of the problem's structure and requirements.

Easier Reasoning and Solution Development: With a simplified view of the problem, developers can reason about the problem more easily and develop solutions more effectively. They can concentrate on the essential aspects of the problem without getting bogged down by unnecessary intricacies.

Common Applications:

Data Modeling: In database design, abstraction is used to create abstract data models that focus on the most critical data entities and their relationships, ignoring implementation details.

Object-Oriented Programming: Abstraction is a fundamental concept in object-oriented programming, where classes and interfaces represent abstract concepts, and specific implementations provide the details.

Algorithm Design: When designing algorithms, developers often abstract the problem by considering its key characteristics, such as input and output requirements, while ignoring implementation-specific details.

Advantages of Abstraction:

Improved Problem Understanding: Abstraction allows developers to understand the problem at a higher level, making it easier to devise an appropriate solution.

Increased Modularity: By focusing on essential concepts, developers can create modular solutions that are easier to maintain and extend.

Reusability: Abstraction often leads to reusable components and solutions that can be applied to similar problems in the future.

In conclusion, abstraction is a valuable problem-solving technique that helps developers manage the complexity of complex problems. By identifying core concepts, suppressing irrelevant details, and creating a simplified view, developers can gain a clearer understanding of the problem and develop more effective and efficient solutions. Abstraction is a crucial skill that empowers developers to tackle intricate challenges with clarity and focus, leading to better software design and development.

Stepwise Refinement:

Stepwise refinement is a systematic problem-solving approach that involves gradually adding more details and refining a solution step by step. Developers start with a basic outline or rough sketch of the solution and iteratively enhance it, adding more specifics and complexities until the full and complete solution emerges. This method allows developers to build upon previously established components, ensuring a cohesive, well-structured, and efficient final solution.

Starting with a Basic Outline: The process begins by outlining the solution at a high level. This initial outline provides a broad overview of the problem and how it might be approached. It may consist of general steps or major components of the solution without delving into specific details.

Iteratively Adding Details: In each iteration, developers gradually add more details to the solution. They break down the high-level steps or components into smaller, more manageable tasks. Each refinement step provides a more detailed understanding of the problem and helps define how each task contributes to the overall solution.

Continuously Improving the Solution: As developers continue the refinement process, they refine the solution's details further, making it more concrete and comprehensive. This iterative improvement allows for a thorough examination of each component, ensuring that nothing is overlooked or missed.

Building on Previously Established Components: The stepwise refinement approach emphasizes building upon previously established components. As each refinement step progresses, developers can take advantage of the work done in earlier stages, ensuring that the solution remains coherent and well-integrated.

Ensuring Cohesive and Well-Structured Solutions: The iterative nature of stepwise refinement ensures that developers thoroughly analyze and design each aspect of the solution. This method helps avoid rushing into a particular approach without fully understanding its implications. By considering various factors and refining the solution incrementally, the final result is more likely to be cohesive, robust, and well-structured.

Common Applications:

Software Design: Stepwise refinement is frequently used during the software design phase, where developers progressively add details to the overall design, from high-level architecture to detailed component design.

Algorithm Development: When designing algorithms, developers apply stepwise refinement to break down complex problem-solving procedures into smaller and more manageable steps.

Planning and Decision Making: The stepwise refinement approach is also used in various decision-making processes, where complex decisions are broken down into smaller, more manageable steps to arrive at the best solution.

Advantages of Stepwise Refinement:

Gradual Understanding: Stepwise refinement allows developers to understand the problem and the solution's design in a gradual and controlled manner.

Flexibility: The iterative nature of the approach allows developers to adjust the solution as new insights emerge, ensuring that the final solution is flexible and adaptable.

Reduced Complexity: By breaking down the problem into smaller steps, stepwise refinement simplifies the overall problem-solving process, making it easier to manage.

In conclusion, stepwise refinement is a valuable problem-solving technique that promotes a systematic and iterative approach to solution development. By starting with a basic outline and progressively adding more details, developers can create well-structured and cohesive solutions. This method encourages thoughtful analysis and thoughtful design, leading to efficient and effective problem-solving outcomes.

Dividing the Problem into Subproblems for Easier Understanding and Solution Development: Complex problems often consist of interconnected parts that influence each other's behavior. By dividing the problem into smaller subproblems, developers can better understand each component's behavior and its impact on the overall solution. Subproblems are often more straightforward to comprehend, and solving them individually becomes more manageable.

Moreover, breaking the problem into subproblems enhances code modularity. Developers can develop and test individual subproblems independently, making it easier to identify and fix issues. Additionally, modular code is reusable and adaptable, enabling developers to apply the same subproblems in other contexts or extend the solution to address related challenges.

Overall, breaking down complex problems is a powerful problem-solving strategy that simplifies the development process and yields more effective solutions. Through techniques like divide and conquer, abstraction, and stepwise refinement, developers can manage the intricacies of complex problems and create scalable, maintainable, and optimized solutions. By mastering this skill, developers can approach any challenging problem with confidence and deliver robust software solutions that meet the needs of their user

5.1.3 Identifying Inputs, Outputs, and Constraints

Identifying Inputs Required for the Problem-Solving Process

The first step in problem analysis is to determine the necessary inputs required to initiate the problem-solving process. Inputs are the data, variables, or information that the solution relies on to produce the desired output. These inputs can come from various sources, such as user inputs, external data files, or pre-existing data structures.

By identifying the inputs, developers can understand what information is needed to drive the solution. This allows them to plan for data acquisition, validation, and processing during the implementation phase. Accurate identification of inputs ensures that the solution will have the necessary information to perform its tasks effectively. In the problem-solving process, identifying the necessary inputs is a crucial step that lays the foundation for developing an effective solution. Inputs are the data, variables, or information that the solution relies on to perform computations, make decisions, and produce the desired output. Accurate identification of inputs ensures that the solution has all the necessary information to carry out its tasks effectively and successfully.

1. **Sources of Inputs:**

- **User Inputs: In many cases, the solution requires data provided directly by the user. This can include text inputs, numerical values, options selected from a menu, or other forms of user interaction.**
- **External Data Files: Some problems involve processing data stored in external files, such as CSV, JSON, XML, or database files. These files contain the necessary data that the solution needs to analyze and manipulate.**
- **Pre-existing Data Structures: In certain situations, the solution may work with pre-existing data structures, such as arrays, lists, dictionaries, or databases, which already contain relevant information.**

2. **Importance of Accurate Identification:** Accurate identification of inputs is vital as it ensures that the solution has access to all the relevant data it needs to perform its tasks correctly. Missing or incorrect inputs can lead to inaccurate results, errors, or even failure of the solution.
3. **Planning for Data Acquisition and Validation:** Once the inputs are identified, developers can plan for acquiring the required data during the implementation phase. This may involve designing user interfaces to gather user inputs, reading data from external files, or initializing data structures with appropriate values.

Additionally, input data validation is essential to ensure that the solution handles unexpected or invalid inputs gracefully. Validating inputs helps prevent potential errors and enhances the solution's robustness.

1. **Data Processing and Utilization:** With the inputs identified and acquired, the solution can proceed with processing and utilizing the data to achieve its objectives. This may involve performing calculations, applying algorithms, or making decisions based on the input data.

Identifying inputs is not a one-time task; it may require iterative refinement during the problem-solving process. As developers gain a deeper understanding of the problem and the solution's requirements, they may discover additional inputs that need to be considered.

In conclusion, accurately identifying inputs is a critical step in the problem-solving process. By understanding what information, the solution requires and planning for data acquisition and validation, developers can ensure that the solution has the necessary resources to perform its tasks effectively. This sets the stage for successful implementation and a well-functioning solution that produces the desired output.

Defining the Expected Outputs or Desired Results of the Solution

Alongside identifying inputs, problem analysis involves defining the expected outputs or desired results that the solution should produce. Outputs represent the information or results that the solution generates based on the provided inputs and the problem's requirements.

Defining clear and specific outputs is essential as it provides a clear target for the solution's success. Developers can validate the correctness of the solution by comparing its actual output with the expected output. This step ensures that the solution meets the problem's objectives and produces the intended results. In the problem-solving process, defining the expected outputs or desired results is a crucial step that defines the purpose and success criteria of the solution. Outputs represent the information, data, or outcomes that the solution is expected to produce based on the provided inputs and the problem's requirements.

1. **Purpose of Defining Outputs:**
    - **Clear Target for Success: By defining specific and clear outputs, developers set a target for the solution's success. The outputs represent the goals the solution aims to achieve, and their clarity ensures that the solution's objectives are well-defined.**
    - **Verification of Correctness: The defined outputs serve as a reference against which developers can verify the correctness of the solution. During implementation and testing, developers compare the actual output generated by the solution with the expected output to ensure that the solution meets the intended requirements.**
2. **Specificity of Outputs:**
    - **Unambiguous and Quantifiable: To be effective, the defined outputs must be unambiguous and quantifiable. They should be expressed in a way that leaves no room for interpretation, and their measurement or evaluation should be based on concrete criteria.**
    - **Covering All Aspects: The outputs should encompass all the relevant aspects of the problem that need to be addressed. They should reflect the solution's comprehensive**

performance, addressing all key aspects of the problem domain.

3. Validating the Solution:
    - Testing and Validation: By comparing the actual output with the expected output, developers can validate the solution's correctness. This validation process is a critical step in ensuring that the solution functions as intended and meets the problem's objectives.
    - Iterative Refinement: The process of defining and validating outputs may require iterative refinement during the problem-solving process. As developers gain more insights and understanding of the problem, they may refine the expected outputs to better align with the solution's objectives.
4. Communication with Stakeholders:
    - Alignment with Stakeholder Expectations: Clearly defined outputs facilitate effective communication with stakeholders. Stakeholders can understand what results to expect from the solution and evaluate whether the proposed solution aligns with their requirements and expectations.
    - Managing Expectations: Well-defined outputs help manage stakeholders' expectations regarding the solution's capabilities and limitations. If the outputs are realistic and achievable, it sets a foundation for successful collaboration between developers and stakeholders.

In conclusion, defining the expected outputs or desired results of the solution is a vital aspect of problem analysis. Clear and specific outputs provide a target for the solution's success and serve as a basis for validating the correctness of the implementation. By aligning the solution's objectives with the defined outputs, developers can ensure that the solution meets the problem's requirements and produces the intended results, ultimately leading to a successful and effective problem-solving outcome.

Recognizing Any Constraints or Limitations That Need to Be Considered

In problem analysis, it is essential to recognize any constraints or limitations that may impact the solution's design or implementation. Constraints can arise from various sources, such as resource limitations (e.g., time, memory, computational power), technical limitations, or specific requirements imposed by the problem domain or stakeholders.

Understanding constraints is critical to avoid overengineering or developing solutions that are impractical to implement. By recognizing and considering constraints, developers can make informed decisions and design solutions that are feasible within the given limitations. In the problem-solving process, recognizing constraints and limitations is a crucial step that helps developers understand the boundaries and restrictions within which the solution must operate. Constraints can arise from various sources, including resource limitations, technical considerations, legal or ethical requirements, and specific expectations from stakeholders or the problem domain.

1. **Types of Constraints:**
    - **Resource Limitations: Constraints related to**

resources include limitations on time, memory, computational power, storage, or other physical resources. Developers need to consider these constraints to ensure that the solution is efficient and can operate within the available resources.

- Technical Limitations: Technical constraints may be related to the platform, programming language, hardware, or software used to implement the solution. Understanding these limitations is essential for developing a technically feasible solution.
- Legal and Ethical Requirements: Some problems may have legal or ethical constraints that the solution must adhere to. Compliance with laws, regulations, and ethical principles is crucial in developing responsible and socially acceptable solutions.
- Stakeholder Expectations: Constraints can also arise from specific requirements or expectations from stakeholders. These may include functional requirements, user interface preferences, security considerations, or specific deliverables that the solution must meet.

2. Impact on Solution Design:
    - Feasibility: Recognizing constraints is essential to assess the feasibility of the solution. Overlooking constraints may lead to overengineering or proposing solutions that are impractical or impossible to implement.
    - Decision Making: Understanding constraints allows developers to make informed decisions

during the solution design phase. Constraints may influence the choice of algorithms, data structures, or design patterns.
- Scope Management: Identifying constraints helps manage the scope of the solution. Developers can prioritize features and functionalities that align with the constraints and set realistic expectations for the solution's capabilities.

3. Iterative Consideration:
    - Continuous Reevaluation: Constraints may evolve over time or become apparent as the problem-solving process progresses. Thus, developers should continuously reevaluate and consider constraints throughout the development cycle.
    - Trade-offs: In some cases, addressing one constraint may require sacrificing or adjusting other aspects of the solution. Understanding trade-offs is essential in making balanced decisions.
4. Communication with Stakeholders:
    - Transparent Communication: Recognizing constraints and openly communicating them with stakeholders fosters transparency and realistic expectations. This helps manage stakeholders' expectations and avoids potential conflicts in later stages.
    - Collaborative Approach: Involving stakeholders in the constraint recognition process encourages collaboration and allows stakeholders to provide valuable insights and

requirements.

In conclusion, recognizing constraints and limitations is a critical aspect of problem analysis and solution design. By understanding the boundaries and restrictions, developers can develop feasible and effective solutions that align with the problem's requirements and stakeholders' expectations. Embracing constraints with a proactive and adaptive approach leads to well-informed decision-making and ultimately results in successful problem-solving outcomes.

Overall, identifying inputs, defining outputs, and recognizing constraints are essential steps in problem analysis. This process provides developers with a comprehensive understanding of the problem's data requirements, solution goals, and potential challenges. By gaining this insight, developers can plan and design solutions that are well-aligned with the problem's needs and constraints, ultimately leading to successful and effective problem-solving outcomes.

5.1.4 Problem Decomposition Techniques

Problem decomposition is the process of breaking down a complex problem into smaller, more manageable components or subproblems. Effectively decomposing problems allows developers to tackle challenging tasks systematically and facilitates the design of efficient and maintainable solutions. There are various problem decomposition techniques that developers can apply to simplify problem-solving and identify common patterns within larger problems.

1. **Strategies for Decomposing Problems Effectively:**
    - **Top-Down Approach: In the top-down approach, developers start by understanding**

the high-level problem and then progressively break it down into smaller subproblems. This approach allows developers to focus on the big picture and gradually refine the solution by addressing individual components.

- Bottom-Up Approach: In the bottom-up approach, developers start by solving individual subproblems and then combine them to solve the larger problem. This approach is useful when the solution to subproblems can be independently determined and later integrated into the overall solution.
- Divide and Conquer: The divide and conquer technique involves breaking down a complex problem into smaller subproblems that are easier to solve independently. Each subproblem's solution is then combined to form the solution to the original problem. This technique promotes modularity and efficiency in problem-solving.

2. Identifying Common Patterns or Recurring Subproblems:
    - Pattern Recognition: By analyzing different problem instances and solutions, developers can recognize common patterns or recurring subproblems within larger problems. Identifying patterns can lead to the development of reusable algorithms and methodologies.
    - Utilizing Libraries and Frameworks: In some cases, developers can leverage existing libraries or frameworks that provide solutions to

common subproblems. Using well-established solutions can save time and effort in implementing complex functionalities.

3. Applying Decomposition Techniques:
   - Abstraction: Abstraction involves identifying essential concepts and suppressing irrelevant details in a problem. By abstracting away complexities, developers can create a simplified view of the problem, making it easier to reason about and solve.
   - Stepwise Refinement: Stepwise refinement is a process of gradually adding more details and refining the solution step by step. Developers start with a basic outline and iteratively enhance it, adding more specifics until the complete solution emerges.
   - Divide and Conquer: As mentioned earlier, divide and conquer involves breaking down a complex problem into smaller subproblems and solving them independently. This approach simplifies problem-solving by focusing on smaller, manageable parts.
4. Benefits of Problem Decomposition:
   - Improved Problem Understanding: Decomposing a problem allows developers to understand each component in isolation, leading to a better overall understanding of the problem and its intricacies.
   - Modular and Maintainable Code: Problem decomposition promotes modularity, making the solution easier to maintain, extend, and debug. Each subproblem can be implemented

and tested separately before integration.

- **Reusability: By recognizing common patterns and recurring subproblems, developers can create reusable algorithms and components that can be applied to similar problem instances.**

In conclusion, problem decomposition techniques are valuable tools that enable developers to break down complex problems into manageable parts. By applying strategies like top-down or bottom-up approaches and leveraging techniques such as divide and conquer, abstraction, and stepwise refinement, developers can simplify problem-solving, promote code reusability, and design efficient and maintainable solutions. Identifying common patterns and recurring subproblems within larger problems enhances the developer's problem-solving capabilities and leads to effective and elegant solutions.

5.2 Algorithm Design Methodologies

5.2.1 Overview of Algorithm Design Methodologies

Algorithm design methodologies play a fundamental role in computer science and programming as they provide systematic approaches to creating efficient and effective algorithms. An algorithm is a step-by-step procedure used to solve a specific problem or perform a particular computation. Designing algorithms is a critical skill for developers, as the efficiency and correctness of algorithms significantly impact the overall performance of software applications.

Understanding the Significance of Algorithm Design Methodologies:

- Efficient Problem Solving: Algorithm design methodologies aim to develop algorithms that solve problems efficiently in terms of time and space complexity. Efficient algorithms lead to faster execution and better utilization of system resources.
- Scalability: Scalability is crucial for algorithms to handle larger input sizes without a significant decrease in performance. Proper algorithm design ensures that solutions can scale gracefully to meet the demands of growing data.
- Reusability: Well-designed algorithms are often reusable, meaning they can be applied to similar problems in various contexts. This reusability saves time and effort, promoting code optimization and maintainability.
- Maintainability: Algorithms developed using sound methodologies are easier to understand and maintain. Clear design principles lead to code that is less error-prone and more straightforward to modify or extend.
- Correctness and Reliability: Rigorous algorithm design methodologies help ensure that algorithms produce the correct results for all possible inputs and edge cases. This reliability is critical in safety-critical systems and applications.

Exploring Different Approaches and Strategies for Designing Algorithms:

- Brute Force: Brute force algorithms exhaustively try all possible solutions to a problem, typically by iterating through all possible combinations. While straightforward, this approach can be inefficient for large input sizes.

- Greedy Algorithms: Greedy algorithms make locally optimal choices at each step with the hope of finding a global optimum. They do not always guarantee the best solution, but they can be efficient and provide reasonable approximations.
- Divide and Conquer: As mentioned earlier, divide and conquer involves breaking down a complex problem into smaller subproblems that can be solved independently. The subproblem solutions are then combined to form the solution to the original problem.
- Dynamic Programming: Dynamic programming is an optimization technique used to solve problems with overlapping subproblems. It breaks down the problem into smaller overlapping subproblems and stores their solutions to avoid redundant computations.
- Backtracking: Backtracking is a systematic way of searching for solutions to problems, exploring all possible paths until a solution is found or proven impossible. It is commonly used in problems with multiple choices or constraints.
- Randomized Algorithms: Randomized algorithms use randomization to make choices during their execution. They often provide approximate solutions but are useful in scenarios where exact solutions are challenging or computationally expensive.
- Heuristic Methods: Heuristic algorithms are practical approaches that aim to find good solutions in a reasonable time. They do not guarantee optimality but are useful for problems where finding an optimal solution is infeasible.

In conclusion, algorithm design methodologies are essential for creating efficient, correct, and maintainable solutions to various computational problems. By understanding the significance of algorithm design and exploring different approaches and strategies, developers can select the most appropriate methods to tackle specific problems efficiently. Algorithm design is a dynamic and creative process, where developers continuously evaluate and refine their solutions to meet the ever-changing demands of modern computing.

5.2.2 Sequential, Selection, and Iteration

In algorithm design, sequential, selection, and iteration are fundamental constructs that govern the flow and logic of algorithms. These constructs play a crucial role in controlling the order of execution and making decisions based on specific conditions. Understanding these constructs is essential for creating effective and well-structured algorithms to solve various computational problems.

1. Sequential:
    - Sequential construct represents the default flow of an algorithm, where instructions are executed in a sequential order, one after the other. Each step follows the previous one, and the algorithm progresses linearly.
    - In a sequential construct, actions are performed in the order they appear in the algorithm, without any conditional checks or repetitions.
    - This construct is the simplest and most straightforward way to express algorithms, and it is suitable for tasks that require a linear sequence of actions without any branching or looping.
2. Selection:
    - Selection, also known as conditional statements,

introduces decision-making into the algorithm. It allows the algorithm to choose between alternative paths based on specific conditions.
   - Common selection constructs include if statements, if-else statements, and switch statements (in some programming languages). These statements evaluate a condition and execute different blocks of code depending on whether the condition is true or false.
   - Selection constructs enable the algorithm to make choices and adapt its behavior based on the inputs or intermediate results.
3. Iteration:
   - Iteration, also known as looping, allows the algorithm to repeat a set of instructions multiple times until a certain condition is met or a specified number of iterations is reached.
   - Common iteration constructs include for loops, while loops, and do-while loops. These loops enable the algorithm to execute a block of code repeatedly, allowing efficient handling of repetitive tasks.
   - Iteration constructs are particularly useful when dealing with collections of data or when a task requires repetitive calculations or operations.

How These Constructs Contribute to the Flow and Logic of an Algorithm:

- Combining Constructs: Algorithms often combine sequential, selection, and iteration constructs to create complex and versatile solutions. By incorporating conditional statements and loops, algorithms can adapt to different situations and efficiently process varying inputs.

- Controlling Flow: These constructs provide mechanisms to control the flow of the algorithm. Selection statements allow the algorithm to make choices and decide which path to follow, while iteration statements control how many times a particular block of code is executed.
- Modularity: Using these constructs helps create modular algorithms, where different parts of the algorithm perform distinct tasks. This modularity enhances code readability, maintainability, and reusability.
- Algorithm Efficiency: Proper use of selection and iteration constructs can significantly impact the efficiency of an algorithm. Making optimal choices and reducing unnecessary repetitions contribute to improved algorithm performance.
- Handling Complexity: Sequential, selection, and iteration constructs provide the necessary tools to handle complex problem-solving scenarios. By breaking down tasks into smaller manageable components, developers can build sophisticated algorithms to address a wide range of challenges.

In conclusion, sequential, selection, and iteration are essential constructs in algorithm design that dictate the order of execution and decision-making within algorithms. These constructs contribute to the flow and logic of the algorithm, enabling it to adapt to different scenarios, efficiently process data, and perform repetitive tasks. By mastering these fundamental constructs, developers can design efficient, flexible, and robust algorithms to solve diverse computational problems.

5.2.3 Top-Down and Bottom-Up Approaches

Top-down and bottom-up approaches are two distinct methodologies used in algorithm design to solve problems by breaking them down into smaller components. Both approaches have their strengths and weaknesses, and their suitability depends on the nature of the problem and the preferences of the developers.

1. **Top-Down Approach:**
    - **Top-down approach, also known as the "stepwise refinement" method, begins by understanding the high-level problem and gradually breaking it down into smaller subproblems.**
    - **Developers start with a broad overview of the problem and then iteratively refine the solution by focusing on smaller components.**
    - **This approach encourages developers to think in terms of the problem's structure and main functionalities before delving into implementation details.**
    - **Advantages:**
        - High-Level Design: The top-down approach emphasizes high-level design, ensuring a clear understanding of the problem's requirements and objectives from the start.
        - Modular Development: Breaking the problem into smaller modules allows for better organization and reusability of code components.
        - Abstraction: Developers can focus on the problem's key aspects while abstracting

away implementation details, which helps manage complexity.

- **Disadvantages:**
  - Delayed Details: The top-down approach may postpone addressing specific implementation details until later stages, which could lead to potential design changes.
  - Less Efficient for Simple Problems: For straightforward problems with limited complexity, the top-down approach might introduce unnecessary overhead.
- **Use Cases:**
  - Complex Problems: The top-down approach is well-suited for tackling complex problems with multiple layers of functionality and intricate interactions.
  - Large Projects: For large-scale projects, the top-down approach facilitates better organization and modular development.

2. **Bottom-Up Approach:**
   - **Bottom-up approach begins by solving individual subproblems and then combines them to form the solution to the overall problem.**
   - **Developers start by identifying smaller components that can be solved independently and incrementally build upon them to address the complete problem.**
   - **This approach encourages developers to focus on the details and work their way up to the larger solution.**

- **Advantages:**
    - Focus on Specifics: The bottom-up approach enables developers to concentrate on specific components and thoroughly address their functionalities.
    - Incremental Progress: Solving smaller subproblems first allows for incremental progress, making it easier to track development and verify correctness.
    - Optimal Solutions: By optimizing individual components, the bottom-up approach can lead to efficient overall solutions.
- **Disadvantages:**
    - Integration Challenges: Integrating individual components into a cohesive whole may pose challenges, especially if dependencies are not well-managed.
    - Overall Design Oversight: The bottom-up approach might lead to overlooking the big picture and potentially missing out on more efficient high-level solutions.
- **Use Cases:**
    - Individual Components: The bottom-up approach is suitable when the problem can be broken down into discrete components with clear functionality.
    - Existing Codebases: When extending existing codebases, the bottom-up approach can be more straightforward, focusing on specific enhancements.

In conclusion, both the top-down and bottom-up approaches have their merits and are valuable tools in algorithm design. The top-down approach emphasizes high-level design and modular development, making it suitable for complex problems and large projects. On the other hand, the bottom-up approach focuses on specific components and incremental progress, making it suitable for problems with well-defined subproblems or when extending existing codebases. Developers can choose the most appropriate approach based on the problem's nature, project requirements, and their preferred problem-solving style.

5.2.4 Stepwise Refinement and Modularization

Stepwise refinement and modularization are essential concepts in algorithm development that contribute to creating clear, organized, and maintainable code. These approaches promote systematic problem-solving and efficient code design, making it easier for developers to understand, modify, and extend algorithms.

1. **Stepwise Refinement:**
    - **Stepwise refinement is a systematic approach to algorithm development that involves starting with a basic outline or rough sketch of the solution and iteratively adding more details until the full solution emerges.**
    - **Developers begin by breaking down the problem into smaller, manageable steps or subtasks. Each step is then refined further by adding more specific instructions or details.**
    - **This iterative process continues until the algorithm's complete solution is achieved, with each refinement step bringing the algorithm closer to its final implementation.**

- **Stepwise refinement enables developers to manage the complexity of a problem by focusing on one aspect at a time, making the development process more organized and structured.**
- **Advantages:**
  - Clear Development Path: Stepwise refinement provides a clear development path, allowing developers to proceed systematically and logically.
  - Debugging and Validation: Refining the algorithm step by step facilitates the detection and resolution of errors or inconsistencies in small, manageable portions.
  - Collaboration: Stepwise refinement promotes teamwork, as different team members can work on refining specific components independently.
- **Disadvantages:**
  - Potential Overdesign: Excessive iterations may lead to overdesign, especially if developers continually refine details that do not significantly impact the solution's efficiency.
  - Time-Consuming: Iteratively refining each step can be time-consuming, especially for complex algorithms.
- **Use Cases:**
  - Complex Algorithms: Stepwise refinement is particularly useful when tackling complex problems, as it allows

developers to break them down into comprehensible parts.

2. **Modularization:**
    - **Modularization involves dividing an algorithm or codebase into separate, independent modules or functions, each responsible for specific tasks or functionalities.**
    - **Modules encapsulate related functionalities, making it easier to understand, maintain, and reuse code. Each module can be developed and tested independently.**
    - **By creating cohesive and loosely coupled modules, modularization promotes code reusability, allowing developers to leverage existing components in other parts of the program.**
    - **Advantages:**
        - Reusability: Modularization leads to reusable code, as well-defined modules can be easily integrated into other projects or utilized multiple times within the same project.
        - Maintainability: Well-organized modules are easier to maintain and modify, as changes in one module have minimal impact on other parts of the codebase.
        - Code Organization: Modularization improves code organization, making it easier to navigate and comprehend the overall structure of the program.
    - **Disadvantages:**

        - Overmodularization: Excessive modularization can lead to a proliferation of small, specialized modules, which may hinder code readability and cohesion.
        - Inter-module Dependencies: Poorly managed dependencies between modules can result in intricate interconnections, making the codebase harder to manage.
    - **Use Cases:**
        - Large Projects: Modularization is particularly useful in large projects, where codebases can become unwieldy without proper organization.
        - Reusable Components: When certain functionalities are required in multiple parts of an application, modularization allows developers to create reusable components.

In conclusion, stepwise refinement and modularization are powerful techniques that aid developers in creating well-structured and maintainable algorithms. Stepwise refinement provides a systematic path to developing complex solutions, breaking them down into manageable steps. Modularization, on the other hand, organizes code into independent modules, promoting reusability and maintainability. Combining these approaches enables developers to build efficient, organized, and extensible algorithms that can handle complex problem-solving scenarios while promoting code reuse and maintainability.

5.3 Pseudocode and Flowcharts

5.3.1 Introduction to Pseudocode

Pseudocode is a language-independent representation of algorithms that uses plain English or a combination of natural language and programming-like constructs to express the logic of an algorithm. It serves as a bridge between the human-readable, high-level understanding of the algorithm and the formal, implementation-specific code.

Understanding Pseudocode as a Language-Independent Representation of Algorithms:

- Pseudocode is not tied to any specific programming language, making it a universal way to express algorithmic logic that can be understood by programmers regardless of their language expertise.
- Instead of focusing on syntax and language-specific rules, pseudocode aims to convey the algorithm's essential steps and decision-making process in a clear and human-readable manner.
- Pseudocode can be used to represent various computational processes, ranging from simple mathematical calculations to complex algorithms with conditionals and iterations.

Exploring the Benefits of Using Pseudocode in Algorithm Design and Communication:

- Clarity and Readability: Pseudocode allows developers to describe the algorithm's logic without getting bogged down in the details of a specific programming language. It emphasizes the algorithm's structure and logic, making it easier to comprehend and analyze.

- Flexibility: As pseudocode is language-independent, it enables developers to communicate ideas and algorithms effectively, regardless of their preferred programming language.
- Algorithm Design and Planning: Pseudocode is an invaluable tool during the initial stages of algorithm design. It enables developers to plan and structure their solutions before writing actual code, facilitating a more organized development process.
- Collaboration: When multiple developers are involved in algorithm design or code review, pseudocode serves as a common ground for communication. It allows team members to discuss and understand the algorithm's logic without being constrained by specific programming languages.
- Algorithm Analysis: Pseudocode makes it easier to analyze and optimize algorithms. Since it focuses on the algorithm's steps and flow, developers can identify potential inefficiencies or areas for improvement before implementing the code.
- Educational Purposes: Pseudocode is often used in educational settings to teach algorithm design and problem-solving. Its language-independent nature helps students grasp fundamental concepts without being overwhelmed by syntax intricacies.

Example of Pseudocode:

```
# Example algorithm to find the maximum value in an array
function findMax(array):
# Assume the array is non-empty
maxVal = array[0]
```

```
for i from 1 to array.length - 1:

  if array[i] > maxVal:
  maxVal = array[i]

return maxVal
```

In this pseudocode example, we have an algorithm to find the maximum value in an array. It is expressed in a language-independent manner, focusing on the logic of iterating through the array and updating the **maxVal** variable when a larger element is found. The actual implementation in a specific programming language would depend on the target language's syntax and data structures.

In conclusion, pseudocode serves as a valuable tool in algorithm design, communication, and education. Its language-independent nature enables developers to focus on the algorithm's logic and structure, promoting clarity, collaboration, and better planning. Pseudocode is a powerful aid for both beginners learning algorithmic concepts and experienced developers discussing and designing algorithms.

5.3.2 Writing Pseudocode

Writing pseudocode requires clarity, precision, and consistency to effectively express algorithmic logic without being tied to any specific programming language. Following certain guidelines helps ensure that the pseudocode is easy to understand, implement, and communicate to others.

Guidelines for Writing Pseudocode to Express Algorithmic Logic Clearly:

1. Use Indentation: Indentation helps in visually representing the block structure of the algorithm. Use consistent indentation to indicate nested statements or loops.
2. Keep It Simple and Concise: Pseudocode should capture

the essence of the algorithm without unnecessary details. Focus on expressing the core steps and decision-making logic.

3. Be Language-Independent: Avoid using specific syntax or constructs that are unique to a particular programming language. The goal is to make the pseudocode easily understandable by developers from various language backgrounds.
4. Use Descriptive Names: Choose descriptive names for variables, functions, and other elements to convey their purpose clearly. This enhances readability and reduces ambiguity.
5. Comment Complex Steps: For complex or intricate parts of the algorithm, consider adding comments to explain the thought process behind each step.
6. Describe Control Flow: Clearly indicate control flow using conditional statements (if, else if, else) and looping constructs (for, while, do-while).
7. Use Appropriate Notations: Use common notations such as arrows or symbols to represent operations like assignment, comparison, and arithmetic.
8. Be Consistent with Notation: Maintain consistency throughout the pseudocode. For example, use the same symbols for similar operations and keep a consistent style for variable names.
9. Focus on Logic, Not Optimizations: Pseudocode should prioritize expressing the logic of the algorithm rather than focusing on specific optimizations. Optimization concerns can be addressed during the implementation phase.
10. Test Your Pseudocode: Before proceeding with the actual implementation, test your pseudocode on paper or mentally walk through the steps to ensure it produces the

expected output.

Using Pseudocode to Describe Algorithmic Steps, Control Flow, and Data Manipulation:

1. Algorithmic Steps: Pseudocode should clearly describe each step of the algorithm in a language-independent manner. For example, use descriptive verbs like "initialize," "compute," "iterate," "update," and "return" to outline the actions performed by the algorithm.
2. Control Flow: Pseudocode should use if-else and loop constructs to represent decision-making and iterative processes. Clearly indicate the conditions that control the flow of the algorithm.
3. Data Manipulation: Pseudocode should show how data is manipulated throughout the algorithm. Use assignment statements and arithmetic operations to demonstrate data transformations and updates.

Example of Pseudocode for Bubble Sort Algorithm:

```
# Bubble Sort Algorithm pseudocode
function bubbleSort(array):

  n = length of array
  for i from 0 to n - 1:
  for j from 0 to n - i - 1:
  if array[j] > array[j + 1]:
  swap array[j] and array[j + 1]

return array
```

In this example, the pseudocode demonstrates the steps of the Bubble Sort algorithm using loops and comparisons to sort an array of elements.

In conclusion, writing pseudocode requires adherence to clear guidelines and a focus on expressing algorithmic logic independently of any specific programming language. Using pseudocode effectively describes the steps, control flow, and data manipulation of the algorithm, making it a valuable tool for algorithm design, communication, and comprehension. Pseudocode serves as a bridge between high-level ideas and formal code implementation, facilitating the development process and encouraging collaboration among developers.

5.3.3 Flowcharts

Flowcharts are visual representations of algorithms and processes, using symbols and connecting lines to illustrate the flow of control and data within a system. They provide an intuitive way to understand the logic of an algorithm, making it easier for developers and non-technical stakeholders to visualize and analyze complex processes.

Introduction to Flowcharts as Visual Representations of Algorithms:

- Flowcharts use graphical symbols to represent various steps, decisions, and actions involved in an algorithm or process.
- They offer a clear and concise way to communicate the logical flow of a program, making it easier to understand, design, and optimize algorithms.
- Flowcharts are language-independent, meaning they can be understood by individuals with different programming language backgrounds.
- They are widely used in software development, system design, process modeling, and project planning.

Understanding the Symbols and Conventions Used in Flowchart Diagrams:

1. Terminal (Oval): The terminal symbol represents the start and end points of a flowchart. It is used to indicate the beginning and end of an algorithm or process.
2. Process (Rectangle): The process symbol represents an action or operation performed in the algorithm. It signifies a computation, calculation, or task carried out during program execution.
3. Decision (Diamond): The decision symbol is used to represent a conditional statement that results in a binary outcome (true or false). It represents decision-making points in the algorithm where different paths can be taken based on a condition's evaluation.
4. Input/Output (Parallelogram): The input/output symbol is used to indicate data input or output from the algorithm. It represents interaction with external entities, such as user input or data storage.
5. Connector (Circle): The connector symbol is used to indicate a connection between different parts of the flowchart, allowing the flow to continue from one point to another.
6. Control Flow Arrows: Arrows connecting the flowchart symbols represent the direction of control flow in the algorithm. They show the sequence in which steps are executed and the logical order of operations.
7. Off-Page Connector (Circle with a Letter): The off-page connector symbol is used to connect different parts of a large flowchart that do not fit on a single page. It is labeled with a letter for easy reference to the corresponding off-page connector on another page.

8. Predefined Process (Rectangle with Double Striped Sides): The predefined process symbol represents a sub-routine or a sequence of operations that are predefined and used multiple times within the algorithm.
9. Loop (Rectangle with Double Rounded Corners): The loop symbol represents a loop or iterative structure in the algorithm. It indicates that a set of instructions will be repeated until a certain condition is met.
10. Annotation (Note): Annotations are used to provide additional information or comments within the flowchart to explain specific steps or decision points.

Flowcharts are versatile tools that facilitate communication and understanding of algorithms, making them a valuable asset during the design, analysis, and documentation phases of software development projects. By leveraging flowcharts, developers can easily visualize the logic of complex algorithms, identify potential issues, and collaborate effectively with team members and stakeholders.

5.3.4 Creating Flowcharts

Flowcharts are effective tools for visually representing algorithmic steps and decision-making processes. They provide a clear and structured way to illustrate the flow of control and data within an algorithm. Here are the steps for creating flowcharts to effectively represent algorithms:

Steps for Creating Flowcharts to Represent Algorithmic Steps and Decision-Making Processes:

1. Identify the Start and End Points:
    - Begin the flowchart with a terminal symbol (oval) to represent the start point of the algorithm.
    - End the flowchart with another terminal symbol

to indicate the algorithm's end.

2. Define the Process Steps:
    - Use process symbols (rectangles) to represent the individual steps or actions in the algorithm.
    - Clearly label each process symbol to describe the action being performed.
3. Incorporate Decision Points:
    - Use decision symbols (diamonds) to represent conditional statements or decision-making points in the algorithm.
    - Label the decision symbols with a question or condition to be evaluated.
4. Determine the Control Flow:
    - Connect the symbols with arrows to indicate the flow of control and data between different parts of the algorithm.
    - Use arrows to show the sequence of steps and the logical flow of operations.
5. Use Proper Flow Control:
    - Utilize connectors (circles) to show the continuation of the flowchart on a different page when the flowchart becomes too large to fit on a single page.
    - Use off-page connectors labeled with letters (A, B, C, etc.) to link to the corresponding connector on another page.
6. Indicate Input/Output:
    - Include input/output symbols (parallelograms) to represent data input or output operations within the algorithm.
7. Consider Modularization:
    - For complex algorithms, consider breaking them

    down into modular components using predefined process symbols (rectangles with double striped sides).
    - Use predefined process symbols to represent subroutines or sequences of operations that are used multiple times within the algorithm.
8. Ensure Clarity and Readability:
    - Keep the flowchart simple, concise, and easy to understand.
    - Use descriptive labels and clear symbols to convey the algorithm's logic.

Using Flowcharts to Illustrate the Flow of Control and Data in an Algorithm:

- Flowcharts provide a visual representation of the algorithm's control flow, showing the sequence of steps and decision points that the algorithm follows during execution.
- Arrows connecting the symbols indicate the flow of control, showing the order in which the algorithm's steps are executed.
- Decision symbols represent conditional statements, and the flow of control branches based on the evaluation of these conditions.
- Flowcharts also illustrate the flow of data within the algorithm, showing how data is input, processed, and output at different stages of the algorithm.

Example Flowchart for a Simple Algorithm (Addition of Two Numbers):

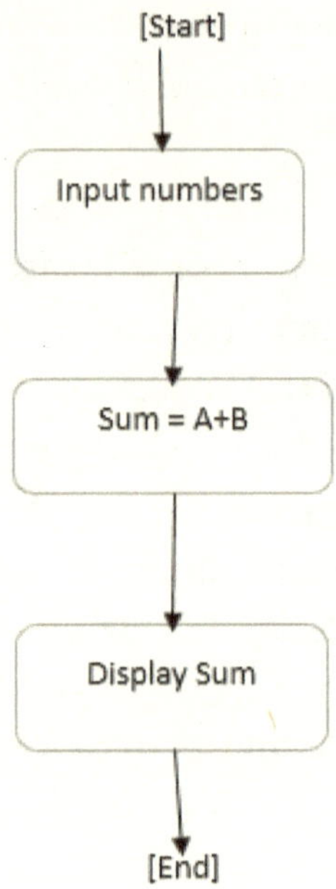

In this example, the flowchart represents a simple algorithm that takes two numbers as input, calculates their sum, and displays the result as output. The process symbols (rectangles) represent the addition of two numbers, and the input/output symbols (parallelograms) represent data input and output operations.

In conclusion, flowcharts are powerful tools for visualizing and illustrating algorithmic steps and decision-making processes. By following the steps for creating flowcharts and using appropriate symbols, developers can create clear, comprehensive, and easily understandable flowcharts that effectively represent the flow of control and data within their algorithms. Flowcharts aid in algorithm design, analysis, and documentation, promoting efficient problem-solving and facilitating effective communication among developers and stakeholders.

Chapter 6: Data Representation

Data representation is a fundamental concept in programming and computer science. It involves understanding how data is stored and manipulated within a computer system. This chapter explores various number systems, conversion between them, and bitwise operations.

6.1 Binary, Decimal, and Hexadecimal Systems

Understanding the fundamental number systems used in computing is essential for effective data representation. This section introduces the binary, decimal, and hexadecimal systems and their significance in representing different types of data.

6.1.1 Binary System

The binary number system lies at the core of modern computing, serving as the fundamental language of computers. It employs just two digits, 0 and 1, to represent all kinds of data and instructions. This section provides a comprehensive overview of the binary system, its role in computing, and its application in basic arithmetic operations.

Explanation of the Binary Number System The binary system, also known as base-2, is a positional numeral system that employs two symbols: 0 and 1. In contrast to the decimal system's ten symbols (0 to 9), the binary system's simplicity is a perfect match for the electronic nature of computers. Each digit in a binary number is called a "bit," short for binary digit.

Computers store and process information in binary form because electronic devices can distinguish between two states: high voltage (1) and low voltage (0). The binary system's positional notation allows for the representation of larger numbers using a combination of bits.

How Computers Use Binary to Represent Data and Instructions Inside a computer's memory and storage, all data—numbers, text, images, and instructions—are stored in binary format. This section explores the connection between the binary system and the inner workings of computers:

1. **Data Representation**: Computers utilize binary to represent everything. For instance, a character from the alphabet is encoded as a unique binary sequence, enabling computers to store and manipulate text.
2. **Machine Code**: Computers execute instructions in machine code, which consists of binary patterns representing operations like addition, comparison, or data movement.
3. **Digital Circuits**: Computers' internal components, such as CPUs and memory, rely on binary signals to perform calculations and manage data.

Binary Arithmetic, Including Addition and Multiplication Binary arithmetic is an essential skill for understanding how computers perform calculations. This section delves into binary addition and multiplication:

1. **Binary Addition**: Adding binary numbers involves a process similar to decimal addition. Carry-over digits occur when the sum of two bits is greater than or equal to 2. For instance, 1 + 1 in binary equals 10 (2 in decimal).
2. **Binary Multiplication**: Binary multiplication employs principles akin to decimal multiplication, albeit with fewer possibilities (0 and 1). It includes aligning numbers and performing additions and shifts.

Understanding binary arithmetic is crucial not only for understanding the inner workings of computers but also for optimizing code and solving computational challenges.

By mastering the concepts of the binary system, its role in computing, and basic binary arithmetic, you'll gain insights into the foundation of data representation and how computers process and manage information. This knowledge is invaluable for programming, system design, and a deeper understanding of the digital world.

6.1.2 Decimal System

The decimal number system, also known as base-10, is the system most familiar to humans due to its everyday use. This section introduces the decimal system, compares it to the binary system, and explores the conversion techniques between the two systems.

Introduction to the Decimal Number System The decimal system employs ten unique digits, 0 through 9, to represent all numbers. Each digit's positional value depends on its position within the number. For example, in the decimal number 352, the digit 2 represents units, the digit 5 represents tens, and the digit 3 represents hundreds.

Comparison of Binary and Decimal Systems in Real-World Applications While the binary system is the foundation of computing, the decimal system dominates human interactions and everyday calculations. This section highlights the practical differences between the two systems:

1. **Human vs. Computer Interaction**: Humans are more comfortable using the decimal system, while computers efficiently process and store data in binary.
2. **Data Representation**: Computers convert decimal numbers to binary for internal processing. Decimal numbers are often represented using the ASCII (American

Standard Code for Information Interchange) encoding.

3. **Real-World Examples**: While binary is ideal for digital devices, the decimal system shines in applications like finance, measurements, and human communication.

Decimal-to-Binary and Binary-to-Decimal Conversion Techniques Converting between the decimal and binary systems is essential for programming and understanding data representation:

1. **Decimal to Binary**: This conversion involves repeatedly dividing the decimal number by 2 and recording the remainders. The binary representation is obtained by reading the remainders in reverse order.
2. **Binary to Decimal**: To convert binary to decimal, multiply each binary digit by 2 raised to the power of its position and sum the results.

These conversion techniques provide a bridge between human-friendly decimal numbers and the binary language of computers.

By grasping the decimal system's fundamentals, its comparison to the binary system, and the techniques for converting between the two, you'll enhance your ability to navigate between human-oriented calculations and the binary world of computers. This knowledge is invaluable for tasks ranging from programming and data manipulation to understanding the broader implications of digital systems in various domains.

6.1.3 Hexadecimal System

The hexadecimal system, often referred to as "hex," is another essential numeral system used in computing. It serves as a bridge between binary and human-readable representations. This section provides a comprehensive overview of the hexadecimal system, its advantages in representing binary values, and techniques for converting between hexadecimal, binary, and decimal systems.

Overview of the Hexadecimal System The hexadecimal system employs sixteen unique symbols: the digits 0 to 9 and the letters A to F. This system's base-16 nature allows for concise representation of binary values. Hexadecimal is widely used in programming, especially for memory addresses, color codes, and binary data manipulation.

How Hexadecimal Is Used to Represent Large Binary Values Concisely Hexadecimal is an efficient way to represent large binary values, making it more manageable for humans to read and write. Each hexadecimal digit corresponds to a group of four binary digits (bits). For instance, the binary number 11011011 is represented as DB in hexadecimal, where D corresponds to 1101 and B corresponds to 1011.

This compact representation is invaluable when dealing with memory addresses or binary data, as it simplifies the representation without losing accuracy.

Conversion Between Hexadecimal and Binary/Decimal Systems Converting between hexadecimal, binary, and decimal systems is essential for various programming tasks:

1. **Hexadecimal to Binary**: Divide each hexadecimal digit into its corresponding four-bit binary representation. Combine the binary groups to obtain the complete binary representation.
2. **Binary to Hexadecimal**: Group the binary digits in sets of four, starting from the right. Convert each group to its hexadecimal equivalent.
3. **Hexadecimal to Decimal**: Convert each hexadecimal digit to its decimal value. Multiply each digit's value by 16 raised

to the power of its position and sum the results.

4. **Decimal to Hexadecimal**: Divide the decimal number by 16 repeatedly to obtain remainders. Convert the remainders to hexadecimal digits, and read them in reverse order.

These conversion techniques allow for seamless communication between different numeral systems and are particularly valuable in scenarios where different systems interact, such as in memory addressing and color representation.

By mastering the hexadecimal system's intricacies, its role in compactly representing binary values, and the art of converting between different systems, you'll gain a versatile toolkit for various programming tasks. This knowledge enhances your ability to work with data representation, memory management, and system-level programming.

6.2 Conversion Between Number Systems

Converting between different number systems is a valuable skill for programmers. This section delves into techniques for converting numbers from one base to another.

6.2.1 Binary to Decimal and Decimal to Binary

Converting between binary and decimal numbers is a fundamental skill in computing. This section outlines step-by-step processes for performing these conversions and provides real-world examples to illustrate their significance.

Binary to Decimal Conversion

Converting binary numbers to decimal involves understanding the positional value of each bit in the binary representation.

1. **Write the Binary Number**: Start by writing down the binary number you want to convert.
2. **Assign Positions**: Assign positional values to each bit from right to left, starting with 2^0 (1) for the rightmost bit and doubling the value for each subsequent bit.
3. **Calculate**: Multiply each binary digit by its corresponding positional value and sum the results.
4. **Example**: Binary number: 101101 Calculation: (1 * 2^5) + (0 * 2^4) + (1 * 2^3) + (1 * 2^2) + (0 * 2^1) + (1 * 2^0) = 32 + 0 + 8 + 4 + 0 + 1 = 45 (decimal)

Decimal to Binary Conversion

Converting decimal numbers to binary involves repeatedly dividing the decimal number by 2 and recording the remainders.

1. **Write the Decimal Number**: Start by writing down the decimal number you want to convert.
2. **Divide and Record**: Divide the decimal number by 2 and record the remainder. Continue this process, dividing the quotient by 2 each time, until the quotient becomes 0.
3. **Read in Reverse**: Read the remainders in reverse order to obtain the binary representation.
4. **Example**: Decimal number: 27 Calculation:
    - 27 ÷ 2 = 13 remainder 1
    - 13 ÷ 2 = 6 remainder 1
    - 6 ÷ 2 = 3 remainder 0

- $3 \div 2 = 1$ remainder 1
- $1 \div 2 = 0$ remainder 1 Binary representation: 11011

Real-World Examples of Conversions

1. **Example 1 - Binary to Decimal**: Binary number: 101010 Conversion: (1 * 2^5) + (0 * 2^4) + (1 * 2^3) + (0 * 2^2) + (1 * 2^1) + (0 * 2^0) = 32 + 0 + 8 + 0 + 2 + 0 = 42 (decimal)
2. **Example 2 - Decimal to Binary**: Decimal number: 79 Conversion: $79 \div 2 = 39$ remainder 1
    - $39 \div 2 = 19$ remainder 1
    - $19 \div 2 = 9$ remainder 1
    - $9 \div 2 = 4$ remainder 1
    - $4 \div 2 = 2$ remainder 0
    - $2 \div 2 = 1$ remainder 0
    - $1 \div 2 = 0$ remainder 1 Binary representation: 1001111

Mastering binary-to-decimal and decimal-to-binary conversions is essential for programming tasks involving different numeral systems. These skills enhance your ability to work with data manipulation, memory addressing, and understanding the core principles of data representation.

6.2.2 Binary to Hexadecimal and Hexadecimal to Binary

Converting between binary and hexadecimal numbers is a crucial skill for programmers, particularly when dealing with memory addresses, data manipulation, and compact data representation. This section presents techniques for converting between binary and hexadecimal and provides insights into practical scenarios where these conversions are invaluable.

Binary to Hexadecimal Conversion

Converting binary numbers to hexadecimal involves grouping binary digits into sets of four and then associating each group with its corresponding hexadecimal digit.

1. **Write the Binary Number**: Start by writing down the binary number you want to convert.
2. **Group into Sets of Four**: Group the binary digits from right to left into sets of four. If the leftmost group has fewer than four digits, pad it with zeros on the left.
3. **Associate with Hex Digits**: Replace each group of binary digits with its corresponding hexadecimal digit.
4. **Example**: Binary number: 101101110110 Groups: 1011 0111 0110 Hexadecimal representation: B76

Hexadecimal to Binary Conversion

Converting hexadecimal numbers to binary involves replacing each hexadecimal digit with its corresponding four-digit binary representation.

1. **Write the Hexadecimal Number**: Start by writing down the hexadecimal number you want to convert.
2. **Replace with Binary**: Replace each hexadecimal digit with its corresponding four-digit binary representation.
3. **Example**: Hexadecimal number: 2F8 Binary representation: 0010 1111 1000

Practical Scenarios Where Hexadecimal Conversion Is Useful

1. **Memory Addresses**: Memory addresses in computers are often represented in hexadecimal, making it easier to manage and communicate complex addresses.
2. **Color Codes**: Hexadecimal is widely used to represent colors in web design and graphics. Each color component (red, green, blue) is represented by a two-digit hexadecimal number.
3. **Binary Data Representation**: Hexadecimal provides a compact representation of binary data, making it more readable for humans. It is commonly used in fields like data storage and network protocols.
4. **Debugging**: Hexadecimal is useful for debugging low-level programming and system issues. It allows programmers to examine memory contents and data structures in a more manageable format.

By mastering binary-to-hexadecimal and hexadecimal-to-binary conversions, you'll be equipped to work with various numeral systems and efficiently manipulate data in a wide range of programming tasks. This knowledge is especially valuable for system-level programming, data analysis, and fields involving low-level interactions with computer systems.

6.2.3 Decimal to Hexadecimal and Hexadecimal to Decimal

Converting between decimal and hexadecimal numbers is a vital skill for programmers, particularly when working with memory addresses, data encoding, and various numeric representations. This section presents techniques for converting between decimal and hexadecimal and explores practical scenarios where these conversions play a pivotal role.

Decimal to Hexadecimal Conversion

Converting decimal numbers to hexadecimal involves dividing the decimal number by 16 repeatedly and recording the remainders. The remainders are then associated with their corresponding hexadecimal digits.

1. **Write the Decimal Number**: Start by writing down the decimal number you want to convert.
2. **Divide and Record**: Divide the decimal number by 16 and record the remainder. Continue this process, dividing the quotient by 16 each time, until the quotient becomes 0.
3. **Associate with Hex Digits**: Replace each remainder with its corresponding hexadecimal digit.
4. **Example**: Decimal number: 789 Calculation:
    - 789 ÷ 16 = 49 remainder 5 (5 in hexadecimal is 5)
    - 49 ÷ 16 = 3 remainder 1 (1 in hexadecimal is 1)
    - 3 ÷ 16 = 0 remainder 3 (3 in hexadecimal is 3) Hexadecimal representation: 315

Hexadecimal to Decimal Conversion

Converting hexadecimal numbers to decimal involves multiplying each hexadecimal digit by 16 raised to the power of its position and summing the results.

1. **Write the Hexadecimal Number**: Start by writing down the hexadecimal number you want to convert.

2. **Convert Hex to Decimal**: Convert each hexadecimal digit to its decimal value. Multiply each digit's value by 16 raised to the power of its position and sum the results.
3. **Example**: Hexadecimal number: 1A7 Conversion:
    - 1 * 16^2 = 256
    - A (10 in decimal) * 16^1 = 160
    - 7 * 16^0 = 7 Decimal representation: 423

Use Cases for Decimal-to-Hexadecimal and Hexadecimal-to-Decimal Conversions

1. **Memory Addresses**: Memory addresses are often represented in hexadecimal, as it provides a compact and readable way to express large numbers.
2. **Data Encoding**: In data storage and communication protocols, hexadecimal is used to encode binary data in a more manageable form.
3. **Color Representation**: Hexadecimal is used to represent colors in various fields, including graphics, web design, and image processing.
4. **Network Addressing**: IP addresses in networking are often represented in hexadecimal for easier human comprehension.

By mastering decimal-to-hexadecimal and hexadecimal-to-decimal conversions, you'll enhance your ability to work with various numeral systems, handle data encoding, and understand memory structures. This knowledge is particularly valuable for system-level programming, data manipulation, and fields that require a deep understanding of numeric representations.

6.3 Bitwise Operations

Bitwise operations manipulate individual bits within binary numbers. This section explores how these operations are used for data manipulation and optimization.

6.3.1 AND, OR, XOR, and NOT Operations

Bitwise operations are fundamental in low-level programming and data manipulation. This section introduces four essential bitwise operations—AND, OR, XOR, and NOT—and explores their applications in tasks like setting or clearing specific bits.

Explanation of Bitwise AND, OR, XOR, and NOT Operations

1. **Bitwise AND** (&): The AND operation compares each pair of corresponding bits in two numbers. If both bits are 1, the result is 1; otherwise, it's 0.
2. **Bitwise OR** (|): The OR operation compares each pair of corresponding bits in two numbers. If either bit is 1, the result is 1; otherwise, it's 0.
3. **Bitwise XOR** (^): The XOR operation compares each pair of corresponding bits in two numbers. If the bits are different (one is 0 and the other is 1), the result is 1; otherwise, it's 0.
4. **Bitwise NOT** (~): The NOT operation flips the bits of a number, turning 1s into 0s and vice versa.

Applications of Bitwise Operations

1. **Setting Specific Bits**: Bitwise OR is often used to set specific bits in a number to 1 while leaving the rest unchanged. This is achieved by performing a bitwise OR

operation with a number containing the desired bit pattern.
2. **Clearing Specific Bits**: Bitwise AND is used to clear specific bits in a number, setting them to 0 while leaving the other bits unchanged. This is done by performing a bitwise AND operation with a number containing the complement of the desired bit pattern.
3. **Toggling Bits**: Bitwise XOR can toggle specific bits, changing 1s to 0s and vice versa. This is achieved by performing a bitwise XOR operation with a number containing the desired bit pattern.
4. **Checking Bit Status**: Bitwise AND can be used to check the status of specific bits. By performing a bitwise AND operation with a mask that has 1s in the positions of the bits you want to check, you can determine whether those bits are set or cleared.

These bitwise operations are invaluable for tasks like manipulating hardware registers, working with flags or status bits, and performing efficient data compression or encryption. They provide a level of granular control over individual bits that is essential in low-level programming and certain specialized applications.

6.3.2 Bit Shifting

Bit shifting is a fundamental operation in computer programming that involves moving the bits of a binary number to the left or right. This section explores left and right bit shifting operations and highlights practical applications of bit shifting.

Understanding Left and Right Bit Shifting Operations

1. **Left Bit Shifting (<<)**: Left shifting a binary number

involves moving its bits to the left by a specified number of positions. This is equivalent to multiplying the number by 2 raised to the power of the shift count.

Example:
010101 << 2 = 01010100 (42 << 2 = 168)

1. **Right Bit Shifting** (>>): Right shifting a binary number involves moving its bits to the right by a specified number of positions. This is equivalent to dividing the number by 2 raised to the power of the shift count.

Example:
110010 >> 3 = 000110 (50 >> 3 = 6)

Practical Applications of Bit Shifting

1. **Multiplying or Dividing by Powers of Two**: Bit shifting is an efficient way to multiply or divide a number by powers of two. Left shifting by **n** is equivalent to multiplying by 2^n, and right shifting by **n** is equivalent to dividing by 2^n.

Example:
5 << 3 = 5 * 2^3 = 40 32 >> 2 = 32 / 2^2 = 8

1. **Data Packing and Unpacking**: Bit shifting is used to pack multiple pieces of information into a single data structure or to extract individual components from a packed structure.
2. **Creating Masks and Flags**: Bit shifting is used to create masks for isolating specific bits or sets of bits within a larger number. It's also used to set or clear individual flags

within a binary representation.

3. **Efficient Storage**: Bit shifting is employed in compression algorithms and data storage methods where space efficiency is crucial.
4. **Encryption and Hashing**: Bit shifting is used in certain encryption and hashing algorithms to scramble data effectively.
5. **Graphics and Image Processing**: Bit shifting is used in various graphical operations, such as color manipulation and pixel value extraction.

Understanding bit shifting is essential for optimizing code, performing low-level operations, and efficiently managing data. It empowers programmers to work with data at the binary level and exploit the benefits of hardware-level manipulation.

6.3.3 Bitwise Operations in Data Manipulation

Bitwise operations are powerful tools in data manipulation, allowing precise control over individual bits within binary data. This section explores practical applications of bitwise operations, including setting flags, toggling bits, and checking the status of specific bits.

Setting Flags

Bitwise OR (|) is commonly used to set flags within a binary number. By performing a bitwise OR operation with a number containing the flag pattern, specific bits can be set to 1 while leaving other bits unchanged. This is useful for representing multiple boolean conditions in a compact form.

Example:
Flags: 0000
Flag A: 0001

Flag B: 0010
Flag C: 0100
Flags = Flags | Flag B; // Sets Flag B
Result: 0110

Toggling Bits

Bitwise XOR (^) is used to toggle specific bits. By performing a bitwise XOR operation with a number containing the desired bit pattern, the target bits can be inverted (0s become 1s and vice versa).

Example:
Value: 101001
Toggle: 110000
Value = Value ^ Toggle; // Toggles specific bits
Result: 011001

Checking Bit Status

Bitwise AND (&) is used to check the status of specific bits. By performing a bitwise AND operation with a mask that has 1s in the positions of the bits you want to check, you can determine whether those bits are set or cleared.

Example:
Value: 101011
Mask: 001010
Check = Value & Mask; // Checks specific bits
Result: 001010

If the result is equal to the mask, the checked bits are set; otherwise, they are cleared.

These operations are fundamental in handling flags, conditional logic, and efficient data representation. They are particularly valuable in scenarios where memory usage and computational efficiency are critical, such as embedded systems programming and data compression.

By mastering the concepts in this chapter, you'll develop a strong foundation in data representation, which is crucial for efficient programming, memory management, and understanding the inner workings of computer systems.

Chapter 7: Arrays and Strings

Arrays and strings are essential data structures in programming, enabling efficient storage and manipulation of collections of elements and text. This chapter delves into various aspects of arrays and strings, including manipulation, traversal, and working with multidimensional arrays.

7.1 Array Manipulation and Traversal

Arrays are ordered collections of elements that allow efficient storage and retrieval of data. This section explores techniques for manipulating and traversing arrays, including common operations and algorithms.

7.1.1 Introduction to Arrays

Arrays are fundamental data structures in programming that provide a way to store multiple elements of the same data type under a single identifier. They play a crucial role in organizing and managing data efficiently, making them an essential concept for every programmer to understand.

Understanding the Concept of Arrays

At its core, an array is a collection of elements, each identified by an index or a key. The elements in an array are typically of the same data type, such as integers, floating-point numbers, characters, or even more complex objects. Arrays provide a systematic way to store related data, making it easier to access and manipulate them as a group.

Arrays are often visualized as a sequence of boxes, with each box containing an element. The index indicates the position of an element within the array, starting from 0 for the first element.

Exploring Use Cases and Benefits of Arrays

Arrays offer several key benefits that make them indispensable in programming:

1. **Efficient Data Storage**: Arrays provide a compact way to store and manage a large number of elements. This efficiency is crucial in situations where memory usage is a concern.
2. **Quick Access**: Elements in an array can be accessed directly using their index, allowing for fast retrieval of data. This is particularly useful when dealing with large datasets.
3. **Uniform Data Handling**: Since all elements in an array are of the same data type, you can apply the same operations to each element in a uniform manner.
4. **Iteration and Traversal**: Arrays simplify iteration through elements using loops, enabling repetitive tasks to be performed efficiently.
5. **Data Organization**: Arrays are often used to organize related data, such as scores in a game, sensor readings, or user information.
6. **Algorithm Implementation**: Many algorithms involve processing a collection of data. Arrays provide a natural representation for these data collections.
7. **Mathematical and Scientific Computing**: Arrays are extensively used in mathematical and scientific computations, such as matrix operations and signal processing.

8. **Graphical Representations**: Arrays are the foundation for representing images, audio signals, and other graphical data.
9. **Database Operations**: Arrays are used in database systems to efficiently manage and retrieve records.

As you delve into programming, understanding arrays will empower you to work with data in a structured and organized manner. Whether you're building simple programs or complex applications, arrays will likely be a central component of your coding journey. Mastering arrays lays the groundwork for more advanced data structures and algorithms, enabling you to create efficient and robust solutions to a wide range of problems.

7.1.2 Array Declaration and Initialization

Arrays are versatile data structures that allow you to store multiple values of the same data type. This section explains how to declare arrays in various programming languages and how to initialize them with values.

Syntax for Declaring Arrays in Different Programming Languages

The syntax for declaring arrays can vary depending on the programming language you're using. Here are examples of array declarations in some common programming languages:

1. **C and C++**:

```
data_type array_name[array_size];
Example:
int numbers[5]; // Declares an integer array of size 5
```

1. **Java:**

data_type[] array_name = new data_type[array_size];
Example:
int[] numbers = new int[5]; // Declares an integer array of size 5

1. **Python:**

Python uses lists as its primary data structure. Lists can store elements of different data types.
array_name = [value1, value2, value3, ...]
Example:
numbers = [1, 2, 3, 4, 5] # Creates a list containing integers

1. **JavaScript:**

JavaScript arrays can also hold values of different types.
let array_name = [value1, value2, value3, ...];
Example:
let numbers = [1, 2, 3, 4, 5]; // Creates an array containing numbers

Initializing Arrays with Values

Arrays can be initialized with values during declaration. Here's how:

1. **C and C++:**

int numbers[5] = {1, 2, 3, 4, 5};

1. **Java:**

int[] numbers = {1, 2, 3, 4, 5};

1. **Python:**

```
numbers = [1, 2, 3, 4, 5]
```

1. **JavaScript:**

```
let numbers = [1, 2, 3, 4, 5];
```

You can also initialize arrays with default values or using loops, which is particularly useful when dealing with large arrays.

Default Values:

Arrays are usually initialized with default values based on their data type. For example, integers are initialized to 0, and strings are initialized to an empty string.

Using Loops:

Loops can be used to initialize arrays with specific patterns or calculations. This is especially helpful when you want to generate array values dynamically.

Understanding array declaration and initialization is essential for effectively using arrays in your programs. It provides you with the foundation to store and manage data in a structured and organized manner.

7.1.3 Accessing Array Elements

Accessing array elements is a fundamental operation in programming, allowing you to retrieve and manipulate individual values stored within an array. This section covers indexing arrays, accessing elements, and dealing with array indices and boundaries.

Indexing Arrays and Accessing Individual Elements

Arrays are zero-indexed, which means that the first element is at index 0, the second element is at index 1, and so on. To access an element in an array, you specify its index within square brackets.

Example (using a zero-indexed array):

Array: [10, 20, 30, 40, 50] Index: 0 1 2 3 4

To access the second element (20) in the array, you would use:

array[1] // Index 1 corresponds to the second element

Handling Array Indices and Boundaries

When working with arrays, it's important to handle array indices and boundaries carefully to avoid errors and unexpected behavior.

1. **Out-of-Bounds Access**: Accessing an index that is outside the valid range of indices for the array can lead to runtime errors or undefined behavior. Always ensure that the index is within the array's bounds.
2. **Bounds Checking**: Some programming languages perform bounds checking automatically and raise an error if an out-of-bounds access is detected. Others, like C and C++, may not perform bounds checking by default, so it's the programmer's responsibility to ensure valid indices.
3. **Loop Iteration**: When using loops to iterate through an array, ensure that the loop variable remains within the valid range of indices. A common pattern is to use a loop variable that goes from 0 to **array.length - 1**.

Example (using a loop to iterate through an array):

for (int i = 0; i < array.length; i++) { // Access and process array[i] }

1. **Array Length**: The length of an array is the total number of elements it can hold. In some programming languages, you can use the **length** property or method to retrieve the length of an array.

Using Arrays in Algorithms and Operations

Arrays are commonly used in algorithms for tasks like searching, sorting, and data manipulation. Understanding how to access array elements accurately is crucial for the correctness and efficiency of these algorithms.

By mastering the techniques of indexing and accessing array elements, you gain the ability to work with collections of data effectively and create algorithms that process data efficiently.

7.1.4 Array Manipulation

Array manipulation involves various operations that allow you to modify the contents of an array. This section explores common array manipulation techniques, including insertion, deletion, updating of elements, and dynamic resizing.

Performing Operations such as Insertion, Deletion, and Updating of Array Elements

1. **Insertion**:

Inserting an element into an array means adding a new value at a specific index while shifting the existing elements to accommodate the new element.

Example (Java):

```
int[] array = {10, 20, 30, 40, 50};
int newValue = 25;
```

```
int insertIndex = 2;
// Shift elements to make space for the new element
for (int i = array.length - 1; i > insertIndex; i—) {
array[i] = array[i - 1];
}
// Insert the new value
array[insertIndex] = newValue;
```

1. **Deletion:**

Deleting an element from an array involves removing the element at a specific index and shifting the remaining elements to fill the gap.

Example (Python):

```
array = [10, 20, 30, 40, 50]
delete_index = 2
# Shift elements to fill the gap left by the deleted element
for i in range(delete_index, len(array) - 1):
array[i] = array[i + 1]
# Resize the array to remove the last element
array.pop()
```

1. **Updating:**

Updating an element means modifying the value at a specific index.

Example (C++):

cppCopy code

```
int array[] = {10, 20, 30, 40, 50};
int updateIndex = 2;
int newValue = 35;
array[updateIndex] = newValue;
```

Techniques for Resizing Arrays Dynamically

Arrays in some programming languages, such as C and C++, have a fixed size once they're declared. However, you can achieve dynamic resizing using techniques like dynamic memory allocation and reallocating memory.

1. **Dynamic Memory Allocation (C and C++)**:

You can use functions like **malloc**() and **free**() in C or **new** and **delete** in C++ to allocate memory for an array dynamically. This allows you to resize the array during runtime.

1. **ArrayList (Java)**:

Java provides the **ArrayList** class, which is a dynamic array implementation. It automatically resizes itself as needed.

1. **List (Python)**:

In Python, lists are dynamic arrays that automatically adjust their size as elements are added or removed.

1. **Vector (C++)**:

The **std::vector** container in C++ provides a dynamic array that can grow or shrink based on the elements added or removed.

Dynamic resizing enables you to handle scenarios where the size of the array needs to change based on the program's requirements. This flexibility comes at the cost of potential overhead due to memory reallocation.

Understanding array manipulation techniques is essential for creating algorithms that manipulate data efficiently. Whether you're building data processing systems or implementing algorithms, mastering array manipulation empowers you to work with data effectively.

7.1.5 Array Traversal

Array traversal involves systematically visiting each element in an array to perform specific operations. This section covers using loops to iterate through array elements and implementing algorithms for searching, sorting, and processing array elements.

Using Loops to Iterate Through Array Elements

Loops are a powerful tool for traversing arrays and performing operations on their elements.

1. **For Loop**:

A **for** loop is commonly used to iterate through an array. The loop variable starts from the first index and increments until it reaches the last index.

Example (Python):

```
array = [10, 20, 30, 40, 50]
for i in range(len(array)):
print(array[i]) # Access and process each element
```

1. **Enhanced For Loop (Java, C#)**:

Some languages provide an enhanced **for** loop (also known as a **foreach** loop) that simplifies array traversal.

Example (Java):

```
int[] array = {10, 20, 30, 40, 50};
for (int num : array) {
```

```
System.out.println(num); // Access and process each element
}
```

1. **While Loop**:

A **while** loop can also be used for array traversal. The loop continues until a specified condition is met.

Example (C++):

```
int array[] = {10, 20, 30, 40, 50};
int i = 0;
while (i < sizeof(array) / sizeof(array[0])) {
cout << array[i] << endl; // Access and process each element
i++;
}
```

Implementing Algorithms to Search, Sort, and Process Array Elements

Arrays are at the core of many algorithms that involve data manipulation. Here are a few common algorithms:

1. **Searching Algorithms**:
    - **Linear Search**: Iterate through the array to find a specific element.
    - **Binary Search**: Requires the array to be sorted. Divide and conquer approach to find an element efficiently.
2. **Sorting Algorithms**:
    - **Bubble Sort**: Repeatedly swap adjacent elements if they are in the wrong order.
    - **Selection Sort**: Select the smallest (or largest) element and move it to its correct position.
    - **Insertion Sort**: Build a sorted array one element at a time by inserting elements in their proper

place.

3. **Processing Algorithms**:
    - **Sum and Average**: Calculate the sum or average of all elements in the array.
    - **Maximum and Minimum**: Find the maximum and minimum values in the array.
    - **Frequency Count**: Count the occurrences of each element in the array.

Array traversal and algorithm implementation are foundational skills for a programmer. They provide the ability to work with and manipulate data efficiently, making them crucial for a wide range of programming tasks.

7.1.6 Searching and Sorting Algorithms

Searching and sorting are fundamental operations in programming that involve finding specific elements within an array and arranging array elements in a specific order. This section provides an overview of popular searching and sorting algorithms.

Searching Algorithms

1. **Linear Search**:

Linear search is a simple algorithm that iterates through the array, element by element, until it finds the target element. It is suitable for unsorted arrays.

1. **Binary Search**:

Binary search is an efficient algorithm for finding an element in a sorted array. It repeatedly divides the search interval in half, narrowing down the search range.

Sorting Algorithms

1. **Bubble Sort**:

Bubble sort repeatedly steps through the array, compares adjacent elements, and swaps them if they are in the wrong order. This process is repeated until the entire array is sorted.

1. **Insertion Sort**:

Insertion sort builds the sorted array one element at a time. It takes an unsorted element and places it in its correct position within the sorted part of the array.

1. **Selection Sort**:

Selection sort works by repeatedly selecting the minimum (or maximum) element from the unsorted part of the array and placing it in the sorted part.

1. **Quicksort**:

Quicksort is a divide-and-conquer algorithm. It selects a "pivot" element and partitions the array into two subarrays – elements less than the pivot and elements greater than the pivot. It then recursively sorts the subarrays.

When to Use Which Algorithm

- Use linear search when dealing with small unsorted arrays or when the array is not sorted, as it has a linear time complexity.
- Use binary search when the array is sorted, as it has a logarithmic time complexity.
- For sorting, bubble sort and insertion sort are simple but less efficient for large arrays. They are suitable for educational purposes and small datasets.
- Selection sort is easy to understand but not very efficient for large arrays.
- Quicksort is a fast sorting algorithm and is often used in practice.

Choosing the right algorithm depends on the specific requirements of your task, the size of the data, and the desired time complexity.

Understanding searching and sorting algorithms is essential for optimizing data manipulation and retrieval in your programs. These algorithms are building blocks for more advanced data processing and analysis tasks.

7.2 String Manipulation and Processing

Strings are sequences of characters that are fundamental for representing and processing textual data. This section explores techniques for manipulating and processing strings.

7.2.1 Introduction to Strings

Strings are a fundamental data type in programming, representing sequences of characters. This section introduces the concept of strings, their importance in various applications, and their role in programming tasks.

Understanding Strings as Sequences of Characters

A string is a collection of characters, which can include letters, digits, symbols, and spaces. Characters within a string are ordered and can be accessed individually. Strings are versatile and are used to represent text in a wide range of contexts, from simple messages to complex documents.

Importance of Strings in Various Applications

Strings play a crucial role in programming due to their applicability in diverse scenarios:

1. **Text Processing**: Strings are extensively used in text processing tasks, such as parsing and analyzing text files, searching for patterns, and modifying textual content.
2. **User Input and Interaction**: Strings are essential for handling user input, whether it's a command, a name, an address, or any other form of text-based interaction.
3. **Data Representation**: Strings are employed to represent data that is naturally text-based, such as phone numbers, dates, and addresses.
4. **Output and Display**: Many programs generate string output that is displayed to users, whether it's messages, reports, or visual elements.
5. **Web Development**: In web development, strings are used to manage URLs, HTML content, and data exchanged with web servers.
6. **File Operations**: Strings are utilized for reading from and

writing to text files, making them indispensable for file handling.

7. **Localization**: In internationalization and localization efforts, strings are used to store translated text for different languages and regions.

Strings often require specialized functions and methods for operations like concatenation, comparison, and manipulation. Modern programming languages provide extensive support for string handling, making it easier to work with text-based data effectively.

Understanding the nature of strings and their significance in programming is essential for developers to build robust and functional software that effectively interacts with and processes textual information.

7.2.2 String Concatenation and Manipulation

String manipulation is a fundamental skill in programming, allowing you to modify and combine strings to create more complex and meaningful data. This section explores string concatenation and various techniques for manipulating strings.

Concatenating Strings to Combine Them

Concatenation involves combining multiple strings to create a single, longer string. This is often used to build sentences, messages, or any composite text-based data.

Example (Python):

```
first_name = "John"
last_name = "Doe"
full_name = first_name + " " + last_name # Concatenate strings with spaces
```

Techniques for Modifying Strings

1. **Replacing Substrings**:

Replacing substrings involves changing occurrences of one substring with another within a larger string.

Example (Java):

```
String sentence = "Hello, world!";
String newSentence = sentence.replace("Hello", "Hi"); // Replace "Hello" with "Hi"
```

1. **Inserting Substrings**:

Inserting a substring involves adding new content at a specific position within a string.

Example (C#):

```
string original = "This is an example.";
string inserted = original.Insert(8, "inserted "); // Insert "inserted " at index 8
```

1. **Removing Substrings**:

Removing substrings involves deleting a portion of a string.

Example (Python):

```
sentence = "This is a sentence."
new_sentence = sentence[:4] + sentence[10:] # Remove "is"
```

1. **Case Conversion**:

Changing the case of a string, such as converting to uppercase or lowercase.

Example (JavaScript):

```
let originalString = "Hello, World!";
```

```
let uppercaseString = originalString.toUpperCase();
```

1. **Trimming:**

Removing leading and trailing whitespace characters from a string.

Example (C++):

```
std::string text = " Some text with spaces ";
text = text.trim(); // Remove leading and trailing spaces
```

String manipulation is essential for tasks like data cleaning, user input processing, and formatting. Being proficient in string manipulation enables you to process and present data effectively, making your programs more versatile and user-friendly.

7.2.3 String Comparison and Searching

String comparison and searching are important operations for analyzing and processing textual data. This section covers techniques for comparing strings and searching for substrings within larger strings.

Comparing Strings for Equality and Ordering

1. **String Equality Comparison:**

Comparing if two strings are equal involves checking whether their content is the same.

Example (Python):

```
string1 = "apple"
string2 = "apple"
if string1 == string2:
print("Strings are equal")
```

1. **String Ordering Comparison:**

Strings can also be compared for their lexicographic (dictionary) ordering.

Example (Java):

```
String string1 = "apple";
String string2 = "banana";
int comparisonResult = string1.compareTo(string2);
if (comparisonResult < 0) {
System.out.println("string1 comes before string2");
}
```

Searching for Substrings Within a Larger String

1. **Finding Substrings:**

To determine if a substring exists within a larger string and find its position.

Example (C#):

```
string sentence = "The quick brown fox jumps over the lazy dog.";
bool containsFox = sentence.Contains("fox"); // Check if "fox" is present
int indexOfFox = sentence.IndexOf("fox"); // Find index of "fox"
```

1. **Counting Occurrences:**

Count the number of occurrences of a substring within a string.

Example (JavaScript):

```
let text = "She sells seashells by the seashore.";
let count = (text.match(/she/gi) || []).length; // Count occurrences of "she" (case-insensitive)
```

1. **Replacing Substrings**:

We covered this earlier in the section on string manipulation. Replacing a substring involves searching for it and replacing it with another string.

Example (Python):

sentence = "I love cats. Cats are wonderful.";

new_sentence = sentence.replace("cats", "dogs"); // Replace "cats" with "dogs"

Understanding string comparison and searching is crucial for tasks like data validation, text analysis, and pattern recognition. These operations are fundamental to effective string processing and manipulation in various programming scenarios.

7.2.4 String Parsing and Tokenization

String parsing and tokenization are techniques used to break down strings into smaller components, often referred to as tokens. This section explores how to split strings using delimiters and extract meaningful data from formatted strings.

Breaking Down Strings into Tokens

1. **Tokenization**:

Tokenization involves splitting a string into smaller segments (tokens) based on specified delimiters. Delimiters are characters that mark the boundaries between tokens.

Example (Python):

sentence = "The quick brown fox jumps over the lazy dog";

words = sentence.split(" "); # Split sentence into words

1. **CSV Parsing**:

Comma-Separated Values (CSV) files often require parsing to extract data into separate fields.

Example (Java):

```
String csvLine = "John,Doe,30,New York";
String[] fields = csvLine.split(",");
```

Extracting Meaningful Data from Formatted Strings

1. **Substrings and Indices**:

Extracting substrings based on specific start and end indices.

Example (C++):

```
std::string sentence = "The cat in the hat";
std::string substring = sentence.substr(4, 7); // Extract "cat"
```

1. **Regular Expressions**:

Regular expressions allow complex pattern matching and extraction.

Example (JavaScript):

```
let text = "Email: contact@example.com";
let email = text.match(/[a-zA-Z0-9._%+-]+@[a-zA-Z0-9.-]+\.[a-zA-Z]{2,}/);
```

1. **Formatted String Extraction**:

Extracting data from strings with a specific format, such as dates or phone numbers.

Example (Python):

```
import re
text = "Date: 2023-06-23";
date_match = re.search(r'\d{4}-\d{2}-\d{2}', text);
```

String parsing and tokenization are essential for data processing, data extraction from various sources, and transforming data into usable formats. These techniques are widely used in tasks like data import/export, text analysis, and handling structured information.

7.3 Working with Multidimensional Arrays

Multidimensional arrays allow the organization of data in multiple dimensions, suitable for tasks such as matrix operations and representing complex data structures.

7.3.1 Introduction to Multidimensional Arrays

Multidimensional arrays are an extension of one-dimensional arrays, allowing you to organize data in multiple dimensions, like rows and columns. This section provides an introduction to multidimensional arrays, their significance, and their application in various contexts.

Understanding the Concept of Multidimensional Arrays

A one-dimensional array represents a list of items. In contrast, a multidimensional array represents a grid or matrix of values, with each element identified by its position in multiple dimensions. Common examples include 2D arrays (rows and columns) and 3D arrays (stacked layers).

Use Cases for Multidimensional Arrays

1. **Matrices and Mathematical Operations**:

Multidimensional arrays are ideal for representing matrices, which have applications in mathematics, physics, and engineering. They are used for tasks like linear transformations, solving systems of equations, and image processing.

1. **Image Representation**:

Images can be represented using multidimensional arrays, where each element stores pixel information (color or intensity). This representation allows manipulation of images, such as filters and transformations.

1. **Game Development**:

In game development, multidimensional arrays can represent game maps, terrains, and other structured data. They are crucial for managing game environments.

1. **Scientific Computing**:

Multidimensional arrays are foundational in scientific simulations, where data is often represented in grid-like structures. This applies to fields like physics, chemistry, and biology.

1. **Tabular Data**:

While not limited to two dimensions, arrays can be used for tabular data, making it easier to manage and process data in rows and columns.

Understanding multidimensional arrays broadens your ability to represent and process structured data efficiently. They offer a powerful tool for tackling problems that involve complex relationships and arrangements of data.

7.3.2 Declaring and Initializing Multidimensional Arrays

Multidimensional arrays allow you to organize data in multiple dimensions, like rows and columns, or even higher dimensions. This section covers how to declare and initialize multidimensional arrays, providing you with the foundation to work with structured data efficiently.

Syntax for Declaring and Initializing Multidimensional Arrays

1. **2D Array Declaration and Initialization (Java):**

int[][] matrix = new int[3][3]; // Declare a 3x3 array
int[][] anotherMatrix = { {1, 2, 3}, {4, 5, 6}, {7, 8, 9} }; // Initialize values

1. **3D Array Declaration and Initialization (C++):**

int threeDArray[2][3][4]; // Declare a 3D array with dimensions 2x3x4

1. **2D Array Declaration and Initialization (Python):**

matrix = [[1, 2, 3], [4, 5, 6], [7, 8, 9]] # Initialize a 3x3 array

Initializing Multidimensional Arrays with Initial Values

1. **2D Array Initialization (C#):**

int[,] grid = { {1, 2, 3}, {4, 5, 6} }; // Initialize a 2D array

1. **3D Array Initialization (JavaScript):**

```
let cube = [
[[1, 2], [3, 4]],
[[5, 6], [7, 8]]
]; // Initialize a 3D array
```

Note: The syntax varies depending on the programming language, but the concept of declaring and initializing multidimensional arrays remains consistent.

Multidimensional arrays provide a structured way to store and access data in multiple dimensions. They are particularly useful for tasks involving grids, tables, or matrices where data has clear relationships.

7.3.3 Accessing and Manipulating Multidimensional Array Elements

Accessing and manipulating elements in multidimensional arrays is essential for working with structured data in various dimensions. This section explores techniques for indexing and performing operations on multidimensional arrays.

Indexing and Addressing Elements in Multidimensional Arrays

1. **2D Array Indexing (Java):**

```
int[][] matrix = { {1, 2, 3}, {4, 5, 6}, {7, 8, 9} };
int element = matrix[1][2]; // Access element at row 1, column 2 (value: 6)
```

1. **3D Array Indexing (C++):**

```
int threeDArray[2][3][4];
int value = threeDArray[1][2][3]; // Access element at layer 1, row 2, column 3
```

1. **2D Array Indexing (Python):**

pythonCopy code
matrix = [[1, 2, 3], [4, 5, 6], [7, 8, 9]] value = matrix[2][0] # Access element at row 2, column 0 (value: 7)

Performing Operations on Matrix-Like Structures

1. **Matrix Addition (C#):**

```
int[,] matrix1 = { {1, 2}, {3, 4} };
int[,] matrix2 = { {5, 6}, {7, 8} };
int[,] result = new int[2, 2];
for (int i = 0; i < 2; i++) {
for (int j = 0; j < 2; j++) { result[i, j] = matrix1[i, j] + matrix2[i, j];
}
}
```

1. **Matrix Multiplication (JavaScript):**

```
let matrix1 = [[1, 2], [3, 4]];
let matrix2 = [[5, 6], [7, 8]];
function matrixMultiply(a, b) {
let result = [];
for (let i = 0; i < a.length; i++) {

 result[i] = [];
 for (let j = 0; j < b[0].length; j++) {
 let sum = 0;
 for (let k = 0; k < a[0].length; k++) {
 sum += a[i][k] * b[k][j];
 }
```

```
result[i][j] = sum;
}

}
return result;
}
let productMatrix = matrixMultiply(matrix1, matrix2);
```

Accessing and manipulating multidimensional array elements enables you to work with structured data efficiently. These operations are fundamental when dealing with grid-like structures, matrices, and higher-dimensional data representations.

7.3.4 Iterating Through Multidimensional Arrays

Iterating through multidimensional arrays is a crucial skill for performing various operations on structured data. This section delves into the use of nested loops and algorithms for tasks involving multidimensional arrays.

Using Nested Loops for Iterating Through Multidimensional Arrays

1. **2D Array Iteration (Java):**

```
int[][] matrix = { {1, 2, 3}, {4, 5, 6}, {7, 8, 9} };
for (int i = 0; i < matrix.length; i++) {
for (int j = 0; j < matrix[i].length; j++) {
int element = matrix[i][j];
// Perform operations on the element
}
}
```

1. **3D Array Iteration (C++):**

```
int threeDArray[2][3][4];
```

```
for (int i = 0; i < 2; i++) {
for (int j = 0; j < 3; j++) {
for (int k = 0; k < 4; k++) {

  int value = threeDArray[i][j][k];
  // Perform operations on the value

}
}
}
```

1. **2D Array Iteration (Python):**

```
matrix = [[1, 2, 3], [4, 5, 6], [7, 8, 9]]
for row in matrix:
for element in row:

  # Perform operations on the element
```

Applying Algorithms for Tasks Like Matrix Multiplication and Traversal

1. **Matrix Multiplication (C#):**

```
int[,] matrix1 = { {1, 2}, {3, 4} };
    int[,] matrix2 = { {5, 6}, {7, 8} };
    int[,] result = new int[2, 2];
    for (int i = 0; i < 2; i++) {
    for (int j = 0; j < 2; j++) {
    int sum = 0;
    for (int k = 0; k < 2; k++) {

      sum += matrix1[i, k] * matrix2[k, j];
```

```
}
result[i, j] = sum;
}
}
```

1. **Matrix Traversal and Sum (JavaScript):**

```
let matrix = [[1, 2, 3], [4, 5, 6], [7, 8, 9]];
let sum = 0;
for (let i = 0; i < matrix.length; i++) {
for (let j = 0; j < matrix[i].length; j++) {

  sum += matrix[i][j];

}
}
```

Iterating through multidimensional arrays enables you to process and manipulate data efficiently. Nested loops are a fundamental tool in working with structured data in various dimensions, and they are essential for performing complex operations like matrix multiplication or traversal.

This chapter equips you with the knowledge and skills to work effectively with arrays and strings, from basic manipulation to advanced algorithms and multidimensional structures. Arrays and strings are foundational data structures that are fundamental in various programming scenarios, making this chapter essential for every programmer's toolkit.

Part III: Programming Paradigms

Chapter 8: Procedural Programming

Procedural programming is a fundamental programming paradigm that focuses on breaking down a program into smaller, reusable functions or procedures. This chapter explores the principles and concepts of procedural programming, providing you with a solid foundation for designing structured and modular code.

8.1 Modular Programming Concepts

8.1.1 Understanding Modules

Modules are a cornerstone of modular programming, representing self-contained units of code that serve specific functionalities. This section introduces the concept of modules and highlights the benefits they bring to the development process.

Introduction to Modules as Self-contained Units of Code

In programming, a module refers to a self-contained unit of code that encapsulates a specific set of functionalities. It can consist of functions, variables, classes, or any combination of these elements. Modules are designed to encapsulate related code, making it easier to manage, reuse, and maintain.

Modules provide the following key advantages:

1. **Modularity:** Modules break down complex programs into manageable parts. Each module handles a specific task, promoting code organization and making the overall program structure more understandable.

2. **Code Reusability:** Once a module is created, it can be reused across different parts of the program or even in other projects. This reusability saves time and effort, as developers don't need to reinvent the wheel for common functionalities.
3. **Maintainability:** Modular code is easier to maintain. If a bug or improvement is needed, developers can focus on a single module without affecting the entire program. This isolation minimizes the risk of unintended consequences.
4. **Collaboration:** Modular programming supports collaborative development. Different team members can work on separate modules simultaneously, as long as the module interfaces are well-defined. This speeds up development and reduces conflicts.
5. **Scalability:** As programs grow in complexity, modular design allows for better scalability. New features or changes can be implemented by adding or modifying modules, rather than overhauling the entire codebase.

Benefits of Modular Programming: Code Reusability, Maintainability, and Organization

- **Code Reusability:** Modules encapsulate specific functionalities, enabling developers to reuse well-defined components across different parts of the program or in different projects. This practice saves time, enhances consistency, and improves development efficiency.
- **Maintainability:** By isolating functionalities in separate modules, the maintenance process becomes more manageable. Updates, bug fixes, and improvements can be applied to individual modules without affecting the entire program.

- **Organization:** Modules organize code into logical units, making it easier to navigate and understand. This is especially beneficial in larger projects, where keeping track of different functionalities can become challenging.

In summary, modules offer a structured approach to designing programs, promoting reusability, maintainability, and a clear code organization. Understanding how to create and effectively use modules is a key skill for developers aiming to build robust and scalable software.

8.1.2 Encapsulation and Abstraction

Encapsulation and abstraction are essential principles in modular programming that contribute to well-structured and maintainable code. This section explores these concepts and their significance in creating effective modules.

Using Encapsulation to Hide Internal Implementation Details

Encapsulation involves bundling data (variables) and the methods (functions) that operate on the data into a single unit, known as a class or module. The key idea is to hide the internal details of how a module works, exposing only a well-defined interface to the outside world. This provides several benefits:

- **Data Protection:** Encapsulation prevents unauthorized access to the internal data of a module. By controlling access through methods, you ensure data integrity and avoid unintended modifications.
- **Modularity:** Modules that use encapsulation are modular and self-contained. Changes made to the internal implementation of a module won't affect other parts of the

program, as long as the interface remains unchanged.
- **Code Organization:** Encapsulation promotes clear separation between different parts of the program. Modules that interact with each other only need to know the exposed interface, reducing the complexity of inter-module communication.

Achieving Abstraction by Exposing Only Essential Features

Abstraction is the process of simplifying complex reality by modeling classes of objects with relevant characteristics. In the context of modular programming, abstraction is achieved by exposing a clear and concise interface while hiding the implementation details.

- **Interface Focus:** Abstraction focuses on what a module does rather than how it does it. This allows developers to work with high-level concepts without getting bogged down in low-level details.
- **Reduced Complexity:** By abstracting away unnecessary details, modules become easier to understand and use. Developers can work with the module's interface without needing to know its internal intricacies.
- **Maintenance and Flexibility:** Abstraction enables changes to the internal implementation without affecting the module's interface. This promotes flexibility and adaptability in response to evolving requirements.

In summary, encapsulation and abstraction are powerful tools in modular programming. Encapsulation hides internal complexities and protects data, while abstraction simplifies interactions by focusing on essential features. By applying these principles, developers create modules that are easier to use, maintain, and extend.

8.1.3 Dependency Management

Effective dependency management is crucial in modular programming to ensure modules interact seamlessly while maintaining flexibility and reusability. This section delves into strategies for managing dependencies and reducing coupling between modules.

Handling Dependencies Between Modules

Dependencies occur when one module relies on another module to perform a certain task or provide specific functionality. While dependencies are inevitable, managing them well is essential to avoid creating tightly coupled and inflexible code.

- **Dependency Types:** Understanding different types of dependencies, including direct and transitive dependencies, and recognizing their impact on the program's architecture.
- **Dependency Chains:** Identifying chains of dependencies and assessing the potential ripple effects of changes in one module on others.
- **Dependency Injection:** Introducing the concept of dependency injection, where dependencies are provided to a module from the outside rather than being created internally.

Techniques for Managing Module Interactions and Reducing Coupling

Reducing coupling between modules is a key goal in modular programming. Lower coupling increases the independence of modules, making them more maintainable and adaptable.

- **Interface Design:** Creating clear and well-defined interfaces for modules that specify how they interact with each other. This minimizes direct interactions between modules and promotes modularity.
- **Loose Coupling:** Striving for loose coupling by designing modules that depend on abstractions rather than concrete implementations. This allows modules to be swapped out or replaced without affecting others.
- **Dependency Inversion Principle:** Introducing the dependency inversion principle, which suggests that high-level modules should not depend on low-level modules, but both should depend on abstractions.
- **Dependency Management Tools:** Exploring tools and frameworks that help manage dependencies and promote loose coupling, such as dependency injection containers.

In summary, managing dependencies and reducing coupling between modules are essential practices for building flexible, maintainable, and scalable software. By carefully designing module interactions and utilizing techniques like dependency injection and loose coupling, developers can create a modular architecture that can evolve and adapt to changing requirements.

8.2 Functions and Parameter Passing

8.2.1 Function Definition and Declaration

Functions are a fundamental building block of procedural programming, allowing developers to encapsulate a set of instructions into a reusable unit. This section covers the syntax for defining functions in various programming languages and emphasizes the importance of creating functions with meaningful names and clear purposes.

Syntax for Defining Functions in Various Programming Languages

The syntax for defining functions can vary across programming languages, but the general structure includes the following elements:

1. **Function Header:** This includes the function's name, return type (if applicable), and parameter list enclosed in parentheses.
2. **Function Body:** The body contains the instructions or statements that define the function's behavior. It is enclosed in curly braces {}.
3. **Return Statement:** If the function returns a value, the return statement specifies the value to be returned to the caller.

Examples of function definition syntax in different languages:

- In C++:

```
return_type function_name(parameter_type parameter_name)
{
```

```
// function body
return value; // if applicable
}
```

- In Python:

```
def function_name(parameter_name):
# function body
return value # if applicable
```

- In Java:

```
return_type function_name(parameter_type parameter_name)
{
// function body
return value; // if applicable
}
```

Creating Functions with Meaningful Names and Clear Purposes

When designing functions, it's essential to follow these principles:

- **Descriptive Naming:** Choose names that accurately reflect the purpose of the function. A well-named function should provide a clear indication of what it does without needing to dive into the implementation details.
- **Single Responsibility:** Functions should have a single, well-defined responsibility. Avoid creating functions that perform multiple unrelated tasks, as this can lead to confusion and reduced code maintainability.
- **Modularity:** Functions should encapsulate specific functionality and provide a clear interface for the caller. This promotes modularity and reusability.

- **Documentation:** Include comments or documentation that describe the function's purpose, parameters, and return value. This helps other developers understand how to use the function correctly.

Creating functions with meaningful names and clear purposes contributes to code readability, maintainability, and reusability. Well-designed functions enhance the overall structure of your program and make it easier for both you and other developers to work with the codebase.

8.2.2 Return Values

Return values play a crucial role in functions, allowing them to provide results or data back to the calling code. This section explores the significance of return values and demonstrates how return statements are used to pass data back to the caller.

Understanding Return Values and Their Significance

Return values are the mechanism by which functions communicate results or data to the code that called them. When a function completes its execution, it can optionally return a value that can be used in subsequent program logic.

Significance of Return Values:

- **Result Communication:** Functions use return values to convey the outcome of their computation or processing to the calling code. For example, a mathematical function might return the result of a calculation.
- **Data Passing:** Functions can pass data back to the caller for further processing. This is particularly useful when a function performs operations on input data and provides

the modified data as output.

- **Error Handling:** Functions often return specific values or error codes to indicate exceptional cases or error conditions. This allows the caller to handle errors gracefully.

Using Return Statements to Pass Data Back to the Calling Code

The return statement is used within a function to specify the value that should be returned to the calling code. The syntax varies slightly depending on the programming language.

Example of using return statements in different languages:

- In C++:

```
int add(int a, int b) {
return a + b;
}
```

- In Python:

```
def add(a, b):
return a + b
```

- In Java:

```
int add(int a, int b) {
return a + b;
}
```

When a function is called, its return value can be assigned to a variable or used directly in expressions:

```
int result = add(5, 3); // result will hold the value 8
```

Return values enhance the flexibility and utility of functions by enabling them to provide meaningful results or data to the rest of the program. Proper use of return values contributes to clearer and more effective code organization.

8.2.3 Parameter Passing

Parameter passing refers to the process of passing data or values to a function when it is called. This section discusses different methods of parameter passing, including pass by value and pass by reference, and explores the management of function arguments and their scope.

Different Methods of Parameter Passing: Pass by Value and Pass by Reference

1. **Pass by Value:** In this method, the value of the actual argument is copied to the parameter of the function. Changes made to the parameter within the function do not affect the original argument.
2. **Pass by Reference:** In this method, the memory address of the actual argument is passed to the parameter. This means changes made to the parameter within the function directly affect the original argument.

Managing Function Arguments and Their Scope

- **Function Arguments:** Function arguments are the values or variables passed to a function when it is called. Functions use these arguments to perform operations or computations.
- **Parameter Scope:** Function parameters have a local scope within the function. This means they are only accessible within the function's body and are not visible or usable

outside of it.

- **Lifetime of Function Arguments:** Function arguments have a lifetime tied to the function call. When the function call ends, the memory allocated for the arguments is released.
- **Argument Passing and Modifiability:** In pass by value, modifications made to the function parameter do not affect the original argument. In pass by reference, modifications made to the function parameter directly affect the original argument.
- **Passing Expressions as Arguments:** It's common to pass variables or constants as arguments, but expressions can also be passed. The expression is evaluated before being passed to the function.

Proper management of function arguments is essential for writing functions that are clear, efficient, and effective. Choosing between pass by value and pass by reference depends on the desired behavior and the need to modify the original data. Understanding the scope and lifetime of function arguments helps prevent unintended side effects and enhances code predictability.

8.3 Structured Programming Principles

8.3.1 Sequence

Sequence is a fundamental concept in structured programming where code is organized as a sequence of executable statements. This section explores the significance of organizing code in a sequential manner and emphasizes the importance of ensuring a logical flow from one statement to the next.

Organizing Code as a Sequence of Executable Statements

In a procedural programming paradigm, code execution typically follows a sequential order. This means that statements are executed one after another, in the order they are written. This approach to organizing code is intuitive and mirrors the natural flow of actions in many scenarios.

Ensuring Logical Flow from One Statement to the Next

Ensuring a logical flow is crucial to writing readable and maintainable code. Each statement should naturally lead to the next, creating a coherent progression. This logical flow simplifies understanding the code's purpose and makes it easier to track the sequence of actions.

Best Practices for Maintaining Logical Flow:

- **Clear Structure:** Write code in a structured and organized manner. Break down complex tasks into smaller steps, each represented by a separate statement.
- **Meaningful Comments:** Include comments that explain the purpose of each statement or sequence of statements. This helps other developers understand the code's intention.
- **Avoiding Unnecessary Jumps:** Minimize the use of jump statements (like "goto" or equivalents) that can disrupt the natural sequence of statements. Instead, rely on loops and conditional statements for controlled branching.
- **Consistent Indentation:** Indentation helps visualize the code's hierarchy and sequence. Maintain consistent indentation to make it easier to spot the sequence of actions.

- **Logical Grouping:** Group related statements together. For example, if you're opening a file, reading its contents, and then closing it, group these actions together.

In summary, structuring code as a sequence of executable statements and maintaining a logical flow from one statement to the next is vital for code readability and comprehensibility. This approach simplifies understanding the code's behavior, aids in debugging, and enhances collaboration among developers.

8.3.2 Selection (Conditional Statements)

Selection, often implemented through conditional statements, is a crucial aspect of procedural programming. This section delves into the use of if-else and switch statements for decision-making and highlights the significance of structuring code based on conditions and logical branching.

Using if-else and Switch Statements for Decision-Making

- **if-else Statements:** The if-else statement is used to execute a block of code if a certain condition is true and an alternative block if the condition is false. It allows the program to take different paths based on the outcome of the condition.

Example (in Python):

```
if condition:
# code to execute if condition is true
else:
# code to execute if condition is false
```

- **switch Statements (or Equivalent):** The switch statement allows the program to choose from multiple options based on the value of an expression. Different cases are evaluated, and the corresponding block of code is executed.

Example (in C++):

```
switch (expression) {
case value1:

  // code to execute if expression equals value1
  break;
  case value2:
  // code to execute if expression equals value2
  break;

default:

  // code to execute if none of the cases match

}
```

Structuring Code Based on Conditions and Logical Branching

Selection structures allow programs to adapt their behavior based on various conditions or inputs. This logical branching enhances the program's versatility and functionality.

Best Practices for Using Conditional Statements:

- **Clarity:** Write conditions that are easy to understand and interpret. Use descriptive variable names and meaningful comparisons.
- **Avoid Overcomplexity:** Refrain from nesting too many conditional statements within each other. Excessive nesting can make code harder to read and maintain.
- **Consistent Formatting:** Maintain consistent indentation

and formatting for improved readability.

- **Clear Commenting:** If the logic behind a conditional statement is complex or non-obvious, consider adding comments to explain the reasoning.

Conditional statements are essential tools for implementing decision-making processes in code. They enable programs to respond intelligently to different scenarios and are a cornerstone of effective procedural programming.

8.3.3 Repetition (Loops)

Repetition, achieved through loops, is a fundamental concept in procedural programming that allows the execution of a block of code multiple times. This section explores the application of loops, including for, while, and do-while loops, for repetitive tasks. It emphasizes the importance of ensuring controlled iteration and avoiding the pitfalls of infinite loops.

Applying Loops for Repetitive Tasks

Loops are powerful constructs that automate the execution of a set of statements, allowing repetitive tasks to be accomplished efficiently. They are particularly useful when a task needs to be performed a specific number of times or as long as a certain condition is met.

Types of Loops:

- **for Loop:** Executes a block of code for a specific number of iterations.

Example (in Python):

```
for i in range(5):
# code to execute for each iteration
```

- **while Loop:** Repeatedly executes a block of code as long as a specified condition is true.

Example (in C++):
```
while (condition) {
// code to execute while condition is true
}
```

- **do-while Loop:** Similar to a while loop, but it guarantees at least one execution of the block of code, even if the condition is false from the start.

Example (in Java):
```
do {
// code to execute at least once
} while (condition);
```

Ensuring Controlled Iteration and Avoiding Infinite Loops

While loops are powerful tools, they can lead to unintended consequences if not managed carefully. Infinite loops occur when the loop's condition is always true, causing the loop to run indefinitely.

Preventing Infinite Loops:

- **Clearly Defined Exit Condition:** Ensure the loop's exit condition will eventually become false. For example, a loop iterating through an array should have a condition based on the array's length.
- **Initialization and Updates:** In for loops, ensure the loop variable is properly initialized and updated within the loop body to reach the exit condition.
- **Break Statements:** Incorporate break statements to forcefully exit a loop if a specific condition is met.
- **Loop Counters:** In while loops, be cautious with the loop counter's initialization and updates to avoid getting stuck.

Loops are essential tools for automating repetitive tasks and are a key component of procedural programming. When used judiciously and with a clear understanding of the exit conditions, loops enhance code efficiency and functionality.

8.3.4 Avoiding Goto Statements

Goto statements are a controversial feature in programming languages that allow jumping to a different part of the code, often causing unstructured and hard-to-maintain code. This section discusses the pitfalls of using goto statements and highlights alternative approaches for achieving structured control flow.

Understanding the Pitfalls of Using Goto Statements

Goto statements can lead to several issues in code:

- **Unreadable Code:** Goto statements can make code difficult to read and understand, as they disrupt the natural sequence of execution.
- **Difficult Debugging:** Jumping to different parts of the code can make debugging challenging, especially when tracking the flow of execution.
- **Spaghetti Code:** Overuse of goto statements can result in "spaghetti code," where the program's logic becomes tangled and convoluted.

Alternatives to Goto for Structured Control Flow

Modern programming languages and methodologies provide alternative ways to achieve structured control flow:

- **Loops:** Loops, such as for, while, and do-while, offer a structured and readable way to repeat code execution.

- **Conditional Statements:** if-else and switch statements provide ways to make decisions and execute different blocks of code based on conditions.
- **Functions:** Breaking code into functions or subroutines helps modularize the codebase, making it more organized and easier to understand.
- **Exception Handling:** Many languages offer exception handling mechanisms for dealing with errors and exceptional situations in a structured manner.
- **Structured Programming:** Adhering to structured programming principles, which emphasize clear control flow and code organization, leads to more maintainable code.

In most cases, alternatives to goto statements provide clearer, more maintainable code that is easier to understand and debug. As such, it's recommended to avoid goto statements and embrace structured programming practices.

Procedural programming principles equip you with the tools to create well-organized, modular, and maintainable code. Understanding modular programming concepts, mastering functions and parameter passing, and applying structured programming principles are essential steps in becoming a proficient procedural programmer.

Chapter 9: Object-Oriented Programming

9.1 Objects and Classes

9.1.1 Introduction to Objects and Classes

In the realm of software development, a profound paradigm shift occurred with the rise of Object-Oriented Programming (OOP). This shift transformed how programs are conceptualized, designed, and executed. OOP introduced a new way of thinking about software, emphasizing the organization of code around the fundamental building blocks of "objects" and "classes." Let's delve into this pivotal introduction to objects and classes and explore the key concepts that form the bedrock of OOP.

Understanding the Paradigm Shift to Object-Oriented Programming

Object-Oriented Programming emerged as a response to the complexities and challenges inherent in managing and scaling codebases in traditional procedural programming. It introduced a novel way of structuring code by centering it around objects, each representing a real-world entity, concept, or abstraction. This paradigm shift revolutionized software development by enabling developers to model complex systems more naturally, enhance code reusability, and encapsulate data and behavior within self-contained entities.

Key Concepts: Objects, Classes, Methods, Attributes

Objects: At the heart of Object-Oriented Programming are "objects." An object is a tangible or abstract entity that encapsulates both data (attributes) and behaviors (methods). Objects mirror real-world entities or concepts, enabling developers to represent complex systems in a more intuitive and manageable manner. For instance, in a banking application, an object could represent a customer, holding information like their name, account balance, and transaction history.

Classes: A "class" serves as a blueprint or template for creating objects. It defines the structure and behavior that its objects will exhibit. Think of a class as a set of instructions for creating and interacting with objects of a certain type. Using our banking example, a "Customer" class might specify the attributes (name, balance) and methods (deposit, withdraw) that all customer objects will possess.

Methods: Methods are functions associated with a class, defining the actions an object of that class can perform. They encapsulate behaviors and actions that objects can undertake. In our "Customer" class, methods could include actions like depositing funds into an account or checking the account balance.

Attributes: Attributes, also known as fields or properties, represent the data associated with an object. They encapsulate the object's state or characteristics. In the context of our "Customer" class, attributes might encompass the customer's name, account number, and account balance.

As we venture deeper into the world of OOP, the concepts of objects and classes will serve as the bedrock upon which we build sophisticated and efficient software solutions. They empower us to model intricate systems, enhance code modularity, and promote code reusability – ultimately leading to more elegant and maintainable codebases.

9.1.2 Defining Classes and Objects in Programming

In Object-Oriented Programming (OOP), classes and objects form the core components that enable us to model real-world entities and implement their behaviors in code. Let's delve into the process of defining classes and creating objects, which lays the foundation for constructing robust and structured software systems.

Creating Class Definitions

A class serves as a blueprint or template for creating objects with shared attributes and behaviors. Defining a class involves specifying its structure, attributes, and methods. Here's a breakdown of the steps to create class definitions:

1. **Class Declaration**: Declare a class using the **class** keyword, followed by the class name. The class name should be descriptive of the entity or concept it represents.
2. **Attributes (Fields)**: Inside the class definition, specify attributes that represent the data associated with objects of the class. Attributes define the state of the objects. For example, a "Person" class might have attributes like **name**, **age**, and **address**.
3. **Methods (Functions)**: Define methods within the class to encapsulate behaviors that the objects can perform. These methods determine how objects interact with each other and with their environment. A "Car" class might have methods like **start_engine()** and **drive()**.

Instantiating Objects from Classes

Once a class is defined, we can create individual instances of that class, known as objects. An object is an instantiation of a class, representing a specific occurrence of the entity described by the class. Here's how we instantiate objects from classes:

1. **Object Creation**: Use the class name followed by parentheses to create a new object. This process is often referred to as "object instantiation" or "object creation."
2. **Constructor**: During object creation, a special method called the "constructor" is invoked. The constructor initializes the object's attributes and sets its initial state. Constructors ensure that objects are created in a consistent and valid state.
3. **Accessing Attributes and Methods**: Once an object is created, we can access its attributes and methods using dot notation. For example, if **car** is an instance of the "Car" class, we can access its attributes like **car.color** and call its methods like **car.start_engine()**.

Creating classes and instantiating objects enables us to create organized and modular codebases. Classes provide a blueprint for objects, while objects themselves hold the data and behavior that bring our software to life. This encapsulation and structure form the cornerstone of OOP, facilitating code reusability, maintainability, and a more intuitive representation of complex systems.

9.1.3 Creating Instances of Classes (Instantiation)

In the realm of Object-Oriented Programming (OOP), the process of creating instances of classes is fundamental. It involves transforming a class blueprint into a tangible object with its own set of attributes and behaviors. This instantiation process is crucial for modeling real-world entities and enabling interactions within a software system.

Constructing Objects with Constructors

When an instance of a class is created, a special method called a "constructor" is invoked. The constructor method is responsible for initializing the object's attributes and preparing it for use. Constructors are defined within the class and are executed automatically during the instantiation process.

The constructor allows us to set initial values for the object's attributes, ensuring that the object is created in a valid and consistent state. It plays a pivotal role in defining the behavior of the object upon its creation.

Initializing Object Attributes

During the instantiation process, we can initialize the attributes of the object using the constructor. Attributes are the data components that define the state of the object. By setting attribute values in the constructor, we ensure that each object starts with specific characteristics.

For example, consider a "Person" class with attributes like **name**, **age**, and **address**. When we create an instance of this class, we can provide values for these attributes in the constructor:

```
class Person:
def __init__(self, name, age, address):

  self.name = name
  self.age = age
  self.address = address
```

```
# Creating an instance of the Person class
person1 = Person("Alice", 30, "123 Main St")
```

In the above example, the **__init__** method serves as the constructor. It takes parameters (**name, age, address**) to initialize the attributes of the object (**self.name, self.age, self.address**).

The instantiation process, fueled by constructors, allows us to tailor each object to its unique context. By setting attributes and preparing the object for use, we establish a foundation for the object to interact with other components of the software system. This encapsulation of data and behavior within objects enhances code organization, reusability, and maintainability, hallmarks of Object-Oriented Programming.

9.1.4 The Relationship Between Classes and Objects

In Object-Oriented Programming (OOP), classes and objects are intricately connected, forming the bedrock of software design. Understanding the relationship between classes and objects is essential for creating well-structured and organized code that models real-world entities effectively.

Class-Object Relationship and Object Identity

A class serves as a blueprint that defines the structure, attributes, and methods of objects. Objects, on the other hand, are instances of classes, embodying the characteristics and behaviors specified by the class. Each object created from the same class shares the same attributes and methods, but they may have distinct attribute values that differentiate them.

Object identity refers to the unique instance of an object in memory. Even if two objects have the same attribute values, they are distinct entities with separate memory addresses. This concept of identity is crucial for maintaining data integrity and ensuring that interactions with objects are well-defined and consistent.

Reference Variables and Object Interaction

In many programming languages, objects are accessed and manipulated using reference variables. A reference variable is a pointer that "references" or "points to" the memory location of an object. When we create an object, we store its memory address in a reference variable.

Reference variables enable us to interact with objects, call their methods, and access their attributes. Multiple reference variables can point to the same object, allowing for shared access and manipulation.

Consider an example:

```
class Circle:
def __init__(self, radius):

 self.radius = radius
 def area(self):
 return 3.14 * self.radius * self.radius

# Creating instances of the Circle class
circle1 = Circle(5)
circle2 = Circle(10)
# Reference variables pointing to the objects
ref_circle1 = circle1
ref_circle2 = circle2
# Accessing methods and attributes
print(ref_circle1.area()) # Output: 78.5
print(ref_circle2.radius) # Output: 10
```

In this example, **ref_circle1** and **ref_circle2** are reference variables pointing to the objects created from the **Circle** class. Both reference variables allow access to the methods and attributes of their respective objects.

Understanding the relationship between classes, objects, and reference variables empowers developers to design cohesive and modular systems. It facilitates the creation of software that accurately models real-world entities and enables efficient interactions between different components.

9.2 Encapsulation, Inheritance, and Polymorphism

9.2.1 Encapsulation: Data Hiding and Information Bundling

In the realm of Object-Oriented Programming (OOP), encapsulation stands as a fundamental concept that underpins the design of modern software systems. Encapsulation involves bundling data and the methods that operate on that data into a single unit, known as a class. This unit serves as a protective container, shielding the internal details of an object from external interference and manipulation.

Encapsulation as a Fundamental OOP Concept

At its core, encapsulation promotes the principle of information hiding. It emphasizes that the internal implementation details of an object should be hidden from external code. Instead of directly accessing an object's attributes, external code interacts with the object through well-defined methods, often referred to as "getters" and "setters." This controlled access ensures that the object's state remains consistent and valid.

Encapsulation encapsulates both data and behavior within a single entity, promoting modularity and separation of concerns. By encapsulating related data and methods in a class, we create a cohesive and self-contained unit that can be reused across different parts of the software.

Benefits of Encapsulation: Data Security and Abstraction

Encapsulation offers several compelling benefits that contribute to the robustness and maintainability of software systems:

1. **Data Security:** By encapsulating data, we restrict direct access to sensitive information. This enhances data security and prevents unintended modifications that could lead to errors or inconsistencies.
2. **Abstraction:** Encapsulation enables abstraction, allowing external code to interact with an object's essential functionality without needing to know the intricate details of its implementation. This abstraction simplifies complex systems, making them more comprehensible and manageable.
3. **Code Flexibility:** Encapsulated classes can be modified internally without affecting external code that relies on them. This separation between internal implementation and external interaction fosters code flexibility and adaptability.
4. **Code Maintenance:** Encapsulation supports code maintenance by localizing changes. When modifications are needed, they can be made within the encapsulated class, minimizing the impact on the rest of the system.

Consider an example of encapsulation in a **BankAccount** class:

```
class BankAccount:
def __init__(self, balance):

 self.__balance = balance # Encapsulated attribute

 def get_balance(self):
```

```
return self.__balance
def deposit(self, amount):
self.__balance += amount
def withdraw(self, amount):
if self.__balance >= amount:
self.__balance -= amount
else: print("Insufficient funds")

# Creating an instance of the BankAccount class
account = BankAccount(1000)
# Accessing the balance using a getter method
print(account.get_balance()) # Output: 1000
# Depositing money into the account
account.deposit(500)
# Withdrawing money from the account
account.withdraw(200)
```

In this example, the encapsulated attribute **__balance** is hidden from direct access, and interactions with it are mediated through getter and setter methods.

Encapsulation's ability to control data access and ensure data integrity makes it a cornerstone of Object-Oriented Programming. It promotes clean and well-structured code by enforcing a clear separation between implementation details and external interactions.

9.2.2 Access Modifiers: Public, Private, Protected

In Object-Oriented Programming (OOP), access modifiers play a vital role in defining the scope and visibility of class members (attributes and methods). These modifiers determine how members can be accessed and manipulated from within the class itself and from external code.

Control of Member Accessibility

Access modifiers provide control over the accessibility of class members, ensuring that they are appropriately encapsulated and interacted with. Different programming languages offer varying access modifiers, but the three most common ones are:

1. **Public:** Members declared as public are accessible from anywhere, both within the class and from external code. They form the interface through which external code interacts with the class.
2. **Private:** Private members are accessible only within the class where they are defined. They are hidden from external code, promoting encapsulation and preventing direct manipulation.
3. **Protected:** Protected members are accessible within the class where they are defined and within its subclasses. They facilitate controlled inheritance and extension of class functionality.

Balancing Encapsulation and Accessibility

Choosing the appropriate access modifier for each member is crucial for achieving a balance between encapsulation and accessibility. Encapsulation aims to shield internal details, while accessibility ensures that external code can use and extend the class effectively.

By using access modifiers effectively, developers can:

- Prevent unintended modifications to internal data by making attributes private.
- Provide a clear and controlled interface to external code through public methods.

- Enable subclasses to build upon the existing functionality of a base class using protected members.

Consider an example of access modifiers in a **Person** class:

```
public class Person {
private String name; // Private attribute
protected int age; // Protected attribute
public String address; // Public attribute
public Person(String name, int age, String address) {

  this.name = name;
  this.age = age;
  this.address = address;

}
public void displayInfo() {

  System.out.println("Name: " + name);
  System.out.println("Age: " + age);
  System.out.println("Address: " + address);

} // Getter and setter methods omitted for brevity
}
```

In this example, the **name** attribute is private to ensure that it can only be accessed and modified within the class. The **age** attribute is protected, allowing subclasses to access and modify it. The **address** attribute is public, providing unrestricted access to external code.

By carefully choosing access modifiers, developers can control the exposure of class members, maintain encapsulation, and create well-designed and flexible software systems.

9.2.3 Inheritance: Extending and Reusing Classes

Inheritance is a core concept in Object-Oriented Programming (OOP) that enables the creation of new classes based on existing ones. It fosters code reuse, extensibility, and the establishment of hierarchical relationships between classes.

Hierarchical Relationships and Inheritance Hierarchy

Inheritance establishes a hierarchical relationship between classes, where one class (the derived or subclass) inherits attributes and behaviors from another class (the base or superclass). This relationship allows the derived class to reuse and extend the functionality of the base class.

Consider a simple example of an inheritance hierarchy involving an **Animal** base class and **Cat** and **Dog** subclasses:

```
class Animal:
def __init__(self, species):

 self.species = species

 def make_sound(self):
 pass # Placeholder for the method

class Cat(Animal):
def make_sound(self):

 return "Meow"

class Dog(Animal):
def make_sound(self):

 return "Woof"
```

In this example, **Cat** and **Dog** inherit from the **Animal** class, forming an inheritance hierarchy. The **make_sound** method is overridden in the subclasses to provide specific implementations.

Implementing Inheritance with Base and Derived Classes

To create an inheritance relationship, a derived class is defined using the **class** keyword, followed by the name of the derived class and the name of the base class in parentheses. The derived class inherits attributes and methods from the base class, and it can also define its own attributes and methods.

Inheritance offers several benefits:

1. **Code Reuse:** Inheritance allows the reuse of attributes and methods from a base class, reducing redundancy and promoting efficient code organization.
2. **Extensibility:** Derived classes can extend the functionality of the base class by adding new attributes and methods or by overriding existing ones.
3. **Polymorphism:** Inheritance enables polymorphism, where objects of different classes can be treated uniformly through shared base class methods.
4. **Hierarchical Modeling:** Inheritance can represent real-world hierarchical relationships, making the codebase more intuitive and aligned with the problem domain.

Continuing with the **Animal** example:

```
# Creating instances of the derived classes
cat = Cat("Felis catus")
dog = Dog("Canis lupus familiaris")
# Calling the overridden method from the base class
print(cat.make_sound()) # Output: Meow
print(dog.make_sound()) # Output: Woof
```

In this example, the **Cat** and **Dog** subclasses inherit the **species** attribute from the **Animal** base class and provide their own implementations of the **make_sound** method.

Inheritance is a powerful mechanism that supports the creation of modular and maintainable code by promoting code reuse and facilitating the representation of complex relationships between classes. It embodies the essence of object-oriented design principles.

9.2.4 Polymorphism: Abstraction and Flexibility

Polymorphism is a fundamental concept in Object-Oriented Programming (OOP) that allows objects of different classes to be treated as objects of a common superclass. It promotes code flexibility, abstraction, and the ability to create code that works with a variety of objects without needing to know their specific types.

Understanding Polymorphism and Its Types

Polymorphism comes in two main types: compile-time polymorphism (also known as static polymorphism) and runtime polymorphism (also known as dynamic polymorphism).

1. **Compile-Time Polymorphism:** This type of polymorphism is achieved through method overloading. Method overloading allows a class to have multiple methods with the same name but different parameter lists. The appropriate method to call is determined by the method's signature (parameter types and number).
2. **Runtime Polymorphism:** This type of polymorphism is achieved through method overriding. Method overriding occurs when a subclass provides a specific implementation for a method that is already defined in its superclass. The method called is determined by the actual type of the

object at runtime.

Achieving Polymorphism through Method Overloading and Overriding

Method Overloading:

```
class Calculator {
int add(int a, int b) {

  return a + b;

}
double add(double a, double b) {

  return a + b;

}
}
```

In this example, the **Calculator** class demonstrates method overloading. It has two **add** methods—one for integer addition and another for double addition. The appropriate method is called based on the argument types.

Method Overriding:

```
class Shape {
void draw() {

  System.out.println("Drawing a shape");
  }

}
class Circle extends Shape {
@Override
void draw() {
```

```
        System.out.println("Drawing a circle");
    }
}
```

In this example, the **Shape** class has a **draw** method, and the **Circle** subclass overrides this method to provide a specific implementation. When the **draw** method is called on a **Circle** object, the overridden method in the **Circle** class is executed.

Polymorphism enables the creation of flexible and extensible code that can work with different types of objects in a unified manner. It simplifies code maintenance and promotes clean and modular design.

9.3 Object-Oriented Design Principles

9.3.1 Principles of Object-Oriented Design (OOD)

Object-Oriented Design (OOD) principles provide a set of guidelines and best practices for creating robust, maintainable, and flexible software. These principles are essential for crafting well-structured and efficient object-oriented systems.

Guiding Principles for Robust and Maintainable Designs

1. **Single Responsibility Principle (SRP):** Each class should have a single responsibility or reason to change. This principle promotes high cohesion and ensures that a class is focused on a specific task, making it easier to maintain and understand.

Example: Consider a banking application where a **Transaction** class handles both transaction processing and logging. Applying SRP, the class could be split into **TransactionProcessor** and

TransactionLogger classes, each responsible for its own distinct role.

1. **Open/Closed Principle (OCP):** Software entities (classes, modules, functions) should be open for extension but closed for modification. This principle encourages the addition of new features through extension rather than altering existing code, thus minimizing the risk of introducing bugs.

Example: In a drawing application, the introduction of new shapes like triangles and circles shouldn't require modification of existing rendering code. Instead, new shape classes can be added to extend the rendering capability.

1. **Liskov Substitution Principle (LSP):** Subtypes must be substitutable for their base types without affecting the correctness of the program. In other words, derived classes should extend but not alter the behavior of their base classes.

Example: If a **Bird** base class has a **fly()** method, any subclass like **Sparrow** or **Penguin** should be able to substitute for **Bird** without breaking the program's logic.

1. **Interface Segregation Principle (ISP):** Clients should not be forced to depend on interfaces they do not use. This principle encourages the creation of specific interfaces for each client, preventing unnecessary dependencies.

Example: In a library management system, separate interfaces for **Borrowable** and **Printable** could be defined, allowing classes to implement only the relevant interface based on their needs.

1. **Dependency Inversion Principle (DIP):** High-level modules should not depend on low-level modules; both should depend on abstractions. This principle promotes the use of interfaces or abstract classes to decouple classes and improve flexibility.

Example: In a messaging application, the **Messenger** class (high-level) shouldn't directly depend on specific **MessageService** classes (low-level). Instead, both can depend on an abstract **MessageService** interface.

Striving for Modularity and Flexibility in Software

1. **Modularity:** OOD encourages breaking down a complex system into smaller, manageable modules or classes. Each module should encapsulate a specific set of functionalities, promoting code reusability and maintainability.

Example: In a game development framework, different modules can be created for rendering, physics, and audio, allowing developers to work on each aspect independently.

1. **Flexibility:** OOD facilitates the creation of flexible software through polymorphism, abstraction, and encapsulation. Polymorphism allows interchangeable use of different classes, abstraction hides unnecessary details, and encapsulation shields internal complexities.

Example: Consider a media player application where different media types (audio, video) are supported. By using polymorphism, a common interface can be defined for both types, allowing the player to handle them interchangeably.

By adhering to these principles, developers can design software that is adaptable to changes, easy to extend, and less prone to bugs. Object-Oriented Design principles play a crucial role in creating software systems that are both efficient and maintainable over time.

9.3.2 Single Responsibility Principle (SRP)

The Single Responsibility Principle (SRP) is a fundamental concept in object-oriented design that emphasizes the importance of designing classes with a single, well-defined responsibility. This principle states that a class should have only one reason to change, meaning it should encapsulate one and only one functionality or concern.

Designing Classes with a Single Responsibility

When applying the SRP, each class should be designed to handle a specific task or aspect of the system. By focusing on a single responsibility, a class becomes more focused, understandable, and maintainable. It also becomes easier to extend or modify when necessary.

For example, consider a class that handles both database operations and user authentication. This violates the SRP, as changes to either the database structure or authentication mechanism would impact the entire class. Instead, the SRP suggests separating these responsibilities into distinct classes.

Minimizing Coupling and Enhancing Cohesion

Applying the SRP often leads to reduced coupling between classes. Coupling refers to the degree of dependency between classes. When classes have a single responsibility, they are less likely to depend on unrelated or tangential functionalities, resulting in lower coupling.

Additionally, SRP enhances cohesion within classes. Cohesion measures how closely the methods and attributes of a class are related to each other. High cohesion indicates that the class is well-focused on a specific purpose. By adhering to the SRP, classes achieve high cohesion, making them more understandable and easier to maintain.

In essence, the SRP promotes modular design by breaking down complex systems into smaller, specialized components. This not only enhances code organization but also simplifies testing, debugging, and collaboration among developers. By adhering to the SRP, software architects and developers can create systems that are more adaptable to changes and less prone to cascading updates.

9.3.3 Open/Closed Principle (OCP)

The Open/Closed Principle (OCP) is a key principle in object-oriented design that promotes the idea that software entities (classes, modules, functions) should be open for extension but closed for modification. In other words, the behavior of existing code should not be altered when new features or functionalities are added. Instead, new features should be added by extending existing code, rather than changing it.

Extending Functionality Without Modifying Existing Code

The OCP addresses the challenge of maintaining software as it evolves over time. When new requirements arise or features need to be added, the OCP guides developers to create new classes or modules that inherit from existing ones, rather than altering the original source code. This approach prevents unintended consequences and regression issues that can arise from modifying working code.

For example, consider a banking software with different account types. If a new account type needs to be added, the OCP suggests creating a new subclass of the existing account class, rather than modifying the existing account class. This way, the existing account functionalities remain unchanged.

Achieving Extensibility through Abstraction

Abstraction plays a crucial role in achieving the OCP. By designing abstract base classes or interfaces, developers can define a set of common behaviors and contract that derived classes must adhere to. New functionalities can then be introduced by creating new derived classes that implement these interfaces or inherit from the base class.

The OCP encourages a design that anticipates changes and allows for future extensions. While it may require more upfront design and effort, it leads to more maintainable and adaptable systems in the long run. Developers can add new features without risking the stability of existing code, facilitating parallel development and reducing the potential for introducing bugs.

In summary, the Open/Closed Principle fosters software designs that are both stable and extensible. By following the OCP, developers ensure that their codebases can evolve gracefully, accommodating new requirements and features without disrupting existing functionality.

9.3.4 Liskov Substitution Principle (LSP)

The Liskov Substitution Principle (LSP) is a vital concept in object-oriented design that emphasizes the need for subtypes to be substitutable for their base types without affecting the correctness of the program. In other words, if a class is a subclass of another class, it should be capable of replacing the parent class without altering the desirable properties of the program.

Ensuring Subtypes Adhere to Superclass Contracts

The LSP builds on the idea that subclasses should adhere to the contracts established by their parent classes. This contract includes not only method signatures but also the expected behavior and invariants. When a subclass follows this contract, it can be safely used interchangeably with its parent class.

For instance, consider a classic example involving shapes. If a class **Square** inherits from a class **Rectangle**, the LSP implies that any operation that can be performed on a **Rectangle** should be applicable to a **Square** as well, without causing unexpected behavior.

Preserving Behavior Inheritance and Compatibility

The LSP ensures that subclassing maintains the expected behavior and functionality inherited from the superclass. This principle prevents surprises and bugs that could arise when substituting objects. It encourages developers to think carefully about the relationships between classes and the inherent assumptions that can be made when substituting objects.

Adhering to the LSP leads to more robust and maintainable code. It allows for greater flexibility in code usage and promotes the creation of well-defined class hierarchies. When new subclasses are introduced, they are evaluated against the LSP to ensure that they maintain the integrity and consistency of the parent class.

In summary, the Liskov Substitution Principle ensures that subclassing is not merely about inheritance but also about preserving expected behavior. By adhering to this principle, developers create class hierarchies that are reliable, consistent, and easy to work with.

9.3.5 Interface Segregation Principle (ISP)

The Interface Segregation Principle (ISP) is a fundamental guideline in object-oriented design that emphasizes the importance of creating fine-grained, client-specific interfaces. It suggests that clients should not be forced to depend on interfaces they do not use, promoting a more flexible and modular design.

Splitting Interfaces to Avoid Client Overloading

The ISP addresses the problem of interface "fatness," where a single large interface includes methods that may not be relevant to all implementing classes. This can lead to clients being burdened with unnecessary dependencies and functionality they do not require.

By splitting interfaces into smaller, focused units, clients can choose the interfaces that are relevant to their needs. This prevents client classes from being overloaded with methods they do not use, resulting in cleaner, more maintainable code.

Example: Consider a document processing system with different types of users (readers, writers, administrators). Instead of having a monolithic interface that includes all possible document-related methods, the ISP suggests creating separate interfaces for each user role. This way, each user type interacts with the system through an interface that provides precisely the methods they require.

Customizing Interfaces for Specific Client Needs

The ISP encourages developers to tailor interfaces to the specific requirements of clients. This allows clients to interact with objects through interfaces that are closely aligned with their needs, promoting a more intuitive and efficient programming experience.

For example, consider a document processing system with different types of users (readers, writers, administrators). Instead of having a monolithic interface that includes all possible document-related methods, the ISP suggests creating separate interfaces for each user role. This way, each user type interacts with the system through an interface that provides precisely the methods they require.

By adhering to the ISP, developers create interfaces that are lean, cohesive, and meaningful. Clients can interact with objects in a more focused and effective manner, reducing unnecessary coupling and promoting a more modular and maintainable design.

In summary, the Interface Segregation Principle promotes the creation of interfaces that are tailored to specific client needs, enhancing modularity, flexibility, and clarity in object-oriented designs.

9.3.6 Dependency Inversion Principle (DIP)

The Dependency Inversion Principle (DIP) is a crucial concept in object-oriented design that focuses on reducing tight coupling between high-level and low-level modules. It advocates for designing systems in a way that allows high-level modules to depend on abstractions rather than concrete implementations, promoting flexibility, maintainability, and ease of change.

Decoupling High-Level Modules from Low-Level Implementations

Traditionally, software systems are built with high-level modules that depend on low-level modules. This can lead to rigid designs where changes in low-level modules can have a cascading impact on high-level modules. The DIP suggests reversing this dependency by making high-level modules independent of low-level details.

By introducing an abstract layer between high-level and low-level modules, changes in the low-level implementation do not directly affect the high-level modules. This decoupling enhances the system's ability to adapt to changes and makes it easier to replace or modify low-level components without affecting the overall architecture.

Example: Consider a payment processing system. Instead of having high-level modules directly depend on specific payment gateway implementations, the DIP suggests creating an abstract payment gateway interface. High-level modules can then interact with this interface, making them independent of the details of individual payment gateways.

Favoring Abstractions over Concrete Implementations

The DIP encourages developers to rely on abstractions, such as interfaces or abstract classes, rather than concrete implementations when designing systems. High-level modules should depend on these abstractions, allowing them to interact with various implementations without being tightly coupled to any specific one.

For instance, consider a payment processing system. Instead of having high-level modules directly depend on specific payment gateway implementations, the DIP suggests creating an abstract payment gateway interface. High-level modules can then interact with this interface, making them independent of the details of individual payment gateways.

By adhering to the DIP, developers create designs that are more modular, flexible, and easier to maintain. Changes can be localized to specific components, and the system as a whole becomes more adaptable to evolving requirements.

In summary, the Dependency Inversion Principle promotes a design approach where high-level modules are decoupled from low-level implementations and depend on abstractions. This fosters better separation of concerns, reduces coupling, and enhances the overall quality and maintainability of object-oriented systems.

9.3.7 Applying OOD Principles in Real-World Scenarios

Object-Oriented Design (OOD) principles provide a solid foundation for creating well-structured, maintainable, and adaptable software systems. Applying these principles to real-world scenarios can lead to more effective designs and better software outcomes.

Realizing OOD Principles in Software Design

When applying Object-Oriented Design principles in software design, developers aim to create systems that exhibit characteristics such as modularity, reusability, flexibility, and low coupling. These principles guide decisions related to class design, inheritance, encapsulation, and interaction between components.

For example, when designing a complex e-commerce platform, applying the Single Responsibility Principle (SRP) ensures that each class or module has a clear and well-defined purpose. Encapsulation and access modifiers help hide implementation details, exposing only the necessary functionality to other parts of the system. Inheritance and polymorphism enable the creation of flexible and extensible components, facilitating future updates and additions.

Case Studies Illustrating the Benefits of OOP Design

Case studies provide practical insights into the benefits of Object-Oriented Design principles. Let's explore a few scenarios where OOD principles have been effectively applied:

1. **Online Banking System:** By applying the Open/Closed Principle (OCP), developers can extend the functionality of an online banking system without modifying existing code. New features like mobile banking or additional account types can be added as separate modules, minimizing the risk of introducing bugs to the core system.
2. **Video Game Development:** In game development, the Liskov Substitution Principle (LSP) ensures that different game characters can be used interchangeably without affecting the overall gameplay. Characters derived from a common base class adhere to the same contract, preserving behavior inheritance.
3. **Medical Records Management:** The Dependency Inversion Principle (DIP) is crucial in healthcare software, where changes to medical protocols or data storage must not disrupt patient record management. By depending on abstractions instead of concrete implementations, the system remains adaptable to changing medical practices.

Applying Object-Oriented Design principles in these scenarios leads to software that is easier to maintain, modify, and extend. The principles enhance code quality, reduce bugs, and improve collaboration among development teams.

In summary, applying Object-Oriented Design principles in real-world scenarios fosters the creation of software systems that are modular, adaptable, and efficient. By embracing these principles, developers can create software that meets current needs while remaining well-prepared for future enhancements and changes.

This comprehensive outline delves into the core concepts of Object-Oriented Programming, from the fundamentals of objects and classes to the principles that govern encapsulation, inheritance, and polymorphism, along with the guidelines for designing robust and maintainable software using object-oriented design principles.

Chapter 10: Functional Programming

Functional programming is a paradigm that treats computation as the evaluation of mathematical functions, emphasizing immutability and the absence of side effects. This chapter explores fundamental concepts of functional programming, including higher-order functions, immutable data, and recursion.

10.1 Functional Programming Concepts

Functional programming is based on several core concepts that differentiate it from traditional imperative programming. This section introduces these concepts and their significance:

10.1.1 Introduction to Functional Programming

In the realm of programming paradigms, functional programming stands as a distinctive approach that contrasts with the more traditional imperative paradigm. This section introduces the fundamental concepts of functional programming, highlighting its departure from imperative programming and elucidating its philosophy and benefits.

Understanding the Shift from Imperative to Functional Programming Paradigms

Imperative programming, the conventional approach to software development, is centered around statements that explicitly instruct the computer on how to perform a sequence of tasks. It often involves mutable state and explicit control flow, where developers specify how a task should be accomplished step by step.

Functional programming, on the other hand, shifts the focus to functions, treating computation as the evaluation of mathematical functions. Rather than instructing the computer on how to perform a task, functional programming emphasizes describing what a program should achieve. This paradigm leverages function composition, immutability, and declarative expressions to create reliable and predictable software.

Exploring the Philosophy and Benefits of Functional Programming

Functional programming embodies a philosophy that aligns with the principles of mathematics and formal logic. It emphasizes the following core ideas:

- **Immutability**: In functional programming, data is treated as immutable. Once a piece of data is created, it does not change. This approach eliminates the risk of unintended side effects and makes programs more predictable and easier to reason about.
- **First-Class Functions**: Functions are treated as first-class citizens, meaning they can be passed as arguments to other functions, returned as values, and stored in data structures. This facilitates higher-order functions and function composition.
- **Declarative Paradigm**: Functional programs are often expressed in a declarative style, where the focus is on describing what needs to be done rather than specifying how to do it. This leads to more concise and readable code.
- **No Side Effects**: Functional programming seeks to minimize or eliminate side effects, which are changes to the state of a program or the world outside the program. This contributes to code that is easier to test, understand, and maintain.
- **Pure Functions**: Pure functions, a cornerstone of

functional programming, produce the same output for the same input and have no side effects. This property enables referential transparency and makes programs easier to reason about and parallelize.

The benefits of functional programming include enhanced code quality, improved software reliability, easier parallelization, and better support for modularization and code reuse. By embracing functional programming, developers can craft software that is more robust, scalable, and maintainable, paving the way for effective problem-solving in various domains.

10.1.2 Pure Functions

In the realm of functional programming, pure functions emerge as a foundational concept that plays a pivotal role in shaping the paradigm's core principles. This section delves into the essence of pure functions, elucidating their definition, characteristics, and the profound impact they wield over predictability and maintainability within a software system.

Defining Pure Functions and Their Characteristics

At its essence, a pure function is a function that adheres to two crucial principles: determinism and lack of side effects.

1. **Determinism**: A pure function yields the same output for the same set of inputs, regardless of the context in which it is executed. This deterministic behavior ensures consistency, making the function predictable and reliable.
2. **Lack of Side Effects**: A pure function refrains from altering or affecting any external state or data. It doesn't modify global variables, modify data structures, or perform

any other actions that could lead to observable changes outside the function's scope.

In essence, pure functions operate solely based on their inputs, encapsulating their logic within a self-contained environment. This isolation from external influences contributes to their stability and predictability.

Here's an example that illustrates the concept of pure functions in functional programming using Python:

```
# Impure Function Example
global_variable = 10
def impure_add(value):

  global global_variable
  global_variable += value
  return global_variable

result = impure_add(5)
print(result) # Output: 15
# Pure Function Example
def pure_add(a, b):
return a + b
result = pure_add(5, 10)
print(result) # Output: 15
```

In this example, **impure_add** is an impure function because it modifies the global variable **global_variable**, which introduces side effects and makes the function's behavior dependent on external state. On the other hand, **pure_add** is a pure function because it only operates on its input parameters **a** and **b** to produce a result. It doesn't modify any external state, and its output solely depends on its inputs.

Pure functions offer several advantages, including easier testing, reasoning, and parallelization, as they don't rely on shared state and produce consistent results for the same inputs.

Understanding How Pure Functions Contribute to Predictability and Maintainability

The strict adherence to determinism and the avoidance of side effects in pure functions bestow several benefits that significantly elevate the quality and maintainability of software systems.

1. **Referential Transparency**: The deterministic nature of pure functions facilitates referential transparency. This means that a function call can be replaced by its resulting value without altering the program's behavior. This property simplifies reasoning about code and enables optimization opportunities.
2. **Testability**: Pure functions are inherently testable. Since they rely solely on inputs and produce predictable outputs, testing becomes straightforward. Unit tests can be written without worrying about complex setups or external dependencies.
3. **Concurrency and Parallelism**: The absence of side effects in pure functions makes them ideal candidates for concurrent and parallel execution. Multiple invocations of a pure function with the same input will always yield the same output, allowing for efficient parallelization without the risk of race conditions.
4. **Code Maintainability**: The self-contained nature of pure functions reduces interdependencies between different parts of the codebase. Changes made to a pure function won't inadvertently impact other components, leading to

code that is easier to understand, refactor, and maintain.

5. **Functional Composition**: Pure functions are well-suited for functional composition, where multiple functions are combined to create more complex operations. Since pure functions don't modify state, composing them results in a clear and understandable flow of data transformations.

By embracing the principles of pure functions, developers can create codebases that are less error-prone, more comprehensible, and amenable to future modifications. The predictability and maintainability facilitated by pure functions are instrumental in realizing the promises of functional programming, paving the way for robust and dependable software systems.

10.1.3 Immutability

In the realm of functional programming, immutability stands as a cornerstone principle that wields significant influence over code behavior and design. This section delves into the concept of immutability, shedding light on its role in preventing unintended side effects and the manifold benefits it brings to software development.

Exploring Immutability and Its Role in Preventing Unintended Side Effects

Immutability, in the context of functional programming, refers to the property of data that once created cannot be changed. This means that once a piece of data is defined, it remains unchanged throughout its lifetime. This principle stands in stark contrast to mutable data, where values can be altered after creation.

The significance of immutability lies in its ability to prevent unintended side effects that often emerge from mutable data. When data is mutable, it becomes challenging to track changes and predict the state of the program at any given point. Unintended modifications can lead to bugs that are difficult to diagnose and reproduce.

Immutable data, on the other hand, guarantees that once a value is set, it remains constant. This predictability ensures that a value used in one part of the program will not change unexpectedly when accessed from another part, creating a stable and reliable environment for computation.

Here's an example that demonstrates the concept of immutability in functional programming using Python:

```
# Mutable List Example
mutable_list = [1, 2, 3, 4, 5]
def modify_list(lst, value):
lst.append(value)
modify_list(mutable_list, 6)
print(mutable_list) # Output: [1, 2, 3, 4, 5, 6]
# Immutable Tuple Example
immutable_tuple = (1, 2, 3, 4, 5)
def try_to_modify_tuple(tpl, value):

 try:
 tpl[0] = value
 except TypeError as e:
 print(f"Error: {e}")

try_to_modify_tuple(immutable_tuple, 6) # Output: Error: 'tuple' object does not support item assignment
```

In this example, we have a mutable list and an immutable tuple. When we attempt to modify the list using the **modify_list** function, the list is indeed modified. However, when we try to modify the tuple using the **try_to_modify_tuple** function, we encounter a **TypeError**. This showcases how immutability prevents unintended changes to data, ensuring that once a tuple is created, its elements cannot be changed.

Immutability is a powerful concept in functional programming, as it promotes safer and more predictable code by eliminating the risk of unintended side effects caused by data mutation.

Benefits of Working with Immutable Data Structures

Embracing immutability brings forth a myriad of benefits that enhance the quality and maintainability of software systems.

1. **Predictability**: Immutable data structures guarantee that data remains constant, leading to predictable behavior. This predictability simplifies debugging and reasoning about the program's behavior.
2. **Concurrency**: Immutable data structures are inherently thread-safe. Since data cannot change after creation, multiple threads can safely read and share immutable data without the risk of race conditions or synchronization issues.
3. **Debugging**: Bugs caused by unintended modifications become rare in an immutable codebase. When an issue arises, developers can focus on a specific part of the code without worrying about unexpected changes elsewhere.
4. **Functional Composition**: Immutability plays a crucial role in functional composition. Functions that operate on immutable data are easier to reason about, as they don't have side effects that could affect the rest of the program.
5. **Versioning and Undo Operations**: Immutable data structures lend themselves well to versioning and undo operations. Storing snapshots of data at different points in time becomes straightforward, enabling efficient undo and

history tracking.

6. **Caching and Memoization**: Immutable data allows for efficient caching and memoization. Since the data doesn't change, the result of a function can be cached for a given set of inputs, improving performance.

By adopting the principles of immutability, functional programming encourages developers to create systems that are robust, maintainable, and resilient to bugs caused by unintended side effects. Immutable data structures lay the foundation for code that is easier to test, understand, and modify, enabling the development of reliable and high-quality software.

10.1.4 Referential Transparency

In the realm of functional programming, referential transparency stands as a fundamental concept that underpins the predictability and reasoning of code. This section delves into the concept of referential transparency, shedding light on its significance in code reasoning and its implications for optimization.

Understanding Referential Transparency

Referential transparency refers to a property of a function or expression in which its output is solely determined by its input, without any hidden state or side effects. In other words, a referentially transparent function will always produce the same output for the same input, regardless of where or when it is called within a program.

Here's an example illustrating referential transparency:

```
# Non-referentially transparent function
total = 0
def add_to_total(value):
```

```
global total

  total += value
  return total

result1 = add_to_total(5) # Result: 5
result2 = add_to_total(3) # Result: 8
# Referentially transparent function
def add(a, b):

  return a + b

result3 = add(5, 3) # Result: 8 (same as before)
# Another example
def square(x):
return x * x
result4 = square(4) # Result: 16
result5 = square(4) # Result: 16 (always the same)
```

In the non-referentially transparent example, the **add_to_total** function modifies a global variable **total**, which makes its output dependent on external state. In contrast, the **add** and **square** functions are referentially transparent because their outputs are solely determined by their inputs.

Please let me know if you'd like more code examples or if you have any specific concepts you'd like to see exemplified

This concept can be understood as an extension of the principle of immutability. A function is referentially transparent if its behavior is predictable solely based on its arguments and not influenced by external factors, such as global variables or mutable state.

Impact on Code Reasoning

Referential transparency has a profound impact on the reasoning and understanding of code. When functions are referentially transparent, their behavior becomes easily predictable. This predictability simplifies the process of understanding and debugging code. Developers can confidently reason about the behavior of a function without having to consider complex interactions with mutable state or hidden side effects.

Referential transparency also encourages a modular and compositional style of programming. Functions can be combined and composed with confidence, knowing that their behavior will remain consistent regardless of the context in which they are used. This composability is a key aspect of functional programming, enabling the construction of complex systems from smaller, well-understood building blocks.

Implications for Optimization

The concept of referential transparency has important implications for optimization. Since a referentially transparent function's output is solely determined by its input, the function's result can be memoized or cached for a given set of arguments. This optimization technique, known as memoization, can lead to significant performance improvements by avoiding redundant calculations.

Furthermore, referential transparency allows for equational reasoning and substitution. In a referentially transparent expression, portions of code can be safely replaced with their computed values, leading to more efficient evaluation and potential compiler optimizations.

Conclusion

Referential transparency is a core concept in functional programming that fosters predictability, modularity, and composability. By ensuring that functions and expressions produce consistent and predictable results based solely on their inputs, referential transparency enhances the clarity, reasoning, and optimization of code. It empowers developers to create reliable and maintainable software systems, and it plays a pivotal role in the broader paradigm shift towards functional programming.

10.2 Higher-Order Functions

Higher-order functions are functions that can accept other functions as arguments or return them as results. This section delves into higher-order functions and their applications:

10.2.1 Understanding Higher-Order Functions

Higher-order functions are a key concept in functional programming that adds a new layer of flexibility and expressiveness to the way we write and use functions. These functions are not only capable of performing operations on data, but they can also accept other functions as arguments or return functions as their results. This higher-order nature of functions opens up a wide range of possibilities for composing and manipulating code.

Defining Higher-Order Functions

A higher-order function is a function that meets one or both of the following criteria:

1. **Takes Functions as Arguments:** A higher-order function can accept other functions as parameters. This allows you to provide custom behavior to a function, effectively

allowing you to extend its functionality without modifying its core implementation.

2. **Returns a Function:** A higher-order function can also produce and return a new function as its result. This is particularly useful for creating specialized functions on the fly, tailoring them to specific needs.

Exploring the Concept of Functions as First-Class Citizens

In functional programming, functions are treated as first-class citizens. This means that functions are entities of the same status as other data types, such as integers or strings. Just like any other data, functions can be passed as arguments to other functions, returned from functions, and stored in variables.

This concept of treating functions as first-class citizens enables powerful techniques like higher-order functions. You can create functions that generate new functions, transform existing functions, or combine multiple functions to create more complex behavior.

Example:

Consider a scenario where you have a list of numbers and you want to apply different operations to each element of the list. Instead of writing separate functions for each operation, you can create a higher-order function that takes an operation function as an argument and applies it to each element of the list.

```
def apply_operation(operation, numbers):
result = []
for num in numbers:

 result.append(operation(num))
 return result

# Define different operation functions
def square(x):
```

```
return x * x
def double(x):
return x * 2
numbers = [1, 2, 3, 4, 5]
# Using the higher-order function to apply different operations
squared_numbers = apply_operation(square, numbers)
doubled_numbers = apply_operation(double, numbers)
print(squared_numbers) # [1, 4, 9, 16, 25]
print(doubled_numbers) # [2, 4, 6, 8, 10]
```

In this example, the **apply_operation** function is a higher-order function that takes an operation function and applies it to each element of the **numbers** list.

Higher-order functions and the concept of functions as first-class citizens provide a powerful and flexible way to structure and manipulate code in functional programming paradigms. They allow you to write more modular, reusable, and concise code by treating functions as versatile entities that can be dynamically composed and transformed.

10.2.2 Function Composition

Function composition is a powerful technique in functional programming that involves combining multiple functions to create more complex behavior. It enables you to build pipelines of functions where the output of one function becomes the input to another, allowing for seamless data transformation and manipulation.

Composing Higher-Order Functions

When you compose functions, you create a new function by chaining together two or more existing functions. This new function encapsulates the behavior of the composed functions, making it easier to reason about and reuse complex operations.

Example:

Let's say you have two functions: one that doubles a number and another that squares a number. You can compose these two functions to create a new function that doubles a number and then squares the result.

```
def compose(f, g):
return lambda x: f(g(x))
def double(x):
return x * 2
def square(x):
return x * x
# Compose the functions double and square
double_then_square = compose(square, double)
result = double_then_square(3) # Apply double, then square: (3 * 2) * (3 * 2) = 36
print(result)
```

In this example, the **compose** function takes two functions **f** and **g**, and returns a new function that applies **f** to the result of **g**. The **double_then_square** function is created by composing the **square** function with the **double** function. When you call **double_then_square(3)**, it first doubles the number (resulting in 6) and then squares the result (resulting in 36).

Building Pipelines of Functions

Function composition is particularly useful for building pipelines of functions, where data flows through a series of functions, each performing a specific transformation.

Example:

Consider a data transformation pipeline that involves converting a list of temperatures from Celsius to Fahrenheit, rounding the results, and then displaying them.

```
def celsius_to_fahrenheit(celsius):
return (celsius * 9/5) + 32
```

```
def round_to_two_decimal_places(number):
return round(number, 2)
def display_result(value):
print(f"Result: {value}")
temperatures_in_celsius = [0, 25, 100]
# Build a pipeline using function composition
pipeline = compose(display_result, round_to_two_decimal_places)
pipeline = compose(pipeline, celsius_to_fahrenheit)
# Apply the pipeline to each temperature
for temp in temperatures_in_celsius:
pipeline(temp)
```

In this example, the **compose** function is used to create a pipeline of functions. The pipeline first converts temperatures from Celsius to Fahrenheit, then rounds the results to two decimal places, and finally displays the formatted results.

Function composition allows you to create clear and modular data transformation pipelines, making your code more readable and maintainable. It encourages a declarative style of programming, where you define what transformations should be applied rather than focusing on how they are implemented.

Function composition is a valuable technique in functional programming that promotes code reusability, separation of concerns, and concise expression of complex operations. It empowers you to create elegant and efficient data transformation workflows by combining the strengths of multiple functions.

10.2.3 Closures and Lexical Scope

In the realm of functional programming, closures and lexical scope are essential concepts that contribute to the power and flexibility of higher-order functions. These concepts play a pivotal role in creating robust and maintainable code by enabling functions to encapsulate data and maintain their context.

Understanding Closures

A closure is a function that retains access to the variables from its containing scope even after the outer function has finished executing. In other words, a closure "closes over" its lexical scope, preserving the environment in which it was created.

Example:

```
def outer_function(x):
def inner_function(y):

  return x + y
  return inner_function

closure = outer_function(10)
result = closure(5) # The closure remembers x = 10 from the outer_function
print(result) # Output: 15
```

In this example, **inner_function** is a closure that captures the variable **x** from its containing scope (**outer_function**). Even after **outer_function** has finished executing, the closure retains access to **x**, allowing it to be used when **closure** is called later.

Exploring Lexical Scope

Lexical scope refers to the visibility and accessibility of variables within a particular portion of code. In most programming languages, including Python, functions create their own lexical scope, and variables defined within a function are accessible only within that function's scope.

Example:

```
def outer_function():
x = 10 # Variable defined within outer_function
def inner_function(y):

  return x + y
  return inner_function

closure = outer_function()
result = closure(5) # inner_function can access x from outer_function's scope
print(result) # Output: 15
# x is not accessible here (outside of outer_function's scope)
```

In this example, the variable **x** is defined within the lexical scope of **outer_function**. This scope is accessible to the **inner_function** closure created within **outer_function.**

Benefits and Applications

Closures and lexical scope offer several benefits:

1. **Encapsulation**: Closures allow functions to encapsulate data within their scope. This promotes information hiding and prevents unintended modification of data.
2. **Data Persistence**: Closures enable data persistence between function calls. This can be particularly useful when creating factory functions, memoization, or managing private data.
3. **Callback Functions**: Closures are commonly used for callback functions, where a function is passed as an argument and retains access to its defining context.
4. **Partial Application and Currying**: Closures facilitate techniques like partial application and currying, where functions with multiple arguments are transformed into

functions with fewer arguments.

In summary, closures and lexical scope empower developers to create modular, flexible, and expressive code. They enable the creation of self-contained functions with controlled access to external variables, leading to code that is both readable and maintainable.

10.3 Immutable Data and Recursion

Functional programming encourages the use of immutable data structures and recursion for solving problems. This section explores these concepts in depth:

10.3.1 Immutable Data Structures

In the realm of functional programming, immutable data structures play a pivotal role in ensuring code correctness, simplicity, and facilitating efficient concurrency. Immutable data, once created, cannot be modified. Instead of altering existing data, operations on immutable data create new data structures. This concept may seem counterintuitive at first, but it brings a multitude of benefits to software development.

Benefits of Immutable Data

Predictable and Reliable Code

Immutable data brings predictability to code behavior. Since data cannot change after creation, the outcome of operations becomes more deterministic and easier to reason about. This predictability contributes to fewer bugs and more reliable code.

Concurrency and Parallelism

Immutable data structures are inherently thread-safe. In a concurrent or parallel programming context, multiple threads can access and work with the same data structure without the risk of data being modified concurrently. This eliminates a significant class of concurrency-related bugs.

Efficient Memory Management

Since immutable data is not modified in place, the need for defensive copying is reduced. This leads to more efficient memory utilization. Additionally, since multiple instances of immutable data can share common parts, memory usage can be optimized.

Simplified Debugging

Immutable data simplifies debugging by minimizing the potential for unexpected state changes. Once data is created, it remains consistent throughout its lifetime, making it easier to track down the source of errors.

Creating and Working with Immutable Data

Creating and using immutable data structures involves techniques such as:

1. **Copying with Modification**: Instead of modifying existing data, create a copy of the data with the desired changes. This preserves the original data while producing a new version.
2. **Persistent Data Structures**: These data structures optimize copying by reusing unchanged portions of data, reducing memory overhead.
3. **Functional Programming Libraries**: Many functional programming languages and libraries provide built-in support for immutable data structures and operations.

Example: Immutable List in Python

original_list = [1, 2, 3]

new_list = original_list + [4] # Creating a new list with an additional element

print(original_list) # Output: [1, 2, 3]

print(new_list) # Output: [1, 2, 3, 4]

In this example, the + operator creates a new list with the original elements and the additional element, leaving the **original_list** unchanged.

Summary

Immutable data structures contribute to functional programming's emphasis on creating reliable, maintainable, and efficient code. By preventing in-place modifications, immutable data simplifies code behavior, enhances concurrency, and promotes efficient memory management. While working with immutable data may require a shift in mindset, the benefits it brings to software development are substantial.

10.3.2 Recursion and Tail-Call Optimization

Recursion is a fundamental concept in functional programming, allowing functions to call themselves to solve problems. It's a powerful technique that can lead to elegant and concise code. However, without proper optimization, recursion can also result in stack overflow errors and inefficient memory usage. This is where tail-call optimization comes into play.

Recursion in Functional Programming

Recursion is the process of solving a problem by breaking it down into smaller instances of the same problem. In functional programming, recursion is often used as an alternative to iterative loops. It allows for the creation of concise, expressive code that directly reflects the problem-solving approach.

Tail-Call Optimization

In traditional recursion, each recursive call adds a new entry to the call stack, which can lead to stack overflow errors for deep recursive calls. Tail-call optimization (TCO) is a technique that optimizes certain recursive functions by reusing the current function's stack frame for the next function call, effectively avoiding the accumulation of stack frames.

In other words, TCO converts recursion into an iterative process by reusing the current function's memory space for the next call, as long as the last action of the current function is the recursive call itself. This optimization prevents stack overflow errors and reduces memory consumption.

Example: Factorial Calculation

Consider the calculation of the factorial of a number using recursion:

```
def factorial(n):
if n == 0:

  return 1

else:

  return n * factorial(n - 1)
```

This recursive implementation calculates the factorial of **n** by breaking it down into smaller subproblems. However, without TCO, deep recursion for large **n** values can lead to a stack overflow.

Example: Tail-Call Optimized Factorial

With tail-call optimization, the same factorial calculation can be implemented as follows:

```
def factorial(n, accumulator=1):
if n == 0:

  return accumulator

else:

  return factorial(n - 1, n * accumulator)
```

In this tail-call optimized version, the accumulator parameter keeps track of the intermediate result as the recursion progresses. This implementation is more memory-efficient and avoids the risk of stack overflow for large **n** values.

Summary

Recursion is a key technique in functional programming, enabling elegant solutions to complex problems. Tail-call optimization enhances the efficiency of recursive functions by preventing stack overflow errors and reducing memory consumption. While not all programming languages support tail-call optimization, understanding its benefits can lead to better design and more efficient functional code.

10.3.3 Recursive Data Processing

Recursive data processing is a powerful technique in functional programming that involves applying a function to a data structure and its substructures in a recursive manner. It allows for elegant and concise solutions to complex problems by breaking them down into smaller, similar subproblems.

Applying Recursion to Data Structures

Recursive data processing involves defining a function that operates on a data structure and then calls itself on the substructures of that data. This approach is particularly useful for working with hierarchical data structures like trees or nested lists.

For example, consider a recursive function to calculate the sum of all elements in a nested list:

```
def nested_list_sum(lst):
if isinstance(lst, int):

  return lst

else:

  total = 0
  for item in lst:
  total += nested_list_sum(item)
  return total
```

In this example, the function **nested_list_sum** checks if an element is an integer. If it is, it returns the integer itself. Otherwise, it iterates through the nested list, recursively calling itself on each sub-element until the sum of all integers is calculated.

Solving Problems with Recursive Algorithms

Recursive data processing is a natural fit for solving problems that exhibit self-similar substructures. Examples of such problems include traversing binary trees, searching for elements in graphs, and evaluating mathematical expressions.

Consider a recursive algorithm to calculate the nth Fibonacci number:

```
def fibonacci(n):
if n <= 1:

  return n

else:

  return fibonacci(n - 1) + fibonacci(n - 2)
```

In this case, the Fibonacci sequence itself is defined recursively: each number is the sum of the two preceding ones. The **fibonacci** function uses recursion to break down the problem into simpler subproblems, eventually reaching the base cases of **n = 0** and **n = 1**.

Benefits and Considerations

Recursive data processing can lead to elegant and readable code for certain types of problems. However, it's essential to ensure that the recursive function reaches base cases to avoid infinite recursion. Additionally, some programming languages have limitations on the depth of recursion due to stack space.

Understanding the principles of recursive data processing and practicing its application can lead to efficient and elegant solutions for a wide range of problems in functional programming.

10.3.4 Practical Applications of Functional Programming

Functional programming concepts have found diverse and impactful applications in various real-world scenarios, showcasing the advantages of this programming paradigm in solving complex problems and improving software development practices.

Domain-Specific Languages (DSLs)

Functional programming is well-suited for creating domain-specific languages (DSLs), which are specialized languages tailored to specific problem domains. DSLs enable concise and expressive code that closely resembles the problem domain, making it easier for domain experts to understand and work with the software.

For example, SQL (Structured Query Language) is a DSL used for database queries. Its functional-style syntax allows developers to express complex data retrieval operations in a clear and intuitive manner.

Parallel and Concurrent Programming

Functional programming promotes immutability and avoids shared mutable state, making it inherently suitable for parallel and concurrent programming. Immutable data structures reduce the need for locks and synchronization mechanisms, which can lead to more efficient and scalable multi-threaded applications.

In the field of parallel processing, functional programming languages and concepts have been used to develop high-performance software for scientific simulations, data analysis, and rendering.

Data Processing and Analysis

Functional programming lends itself well to data processing and analysis tasks. Higher-order functions and immutable data structures simplify the manipulation of data streams and collections. Libraries and frameworks built on functional principles, like Apache Spark and Apache Flink, are widely used for big data processing and real-time stream processing.

Web Development

Functional programming languages and concepts are increasingly being adopted in web development. Libraries like React (JavaScript) and Elm focus on building user interfaces using a functional approach. These libraries allow developers to express UI components as pure functions of the application's state, making the UI code more predictable and easier to reason about.

Financial Modeling

Functional programming's emphasis on immutability and pure functions has found applications in financial modeling and algorithmic trading. Predictable behavior and minimized side effects are crucial in financial systems, where accuracy and reliability are paramount.

Case Studies

- **Netflix**: Netflix transitioned parts of its recommendation system to functional programming, improving the efficiency of data processing and enabling faster experimentation with algorithms.
- **Twitter**: Twitter migrated parts of its infrastructure to functional programming, resulting in improved performance, better concurrency handling, and reduced development time.
- **WhatsApp**: WhatsApp uses Erlang, a functional programming language, to manage the massive amount of concurrent connections required for real-time messaging.
- **NASA**: NASA's Jet Propulsion Laboratory (JPL) has used functional programming languages like Haskell for certain mission-critical software, taking advantage of their

mathematical rigor and reliability.

In these case studies and many more, functional programming has demonstrated its ability to provide elegant solutions to complex problems, enhance code maintainability, and improve system performance. Its emphasis on immutability, composability, and predictability makes it a valuable tool in various domains of software development.

Functional programming offers a unique perspective on software development, emphasizing clean code, modularity, and expressive data transformations. By mastering the concepts of functional programming, developers can write code that is more concise, predictable, and maintainable, opening up new avenues for solving complex problems.

Part IV: Data Structures and Algorithms

Chapter 11: Introduction to Data Structures

In the world of computer science and programming, data structures play a crucial role in organizing and managing data effectively. They provide the foundation for building efficient algorithms and solving complex computational problems. This chapter introduces some of the fundamental data structures and explores their characteristics, use cases, and operations.

11.1 Arrays

Arrays are fundamental data structures that play a central role in programming and computer science. They provide a systematic way to organize and store a collection of items of the same data type. Arrays are highly efficient for accessing elements and are widely used for various applications.

11.1.1 Key Concepts

Declaration and Initialization of Arrays

Arrays are declared by specifying the data type of the elements they will hold and the number of elements in square brackets. Initialization involves assigning values to the individual elements of the array.

Example in Python:

```
# Declaration and Initialization of an integer array
my_array = [10, 20, 30, 40, 50]
```

Indexing and Accessing Array Elements

Array elements are accessed using their index, which indicates their position in the array. The index starts from 0 for the first element and goes up to **length - 1** for the last element.

Example in C++:

```
int scores[5] = {90, 85, 78, 92, 88};
int first_score = scores[0]; // Accessing the first element
```

Dynamic vs. Static Arrays

Static arrays have a fixed size that is determined at compile-time and cannot be changed during runtime. Dynamic arrays, also known as resizable arrays or lists, can grow or shrink in size as needed during program execution.

Example in Java (Static Array):

```
int[] staticArray = new int[5]; // Static array with size 5
```

Example in Python (Dynamic Array):

```
dynamic_array = [] # Empty list (dynamic array)
dynamic_array.append(10) # Adding an element dynamically
```

Multidimensional Arrays

Arrays can have multiple dimensions, allowing for the creation of matrices and other multi-dimensional data structures.

Example in C:

```
int matrix[3][3] = {
{1, 2, 3},

 {4, 5, 6},
 {7, 8, 9}

};
```

int element = matrix[1][2]; // Accessing an element in the matrix

Arrays are the building blocks for many other data structures and algorithms. They offer a simple yet powerful way to manage and manipulate collections of data, making them an essential concept to grasp in programming.

11.2 Linked Lists

Linked lists are fundamental data structures that provide dynamic memory allocation and efficient insertion and deletion operations. They consist of nodes, each holding a data element and a reference (or link) to the next node in the sequence. Linked lists allow for flexible memory management and are particularly useful when the size of the data structure needs to change dynamically.

11.2.1 Key Concepts

Singly Linked Lists vs. Doubly Linked Lists

Singly linked lists consist of nodes where each node points to the next node in the list. This structure provides a simple and memory-efficient way to store data.

Example of a singly linked list:

Node 1 -> Node 2 -> Node 3 -> null

Doubly linked lists extend the concept of singly linked lists by having each node point to both the next and the previous node.

Example of a doubly linked list:

null <- Node 1 <-> Node 2 <-> Node 3 -> null

Insertion and Deletion Operations in Linked Lists

Insertion and deletion operations in linked lists are efficient compared to arrays. To insert a new node, you simply update the links of adjacent nodes to include the new node. Similarly, to delete a node, you adjust the links to bypass the node to be deleted.

Traversal and Searching in Linked Lists

Traversing a linked list involves moving from one node to another while examining or processing their data. Searching in linked lists typically requires traversing the list until the desired element is found.

Example in Python (Singly Linked List Traversal):

```
class Node:
def __init__(self, data):

 self.data = data
 self.next = None

class LinkedList:
def __init__(self):

 self.head = None

 def traverse(self):
 current = self.head
 while current:
 print(current.data)
 current = current.next
```

Circular Linked Lists

In circular linked lists, the last node points back to the first node, creating a closed loop. They can be both singly and doubly linked.

Example of a circular singly linked list:

Node 1 -> Node 2 -> Node 3 -> Node 1

Linked lists are valuable data structures due to their dynamic nature and efficient insertion and deletion operations. They are widely used in various applications, including implementing stacks, queues, and hash tables. Understanding linked lists is essential for any programmer working with data structures and algorithms.

11.3 Stacks

A stack is a fundamental data structure that follows the Last-In-First-Out (LIFO) principle. It represents a collection of elements with two main operations: push and pop. Elements are added and removed from the top of the stack, much like a stack of plates, where the last plate placed is the first to be removed.

11.3.1 Key Concepts

Push and Pop Operations in Stacks

- **Push**: This operation adds an element to the top of the stack. The new element becomes the top element.
- **Pop**: This operation removes and returns the top element from the stack. The next element becomes the new top.

Stacks are often used in scenarios where the order of elements is crucial, such as managing function calls in programming languages or evaluating mathematical expressions.

Stack-Based Algorithms

Stacks play a crucial role in various algorithms, including:

- **Expression Evaluation**: Stacks are used to evaluate arithmetic expressions, ensuring correct order of operations.
- **Backtracking**: In algorithms like depth-first search, stacks are used to keep track of choices and backtrack when needed.
- **Function Call Management**: Stacks are used by programming languages to manage function calls and return addresses.

Implementing Stacks Using Arrays or Linked Lists

Stacks can be implemented using either arrays or linked lists.

- **Array Implementation**: An array can be used to store stack elements. The top of the stack is tracked using an index. Pushing involves incrementing the top index and placing the element at that index. Popping involves returning the element at the top index and decrementing the top index.
- **Linked List Implementation**: A linked list can also be used to implement a stack. The head of the linked list represents the top of the stack. Pushing involves adding a new node at the head. Popping involves removing and returning the head node.

Example in Python (Stack Implementation using Linked List):

```
class Node:
```

```
def __init__(self, data):

 self.data = data
 self.next = None

class Stack:
def __init__(self):

 self.top = None

 def push(self, data):
 new_node = Node(data)
 new_node.next = self.top
 self.top = new_node

 def pop(self):
 if not self.top:
 return None

popped = self.top.data
self.top = self.top.next
return popped
```

Stacks are versatile and widely used in programming and algorithmic scenarios. They provide an elegant and efficient way to manage elements with a Last-In-First-Out behavior, making them a valuable tool in various applications.

11.4 Queues

A queue is a fundamental data structure that follows the First-In-First-Out (FIFO) principle. It represents a collection of elements with two main operations: enqueue and dequeue. Elements are added at the rear (end) of the queue and removed from the front, resembling a line of people waiting.

11.4.1 Key Concepts

Enqueue and Dequeue Operations in Queues

- **Enqueue**: This operation adds an element to the rear of the queue.
- **Dequeue**: This operation removes and returns the element from the front of the queue.

Queues are commonly used in scenarios where the order of processing matters, such as task scheduling and breadth-first traversal of graphs.

Priority Queues and Their Variants

A priority queue is an extension of the basic queue concept. In a priority queue, each element has an associated priority, and elements are removed from the queue based on their priority. Priority queues are useful in scenarios where tasks with higher priority need to be processed before those with lower priority.

Variants of priority queues include min-priority queues (elements with lower values have higher priority) and max-priority queues (elements with higher values have higher priority).

Implementing Queues Using Arrays or Linked Lists

Similar to stacks, queues can also be implemented using arrays or linked lists.

- **Array Implementation**: An array can be used to store queue elements. The front and rear indices are maintained to keep track of the positions for enqueue and dequeue operations.

- **Linked List Implementation**: A linked list can also be used to implement a queue. In this case, enqueueing involves adding a new node at the rear, and dequeueing involves removing and returning the front node.

Example in Python (Queue Implementation using Linked List):

```
class Node:
def __init__(self, data):
self.data = data
self.next = None
class Queue:
def __init__(self):

  self.front = None
  self.rear = None

  def enqueue(self, data):
  new_node = Node(data)
  if not self.front:
  self.front = new_node
  else:
  self.rear.next = new_node
  self.rear = new_node

def dequeue(self):

  if not self.front:
  return None
  dequeued = self.front.data
  self.front = self.front.next
  return dequeued
```

Queues are essential in managing ordered sequences of elements, making them valuable in a wide range of applications. Whether it's managing tasks or ensuring fair resource allocation, queues provide an efficient and orderly approach to data handling.

11.5 Trees

Trees are fundamental hierarchical data structures that are widely used for organizing and representing hierarchical relationships in various applications. They consist of nodes connected by edges, forming a structure resembling a branching hierarchy.

11.5.1 Key Concepts

Tree Terminology: Root, Nodes, Leaves, Subtrees

- **Root**: The topmost node of a tree, serving as the starting point for traversing the tree.
- **Nodes**: The individual elements in a tree, each containing data and references to child nodes.
- **Leaves**: Nodes that have no children, often representing the end points of a branch.
- **Subtrees**: Hierarchical structures within a tree that have their own root node and children.

Binary Trees and Binary Search Trees (BSTs)

- **Binary Tree**: A tree in which each node has at most two children, referred to as the left child and the right child.
- **Binary Search Tree (BST)**: A binary tree in which the values of nodes in the left subtree are less than or equal to the root value, and the values of nodes in the right subtree are greater than the root value. This property enables

efficient searching, insertion, and deletion operations.

Balanced vs. Unbalanced Trees

- **Balanced Tree**: A tree in which the heights of the subtrees of any node differ by at most one. Balanced trees ensure optimal performance for various operations.
- **Unbalanced Tree**: A tree in which the heights of the subtrees can differ significantly, potentially leading to poor performance.

Tree Traversal Algorithms: In-Order, Pre-Order, Post-Order

- **In-Order Traversal**: Visit nodes in left, root, right order.
- **Pre-Order Traversal**: Visit nodes in root, left, right order.
- **Post-Order Traversal**: Visit nodes in left, right, root order.

Tree traversal algorithms are crucial for accessing and processing tree elements in a specific order, and they have applications in tasks such as searching, printing, and modifying tree data.

Example in Python (Binary Tree and In-Order Traversal):

```
class TreeNode:
def __init__(self, data):

 self.data = data
 self.left = None
 self.right = None

def in_order_traversal(node):
if node:

 in_order_traversal(node.left)
 print(node.data)
```

```
    in_order_traversal(node.right)

# Creating a binary tree
root = TreeNode(10)
root.left = TreeNode(5)
root.right = TreeNode(15)
root.left.left = TreeNode(3)
root.left.right = TreeNode(8)
root.right.left = TreeNode(12)
root.right.right = TreeNode(18)
# In-order traversal
in_order_traversal(root)
```

Trees play a crucial role in organizing and representing hierarchical relationships, providing efficient solutions for various scenarios. Whether it's managing file systems, hierarchical data, or search operations, trees are a fundamental tool in computer science and software development.

11.6 Binary Search Trees (BSTs)

Binary Search Trees (BSTs) are a critical data structure in computer science, particularly for efficient searching and sorting operations. They are a specialized form of binary trees with a key-based ordering property that enables fast access and manipulation of data.

11.6.1 Key Concepts

BST Properties and Ordering

- **Key-Based Ordering**: In a BST, each node has a key, and nodes are ordered such that for each node:
    - All keys in the left subtree are less than the node's key.

    - All keys in the right subtree are greater than the node's key.

Searching, Insertion, and Deletion in BSTs

- **Searching**: BSTs allow for efficient searching. Starting at the root, comparisons are made between the search key and node keys, guiding the search down the left or right subtree until the desired key is found or determined to be absent.
- **Insertion**: To insert a new key, the tree is searched to find the appropriate position, and a new node is created and linked into the structure while maintaining the key-based ordering property.
- **Deletion**: Deleting a node from a BST involves rearranging the tree to maintain the ordering property. Cases include deleting a node with no children, one child, or two children.

Balanced BSTs: AVL Trees and Red-Black Trees

- **Balanced BSTs**: In certain situations, the performance of a BST can degrade if it becomes highly unbalanced, resulting in skewed trees and worst-case time complexity. Balanced BSTs ensure that the tree remains relatively balanced, leading to better performance guarantees.
- **AVL Trees**: AVL trees are a type of self-balancing BST where the heights of the left and right subtrees of any node differ by at most one. Rotations are performed to maintain balance after insertion or deletion operations.
- **Red-Black Trees**: Red-Black trees are another self-

balancing BST variant. They enforce specific properties, including ensuring that the longest path from the root to a leaf is no more than twice as long as the shortest path. Color coding and rotations are used to maintain balance.

Example in Python (BST Insertion and In-Order Traversal):

```
class TreeNode:
def __init__(self, key):

  self.key = key
  self.left = None
  self.right = None

def insert(root, key):
if root is None:

  return TreeNode(key)

if key < root.key:

  root.left = insert(root.left, key)

else: root.right = insert(root.right, key)

  return root

def in_order_traversal(node):
if node:

  in_order_traversal(node.left)
  print(node.key)
  in_order_traversal(node.right)

# Creating a BST
root = None
```

```
keys = [15, 8, 20, 5, 12, 18, 25]
for key in keys:
root = insert(root, key)
# In-order traversal
in_order_traversal(root)
```

Binary Search Trees are essential for various applications, including database indexing, implementing associative arrays (dictionaries), and efficient sorting algorithms. However, maintaining balance is crucial to ensure optimal performance, leading to the development of self-balancing variants like AVL trees and Red-Black trees. By understanding these fundamental data structures and their characteristics, you'll be better equipped to choose the right structure for a given problem and implement efficient algorithms.

Chapter 12: Algorithm Design and Analysis

In the realm of computer science, algorithm design and analysis play a pivotal role in solving complex problems efficiently. This chapter delves into various fundamental algorithms, shedding light on their design, analysis, and practical applications.

12.1 Searching Algorithms

Searching algorithms are essential for finding specific elements within a dataset. This section explores two prominent searching algorithms: linear search and binary search.

12.1.1 Linear Search

Linear search, often referred to as sequential search, is a fundamental searching algorithm used to find a target element within a list or array. This algorithm operates by sequentially checking each element in the list until a match is found or the entire list has been examined. While straightforward to implement, linear search is most suitable for relatively small datasets due to its linear time complexity.

Key Concepts:

- **Basic Idea:** Linear search iterates through each element of the list and compares it with the target element.
- **Time Complexity:** Linear search has a time complexity of O(n), where "n" is the number of elements in the list. In the worst case, the algorithm may need to examine every element.
- **Use Cases:** Linear search is appropriate when the dataset is

small or unsorted. It's a simple and reliable approach but may become inefficient for larger datasets.

- **Advantages:** Easy to understand and implement. Works for both sorted and unsorted datasets.
- **Disadvantages:** Inefficient for large datasets as the search time grows linearly with the size of the dataset.
- **Algorithm:**
    1. Start at the beginning of the list.
    2. Compare the current element with the target element.
    3. If a match is found, return the index of the element.
    4. If no match is found, move to the next element and repeat steps 2-3.
    5. If the end of the list is reached without finding a match, return a "not found" indicator.

Example:

Suppose we have an array of integers: [25, 10, 7, 42, 15, 6, 30]. Let's find the index of the target element 15 using linear search.

1. Start at index 0: Compare $25 \neq 15$.
2. Move to index 1: Compare $10 \neq 15$.
3. Move to index 2: Compare $7 \neq 15$.
4. Move to index 3: Compare $42 \neq 15$.
5. Move to index 4: Compare $15 = 15$. Match found!

The target element 15 is found at index 4.

Linear search is a foundational concept and serves as a starting point for understanding more complex searching algorithms. While its efficiency is limited for large datasets, it provides a basic approach to locating elements within a list.

12.1.2 Binary Search

Binary search is a powerful and efficient searching algorithm used to locate a target element in a **sorted** array or list. This algorithm operates by repeatedly dividing the search interval in half, significantly reducing the number of elements to be examined in each step. Binary search is particularly suitable for large datasets due to its logarithmic time complexity.

Key Concepts:

- **Basic Idea:** Binary search is performed on a **sorted** dataset by repeatedly dividing the search range in half and comparing the middle element with the target.
- **Time Complexity:** Binary search has a time complexity of O(log n), where "n" is the number of elements in the list. With each iteration, the search interval is halved, leading to a dramatic reduction in search time for large datasets.
- **Use Cases:** Binary search is highly efficient for searching in sorted datasets. It is particularly useful when the dataset is large and sorted.
- **Advantages:** Significantly faster than linear search for large datasets. Well-suited for scenarios where the dataset is sorted and changes infrequently.
- **Disadvantages:** Requires the dataset to be sorted prior to searching. If the dataset frequently changes, the overhead of maintaining sorted order might outweigh the benefits of binary search.
- **Algorithm:**
    1. Initialize two pointers, **low** and **high**, to the first and last elements of the sorted list, respectively.
    2. Calculate the middle index as (**low** + **high**) / **2**.

3. Compare the middle element with the target element.
    - If they match, return the index.
    - If the middle element is less than the target, adjust **low** to **mid + 1**.
    - If the middle element is greater than the target, adjust **high** to **mid - 1**.
4. Repeat steps 2-3 until the **low** pointer is greater than the **high** pointer.
5. If the target element is not found, return a "not found" indicator.

Example:

Suppose we have a sorted array of integers: [4, 8, 15, 20, 22, 35, 40, 45, 50, 55]. Let's find the index of the target element 35 using binary search.

1. Initial **low = 0, high = 9**, and calculate **mid = (0 + 9) / 2 = 4.**
2. Compare element at index 4 (22) with target 35. Since 22 < 35, update **low = 5.**
3. Calculate **mid = (5 + 9) / 2** = 7.
4. Compare element at index 7 (45) with target 35. Since 45 > 35, update **high = 6.**
5. Calculate **mid = (5 + 6) / 2 = 5.**
6. Compare element at index 5 (35) with target 35. Match found!

The target element 35 is found at index 5.

Binary search's efficiency makes it a valuable tool for searching in sorted datasets, and its principles extend to more complex search algorithms used in various applications.

12.2 Sorting Algorithms

Sorting algorithms arrange elements in a specific order, facilitating easier data retrieval and analysis. This section delves into sorting techniques such as bubble sort, insertion sort, and merge sort.

12.2.1 Bubble Sort

Bubble Sort is a simple and intuitive sorting algorithm that repeatedly steps through a list, compares adjacent elements, and swaps them if they are in the wrong order. This process is repeated for each element in the list until the entire list is sorted. While easy to understand and implement, Bubble Sort's performance is relatively poor for large datasets due to its quadratic time complexity.

Key Concepts:

- **Basic Idea:** Bubble Sort repeatedly iterates through the list and compares adjacent elements, swapping them if they are in the wrong order. This process is repeated until the entire list is sorted.
- **Time Complexity:** Bubble Sort has an average and worst-case time complexity of O(n^2), where "n" is the number of elements in the list. In each iteration, Bubble Sort compares and possibly swaps all adjacent elements.
- **Use Cases:** Bubble Sort is suitable for small datasets or as an educational tool to understand sorting algorithms.
- **Advantages:** Easy to understand and implement. Requires minimal additional memory.
- **Disadvantages:** Inefficient for large datasets due to its quadratic time complexity. There are more efficient sorting algorithms available.
- **Algorithm:**
    1. Start from the first element and compare it with

the next element.
2. If the next element is smaller, swap them.
3. Move to the next pair of elements and repeat step 2.
4. Continue this process until the end of the list is reached.
5. Repeat steps 1-4 for a total of "n" iterations (where "n" is the number of elements in the list).
6. After each iteration, the largest unsorted element will "bubble up" to its correct position at the end of the list.

Example:

Suppose we have an unsorted array of integers: [5, 2, 9, 1, 5, 6]. Let's use Bubble Sort to sort this array in ascending order.

1. First iteration: [2, 5, 1, 5, 6, 9] (Swap 5 and 2)
2. Second iteration: [2, 1, 5, 5, 6, 9] (Swap 5 and 1)
3. Third iteration: [2, 1, 5, 5, 6, 9] (No swaps)
4. Fourth iteration: [1, 2, 5, 5, 6, 9] (Swap 2 and 1)

The array is now sorted.

While Bubble Sort is not suitable for large datasets due to its inefficiency, it serves as a foundational sorting algorithm that helps build an understanding of sorting concepts. More efficient sorting algorithms like Merge Sort and Quick Sort are often preferred for practical applications.

12.2.2 Insertion Sort

Insertion Sort is a simple sorting algorithm that builds the final sorted array one element at a time. It iterates through the input elements, shifting each element larger than the current value to the right until the correct position is found. Insertion Sort is efficient for small datasets and performs well when the input array is already partially sorted. However, its average-case time complexity is O(n^2), making it less suitable for larger datasets compared to more advanced sorting algorithms.

Key Concepts:

- **Basic Idea:** Insertion Sort maintains a "sorted" and an "unsorted" portion of the array. It iterates through the unsorted portion, removing each element and inserting it into its correct position within the sorted portion.
- **Time Complexity:** Insertion Sort has an average and worst-case time complexity of O(n^2), where "n" is the number of elements in the list. It requires comparing and shifting elements for each element in the list.
- **Use Cases:** Insertion Sort is suitable for small datasets or when the array is already partially sorted.
- **Advantages:** Simple to understand and implement. Efficient for small datasets or nearly sorted arrays.
- **Disadvantages:** Inefficient for larger datasets due to its quadratic time complexity. More advanced sorting algorithms may be preferred for larger data.
- **Algorithm:**
    1. Start with the second element (index 1) and consider it as the "current" element.
    2. Compare the current element with the elements to its left in the sorted portion of the array.
    3. If the current element is smaller, shift the larger elements to the right to make space for the current element.
    4. Repeat steps 2 and 3 until the correct position for

the current element is found.
5. Move to the next unsorted element and repeat steps 2-4.
6. Continue this process until all elements are in the sorted portion.

Example:

Suppose we have an unsorted array of integers: [8, 4, 2, 7, 3]. Let's use Insertion Sort to sort this array in ascending order.

1. First iteration: [4, 8, 2, 7, 3] (Insert 4 into its correct position)
2. Second iteration: [2, 4, 8, 7, 3] (Insert 2 into its correct position)
3. Third iteration: [2, 4, 7, 8, 3] (Insert 7 into its correct position)
4. Fourth iteration: [2, 3, 4, 7, 8] (Insert 3 into its correct position)

The array is now sorted.

Insertion Sort is valuable for educational purposes and for sorting small datasets or nearly sorted arrays efficiently. However, for larger datasets, other sorting algorithms like Merge Sort or Quick Sort are more suitable due to their better average-case time complexity.

12.2.3 Merge Sort

Merge Sort is a highly efficient sorting algorithm that follows the divide-and-conquer paradigm. It divides the input array into smaller subarrays, sorts them, and then merges the sorted subarrays to produce the final sorted array. Merge Sort is known for its consistent and reliable performance, with an average and worst-case time complexity of O(n log n).

Key Concepts:

- **Divide and Conquer:** Merge Sort divides the input array into smaller halves until each subarray contains only one element. It then repeatedly merges adjacent subarrays while ensuring that the merged subarrays remain sorted.
- **Time Complexity:** Merge Sort has an average and worst-case time complexity of O(n log n), making it more efficient than quadratic-time algorithms like Bubble Sort and Insertion Sort for larger datasets.
- **Stability:** Merge Sort is a stable sorting algorithm, which means that the relative order of equal elements is preserved during sorting.
- **Use Cases:** Merge Sort is suitable for sorting large datasets efficiently and is often used as a basis for more advanced sorting algorithms.
- **Advantages:** Consistently good performance, even for large datasets. Suitable for both small and large arrays. Stable sorting.
- **Disadvantages:** Requires additional memory for the temporary storage of subarrays during merging.
- **Algorithm:**
    1. Divide the unsorted array into two halves.
    2. Recursively sort each half.
    3. Merge the sorted halves to produce a single sorted array.

Example:

Suppose we have an unsorted array of integers: [8, 4, 2, 7, 3]. Let's use Merge Sort to sort this array in ascending order.

1. Divide the array: [8, 4, 2, 7, 3] → [8, 4] [2, 7, 3]
2. Recursively sort each half: [8, 4] → [4, 8], [2, 7, 3] → [2, 3, 7]
3. Merge the sorted halves: [4, 8] [2, 3, 7] → [2, 3, 4, 7, 8]

The array is now sorted.

Merge Sort's efficiency and stability make it a popular choice for sorting large datasets and are important features in the design of various algorithms and data manipulation techniques.

12.3 Graph Algorithms

Graph algorithms are essential for analyzing relationships between entities represented as nodes and edges. This section covers two fundamental graph algorithms: Breadth-First Search (BFS) and Depth-First Search (DFS).

12.3.1 Breadth-First Search (BFS)

Breadth-First Search (BFS) is a graph traversal algorithm that systematically explores a graph by visiting all the vertices at the same level before moving to the next level. It is often used to find the shortest path between two nodes and to explore all nodes in a graph. BFS operates like a wave, starting from a selected source vertex and radiating outwards.

Key Concepts:

- **Exploration Order:** BFS explores the graph in layers, starting from the source vertex and moving to its adjacent vertices before moving to the next level of vertices. This ensures that all vertices at the same distance from the source are visited before moving deeper into the graph.

- **Queue:** BFS uses a queue data structure to manage the order of vertex traversal. The source vertex is enqueued initially, and then its neighbors are enqueued, and the process continues in a breadth-first manner.
- **Shortest Path:** BFS can be used to find the shortest path between two nodes in an unweighted graph. The first time the destination vertex is reached, the shortest path is guaranteed to be found.
- **Time Complexity:** The time complexity of BFS is O(V + E), where V is the number of vertices and E is the number of edges. This complexity arises from visiting each vertex and each edge once.
- **Applications:** Shortest path finding, exploring all connected components in a graph, network broadcasting, and puzzle solving.
- **Advantages:** Guarantees the shortest path in unweighted graphs. Can be used to explore all nodes reachable from a source node. Easy to implement using a queue.
- **Disadvantages:** May not work well for very large graphs with dense connectivity.

Algorithm Steps:

1. Enqueue the source vertex into the queue.
2. Mark the source vertex as visited.
3. While the queue is not empty:
    - Dequeue a vertex from the queue.
    - Process the vertex (e.g., print it).

- Enqueue all unvisited neighbors of the vertex and mark them as visited.

Example:

Suppose we have the following undirected graph:

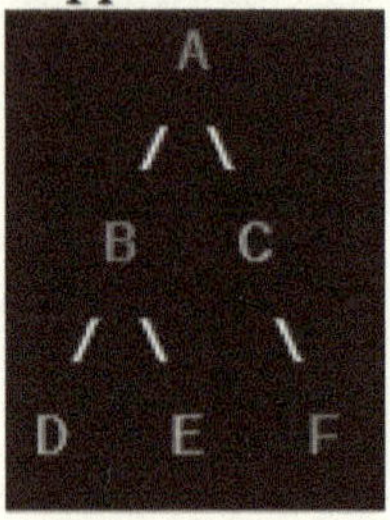

Starting from vertex A, a BFS traversal would visit the vertices in the order: A, B, C, D, E, F.

BFS's ability to find the shortest path and explore the graph layer by layer makes it a fundamental algorithm in graph theory and various applications in computer science and data analysis.

12.3.2 Depth-First Search (DFS)

Depth-First Search (DFS) is a graph traversal algorithm that explores a graph by visiting as far as possible along a branch before backtracking. It is used to traverse or search through a graph or tree data structure. DFS operates by systematically exploring as deeply as possible along each branch before backtracking.

Key Concepts:

- **Exploration Order:** DFS starts at an initial vertex and explores as deeply as possible along each branch before backtracking. It moves deeper into the graph before backtracking to previous levels.
- **Stack:** DFS uses a stack (either explicit or through recursion) to manage the order of vertex traversal. When a vertex is visited, its neighbors are pushed onto the stack to

be visited later.

- **Backtracking:** When a dead-end is reached (i.e., a vertex with no unvisited neighbors), DFS backtracks to the last vertex with unvisited neighbors and continues exploring.
- **Time Complexity:** The time complexity of DFS is O(V + E), where V is the number of vertices and E is the number of edges. Similar to BFS, this complexity arises from visiting each vertex and each edge once.
- **Applications:** Topological sorting, cycle detection, pathfinding, maze solving, and more.
- **Advantages:** Can be more memory-efficient than BFS, especially when the branching factor is high. Can be easily implemented using recursion.
- **Disadvantages:** DFS might not find the shortest path between two nodes. It can get stuck in deep branches before exploring shallow ones.

Algorithm Steps:

1. Start at the initial vertex and mark it as visited.
2. Process the current vertex (e.g., print it).
3. Explore each unvisited neighbor of the current vertex recursively or by pushing them onto the stack.
4. Backtrack (return) when no more unvisited neighbors are available.

Example:
Consider the following graph:

```
    A
   / \
  B   C
 / \   \
D   E   F
```

Starting from vertex A, a DFS traversal would visit the vertices in the order: A, B, D, E, C, F.

DFS's ability to explore deeply into a graph makes it suitable for tasks such as exploring connected components, finding paths, and detecting cycles. It can be applied to various scenarios where exploring different paths through a graph or tree is necessary.

By understanding and applying these searching, sorting, and graph algorithms, programmers can design more efficient and effective solutions to a wide range of computational problems. These algorithms serve as building blocks for various applications, from data analysis to software optimization.

Chapter 13: Advanced Data Structures

In this chapter, we delve into more complex and specialized data structures that offer unique advantages for specific tasks and scenarios. These advanced data structures provide efficient solutions to a wide range of problems, from fast data retrieval to optimal priority management and graph analysis. The goal is to offer a highlight of the other useful data structures and where they are applicable. However, acknowledging the fact that this is a foundation book, we will reserve the detail for a future volume.

13.1 Hash Tables and Hash Functions

Hash tables are versatile data structures that offer fast data insertion, retrieval, and deletion. They work on the principle of hashing, where a hash function converts a data item into an index within an array. This enables constant-time average-case operations for common tasks. Hash tables are commonly used for implementing dictionaries, caches, and database indexing.

Key Concepts:

13.1.1 Hash Function

A hash function is a fundamental element of hash tables, playing a pivotal role in converting complex data into fixed-size values, commonly referred to as hash codes. These hash codes determine the storage location of data items within the hash table. A reliable hash function is essential for the efficiency and performance of hash table operations.

Mapping Data to Hash Codes:

When a hash function receives an input, such as a key or data item, it applies a series of computations to transform this input into an integer value known as the hash code. This hash code serves as the index where the data will be stored in the hash table. The mapping should be deterministic, meaning that the same input will consistently produce the same hash code throughout the lifetime of the hash table.

Uniform Distribution:

One of the key objectives of a well-designed hash function is to ensure the uniform distribution of keys across the available slots in the hash table. An even distribution of keys minimizes the chances of collisions, where different keys end up with the same hash code. When keys are uniformly distributed, the hash table operates efficiently, enabling fast data retrieval and insertion.

Characteristics of a Reliable Hash Function:

A reliable hash function exhibits several important characteristics:

1. **Determinism:** The hash function should be deterministic, meaning that for the same input, it will consistently produce the same hash code. This predictability is vital for maintaining the integrity and coherence of the hash table.

Example: Let's consider a simple hash function that takes a string as input and computes the sum of the ASCII values of its characters. For the string "hello," the hash code would be 104 + 101 + 108 + 108 + 111 = 532.

1. **Efficiency:** An efficient hash function should have a constant time complexity. It must be capable of producing

hash codes quickly, even for large datasets. The efficiency of the hash function directly impacts the overall performance of the hash table.

Example: A common efficient hash function used in programming languages is the "Fowler-Noll-Vo" (FNV) hash function. It employs a series of bitwise operations and prime numbers to generate hash codes with minimal collisions.

1. **Low Probability of Collisions:** While complete avoidance of collisions may be impractical, a good hash function aims to minimize their occurrence significantly. By distributing keys uniformly, the hash function reduces the number of keys that map to the same hash code, thereby decreasing the likelihood of collisions.

Example: Consider a hash function that employs the modulo operation to convert input values into hash codes. This function divides the input value by the size of the hash table and uses the remainder as the hash code. This approach often leads to uniform distribution and reduced collisions.

1. **Handling Varying Input Sizes:** Hash functions should be capable of processing inputs of varying sizes and converting them into a fixed-size hash code. This flexibility allows hash tables to efficiently handle keys or data items of different lengths.

Example: The SHA-256 (Secure Hash Algorithm 256-bit) is a widely used cryptographic hash function that takes variable-length input and generates a 256-bit fixed-size hash code. It is employed in various security applications to ensure data integrity.

1. **Avoiding Predictable Patterns:** A strong hash function is designed to avoid producing predictable patterns or biases in the output. Predictable patterns could lead to clustering of keys around certain indices, increasing the risk of collisions.

Example: The Pearson Hash function is designed to eliminate predictable patterns by employing a fixed lookup table to map each byte of the input to a unique hash code.

In conclusion, a well-crafted hash function is critical for the optimal performance of hash tables. It should efficiently map data to hash codes, ensure uniform distribution, and minimize the likelihood of collisions. By fulfilling these characteristics, the hash function facilitates swift and efficient data retrieval and storage within the hash table, making it an essential component in various applications across computer science.

13.1.2 Collision Resolution

Collisions are an inevitable occurrence in hash tables when two distinct keys produce the same hash code, leading to multiple keys attempting to occupy the same index in the hash table. Efficiently handling collisions is crucial to maintaining the integrity of the hash table and ensuring fast and accurate data retrieval.

Collisions in Hash Tables:

1. **Chaining (Linked Lists):**
    - In chaining, each slot in the hash table contains a linked list data structure.
    - When a collision occurs, the collided key-value pair is appended to the linked list at the corresponding index.

- This allows multiple keys to coexist at the same index, ensuring that data is stored and retrieved correctly.

Example: Consider a hash table with slots indexed from 0 to 9. When keys "apple" and "apricot" both hash to index 4, they are stored as linked list nodes at that index:

Index 0:
Index 1:
Index 2:
Index 3:
Index 4: -> ("apple", value_apple) -> ("apricot", value_apricot)
Index 5:
Index 6:
Index 7:
Index 8:
Index 9:

1. **Open Addressing (Probing):**
   - In open addressing, when a collision occurs, the algorithm searches for the next available slot (probing) to place the collided key.
   - Probing techniques include linear probing, quadratic probing, and double hashing.
   - Open addressing ensures that all keys are stored directly in the hash table, without the need for additional data structures.

Example: Continuing from the previous example, if "orange" also hashes to index 4, linear probing will search for the next available index (index 5) and store "orange" there:

Index 0:
Index 1:

Index 2:
Index 3:
Index 4: ("apple", value_apple) -> ("apricot", value_apricot)
Index 5: ("orange", value_orange)
Index 6:
Index 7:
Index 8:
Index 9:

Comparison of Chaining and Open Addressing:

Pros of Chaining:

- Efficient for handling a high number of collisions, as linked lists can accommodate an arbitrary number of keys at each index.
- Does not require resizing the hash table during collision resolution, reducing overhead.

Cons of Chaining:

- Slightly increased memory overhead due to the need for an additional data structure (linked lists) for each slot in the hash table.
- Linked list traversal might have a slight impact on performance for large linked lists.

Pros of Open Addressing:

- No additional data structures are required, leading to lower memory overhead.
- Better cache performance due to contiguous storage of elements directly in the hash table.

Cons of Open Addressing:

- More challenging to handle a high number of collisions, especially when the table is almost full, as it may lead to clustering and increased probing.
- Resizing the hash table is sometimes necessary when it becomes heavily occupied, which can be computationally expensive.

The choice between chaining and open addressing depends on factors such as the expected number of collisions, the desired memory usage, and the nature of the data being stored. Chaining is generally preferred when collisions are frequent or when memory is not a critical concern. On the other hand, open addressing may be a better choice when memory optimization and cache performance are essential. Ultimately, the selection of a collision resolution technique should be based on the specific requirements of the application using the hash table.

13.1.3 Load Factor

The load factor is a critical parameter that determines the occupancy level of a hash table. It is defined as the ratio of the number of elements (key-value pairs) stored in the hash table to the total number of slots (buckets) available. Understanding and managing the load factor is essential for maintaining efficient hash table operations.

Understanding the Load Factor:

The load factor, often denoted by the symbol "λ" (lambda), is calculated as:

λ = Number of elements / Number of slots

A load factor of 1.0 indicates that the hash table is fully occupied, meaning that there is one element in each slot. In contrast, a load factor of 0.5 means that half of the slots in the hash table are empty.

Effects of Load Factor on Collisions:

The load factor has a direct impact on the occurrence of collisions in a hash table. As the load factor increases, the likelihood of collisions also increases. When the load factor approaches or exceeds 1.0, the hash table becomes densely occupied, making it more challenging to find available slots for new keys, leading to more collisions.

Advantages of a Low Load Factor:

Maintaining a low load factor offers several benefits for the performance of a hash table:

1. **Reduced Collisions:** With fewer elements stored in each slot, the chances of multiple keys mapping to the same slot (collision) decrease. This results in better performance during hash table operations, as fewer collisions mean faster data retrieval and insertion.
2. **Faster Operations:** A lower load factor ensures that searching and insertion operations are generally more efficient. As there are fewer elements in each slot, probing (in the case of open addressing) or traversal of linked lists (in the case of chaining) becomes less time-consuming.

Dynamic Resizing for an Optimal Load Factor:

To maintain an optimal load factor, hash tables often employ dynamic resizing. When the load factor exceeds a predefined threshold, the hash table is resized, typically by doubling or halving the number of slots. This process is known as rehashing.

Techniques for Dynamic Resizing:

1. **Upsizing:**
    - When the load factor exceeds a certain threshold (commonly around 0.7 or 0.8), the hash table is resized to accommodate more elements.
    - Upsizing involves creating a new hash table with more slots and rehashing all existing key-value pairs into the new hash table.
    - The new size of the hash table should be a prime number to help distribute keys uniformly.
2. **Downsizing:**
    - When the load factor falls below a specified threshold (often around 0.2 or 0.3), the hash table is downsized to save memory.
    - Downsizing requires creating a new hash table with fewer slots and rehashing the elements into the new table.
    - Similar to upsizing, the new size of the hash table should be a prime number.

Dynamic resizing allows the hash table to adjust its size based on the number of elements it contains, ensuring an optimal load factor and efficient performance. By avoiding overloading or underutilizing the hash table, dynamic resizing helps strike a balance between memory usage and collision avoidance, providing a smooth and efficient hash table operation in various applications.

13.1.4 Time Complexity

Time complexity is a crucial factor in evaluating the efficiency of data structures and algorithms. For hash tables, the average-case time complexity for common operations like insert, delete, and search is constant, denoted as O(1). This means that these operations take a constant amount of time, irrespective of the size of the hash table.

Average-Case Time Complexity (O(1)):

The constant-time complexity is achievable under the assumption of uniform distribution and a well-designed hash function. When keys are evenly distributed across the hash table and the hash function minimizes collisions, each operation can be executed in constant time.

Worst-Case Time Complexity (O(n)):

However, in the worst-case scenario, the time complexity of hash table operations may degrade to O(n), where n is the number of elements stored in the hash table. This occurs when a large number of keys hash to the same slot due to excessive collisions. As a result, the hash table degenerates into a linear data structure, and operations like search, insert, or delete may require traversing the entire list of elements in that slot.

Mitigating Worst-Case Scenarios:

To ensure that the hash table remains efficient, even in the worst-case scenario, several techniques can be employed:

1. **Well-Designed Hash Functions:**
    - Choosing or designing a good hash function is critical to minimizing collisions and ensuring a uniform distribution of keys.
    - A well-designed hash function should provide a random-like distribution of hash codes, reducing the likelihood of clustering and collisions.
2. **Load Factor Management:**
    - Keeping the load factor at an optimal level is essential for maintaining constant-time

performance.
   - If the load factor is consistently high, it increases the risk of collisions. Therefore, dynamic resizing (upsizing or downsizing) should be employed to adjust the size of the hash table and maintain a low load factor.
3. **Collision Resolution Techniques:**
   - The choice of a collision resolution technique can impact the worst-case time complexity.
   - Chaining (linked lists) generally provides better worst-case performance, as it handles collisions efficiently by maintaining separate lists for collided keys.
   - Open addressing techniques (linear probing, quadratic probing, etc.) may lead to more clustering and longer probe sequences in worst-case scenarios.
4. **Choosing Prime Numbers for Table Size:**
   - When resizing the hash table, it is beneficial to choose a new size that is a prime number.
   - Using prime numbers helps ensure a more even distribution of keys across the resized hash table, reducing the likelihood of clustering.
5. **Rehashing with Different Hash Functions:**
   - In some cases, especially when facing significant data changes or rehashing due to resizing, using a different hash function may improve performance.
   - Changing the hash function can lead to a more balanced distribution of keys, reducing the potential for collisions.

By implementing these techniques and adopting best practices for designing and managing hash tables, the worst-case scenario can be mitigated, maintaining the average constant-time performance that makes hash tables a powerful and efficient data structure for a wide range of applications.

13.1.5 Applications

Hash tables are versatile data structures with widespread applications across various fields in computer science. Their efficient key-value pair storage and retrieval capabilities make them invaluable for optimizing performance in different scenarios.

1. Dictionaries:

Hash tables are commonly used to implement dictionary data structures, where keys correspond to unique words or terms, and values represent their respective definitions or associated data. Due to their constant-time lookup, hash tables provide fast access to definitions, making dictionary searches quick and efficient.

2. Caching:

Hash tables play a significant role in caching frequently accessed data to improve application performance. In caching, hash tables are used to store the most recently accessed data or computed results. This prevents the need to recalculate or fetch data from a slower data source repeatedly. As a result, applications can respond more quickly to user requests, enhancing overall responsiveness and reducing processing overhead.

3. Spell Checkers:

In spell checkers, hash tables are utilized to store and quickly check the existence of valid words in a given dictionary. The dictionary words are hashed, and their hash codes are stored in the hash table. When a user input word needs to be checked for spelling correctness, its hash code is calculated, and a lookup is performed in the hash table. If the hash code is present, the word is considered valid; otherwise, it is flagged as a misspelling.

4. Database Indexing:

Hash tables assist in fast retrieval of data in databases, enhancing query performance. In database indexing, hash functions are used to map keys (such as primary keys or indexed attributes) to specific addresses (buckets) in the hash table. This process allows the database system to efficiently locate and retrieve records matching a given key, significantly reducing query execution time.

Example of Database Indexing:

Suppose we have a database of student records with unique student IDs. To facilitate fast access to student information, the student IDs are used as keys in a hash table. When querying a specific student's details using their ID, the hash function calculates the hash code for that ID and quickly retrieves the corresponding bucket, which holds the student's record.

By leveraging the power of hash tables, applications can achieve significant performance improvements across diverse domains. From providing rapid dictionary lookups and caching frequently accessed data to facilitating spell checking and optimizing database queries, hash tables remain a foundational data structure for solving a wide range of computational challenges.

13.1.6 Conclusion

In conclusion, hash tables and hash functions are powerful data structures that offer efficient data management and retrieval capabilities. Let's recap the key concepts and emphasize the significance of these structures in computer science.

Key Concepts of Hash Tables and Hash Functions:

- **Hash Function:** A hash function is a critical component of a hash table that maps data of variable size to a fixed-size value (hash code). A well-designed hash function ensures uniform distribution of keys, minimizing collisions.

- **Collision Resolution:** Collisions occur when two distinct keys produce the same hash code. Techniques like chaining (linked lists) and open addressing (probing) handle collisions and accommodate multiple keys at the same index.
- **Load Factor:** The load factor represents the ratio of elements stored to the total number of slots in the hash table. Maintaining a low load factor reduces collisions and ensures efficient operations.
- **Time Complexity:** Hash tables offer constant-time average-case operations (O(1)) for insert, delete, and search. However, excessive collisions may lead to worst-case complexity (O(n)).

Efficiency and Versatility of Hash Tables:

Hash tables provide an array of benefits, making them a versatile and powerful data structure:

- **Fast Lookup:** The constant-time complexity for common operations allows rapid retrieval of data, making hash tables ideal for dictionaries and databases.
- **Caching Efficiency:** Hash tables enhance application performance through efficient caching, reducing the need for repeated data retrieval.
- **Spell Checkers:** Hash tables expedite spell checking by quickly verifying the existence of valid words in a dictionary.
- **Database Indexing:** Hash tables improve query performance in databases, enabling fast retrieval of records based on key attributes.

Exploring Further Applications:

As readers delve into the world of hash tables, they will discover numerous other applications across computer science and beyond. From implementing data structures like sets and maps to optimizing algorithms, hash tables find relevance in a wide range of computational problems.

Significance as a Foundational Data Structure:

Hash tables serve as a fundamental building block in computer science due to their efficiency, versatility, and wide-ranging applications. Mastering hash tables enables programmers to design more efficient algorithms, enhance application performance, and solve complex problems with ease.

Encouragement:

In conclusion, we encourage readers to explore further the potential of hash tables and hash functions. Understanding their inner workings and applications opens doors to a world of efficient data management, blazing-fast lookups, and elegant solutions to computational challenges. By harnessing the power of hash tables, individuals can unleash the full potential of their coding prowess and contribute to the ever-evolving landscape of computer science.

In summary, hash tables and hash functions provide an efficient way to manage and retrieve data, making them a foundational data structure in computer science with diverse applications.

13.2 Heaps and Priority Queues

13.2.1 Key Concepts: Heap Property and Operations

Heap Property: A heap is a specialized binary tree with a specific order between parent and child nodes. It can have either the max-heap property, where parent nodes are greater than or equal to their children, or the min-heap property, where parent nodes are smaller than or equal to their children. The heap property ensures that the highest (max heap) or lowest (min heap) priority element is at the root of the tree, allowing for efficient extraction of elements with extreme priorities.

Operations on Heaps: Heaps support efficient insertion and extraction of elements with respect to their priorities. The "insert" operation adds a new element to the heap while maintaining the heap property. The "extract" operation retrieves and removes the highest (max heap) or lowest (min heap) priority element from the heap. These operations are crucial for various algorithms that require maintaining elements in a specific order based on their priorities.

13.2.2 Priority Queue: Introduction and Applications

Introduction to Priority Queue: A priority queue is an abstract data type that allows inserting elements with associated priorities and extracting the element with the highest (max heap) or lowest (min heap) priority. It abstracts the concept of a queue by prioritizing elements based on their values, facilitating efficient access to the most important elements in a data set.

Applications of Priority Queues: Priority queues find applications in various domains, optimizing algorithms and data structures in multiple ways:

1. **Task Scheduling:**
    - Priority queues are used in task scheduling systems to manage tasks based on their priorities.
    - Higher-priority tasks are executed first, ensuring that critical tasks are promptly addressed.
2. **Dijkstra's Algorithm:**
    - Priority queues implemented using heaps are essential for optimizing graph algorithms like Dijkstra's shortest path algorithm.
    - The priority queue efficiently selects the next

vertex with the shortest distance during graph traversal.

3. **Huffman Coding:**
    - Priority queues are integral to data compression algorithms like Huffman coding.
    - They facilitate the efficient construction of the Huffman tree, forming the basis for assigning variable-length codes to characters.

13.2.3 Time Complexity and Efficiency

Time Complexity of Heap Operations: Insertion and extraction operations in heaps have a time complexity of O(log n), where n is the number of elements. The efficient time complexity is a key factor in the popularity of heaps and priority queues, enabling quick access to elements with extreme priorities.

Efficiency of Heaps and Priority Queues: Heaps and priority queues provide an efficient way to manage and retrieve data based on priorities. Their constant-time average-case operations (O(log n)) for insertion and extraction ensure that important elements can be accessed quickly, making them valuable tools in various computational tasks.

In conclusion, understanding the different types of heaps, the key concepts related to the heap property and operations, and the significance of priority queues is crucial for designing efficient algorithms and data structures. By leveraging the power of heaps and priority queues, computer scientists and programmers can enhance the performance of their applications, optimize task management, and efficiently solve a wide range of computational challenges. The efficiency and versatility of heaps and priority queues solidify their position as essential data structures in computer science.

13.3 Graph Representation and Algorithms

(Dijkstra's Algorithm)

Graphs are versatile data structures that model relationships between objects. They consist of vertices (nodes) and edges (connections). Graph algorithms are used to solve problems related to networks, routes, social relationships, and more. Dijkstra's algorithm, in particular, finds the shortest path between nodes in a weighted graph.

13.3.1 Key Concepts: Graph Terminology

Graphs are versatile data structures used to model relationships between objects. Understanding various aspects of graph structure is crucial for designing efficient graph algorithms:

- **Directed and Undirected Graphs:** Graphs can be either directed or undirected. In a directed graph, edges have a direction from one vertex to another, meaning they represent a one-way relationship. In contrast, undirected graphs have edges with no direction, representing bidirectional relationships.
- **Weighted and Unweighted Graphs:** Edges in a graph can be weighted or unweighted. In a weighted graph, edges have numerical values representing distances, costs, or other metrics. These weights represent the "cost" or "distance" to traverse the edge. On the other hand, unweighted graphs have all edges with the same weight, usually representing a binary relationship between vertices.
- **Edges and Vertices:** In a graph, vertices (also known as nodes) represent distinct objects or entities, while edges represent connections or relationships between those objects. The combination of vertices and edges forms the basic components of a graph, allowing it to represent

complex relationships in a structured manner.

Understanding these key concepts of graph terminology lays the foundation for effectively utilizing graphs in various applications, including designing efficient algorithms to solve real-world problems.

13.3.2 Adjacency Matrix and List

Graphs can be represented in different ways, each with its own advantages and disadvantages:

- **Adjacency Matrix:** A 2D matrix representing connections between vertices. It is efficient for dense graphs but can be memory-intensive for sparse graphs since it stores all possible connections.
- **Adjacency List:** A list of vertices and their adjacent vertices. It is memory-efficient for sparse graphs, as it only stores connections that exist.

13.3.3 Dijkstra's Algorithm

Dijkstra's algorithm is a powerful tool for finding the shortest path between nodes in a weighted graph. The algorithm operates based on the following principles:

- **Greedy Approach:** Dijkstra's algorithm follows a greedy strategy by selecting the vertex with the shortest known distance to the source vertex at each step.
- **Priority Queue (Min-Heap):** To efficiently manage vertices based on their tentative distances, Dijkstra's algorithm uses a priority queue (often implemented as a min-heap).

13.3.4 Time Complexity

Dijkstra's algorithm has a time complexity of O((V + E) log V), where V is the number of vertices and E is the number of edges. The use of a priority queue optimizes the process of exploring the graph, making it feasible for large graphs.

Applications

Dijkstra's algorithm finds applications in various domains:

- **Finding Shortest Paths:** In navigation systems, Dijkstra's algorithm is used to find the shortest route between two points, enabling efficient travel planning.
- **Network Routing:** In computer networks, Dijkstra's algorithm plays a crucial role in determining optimal paths for data transmission, minimizing delays and packet losses.
- **Recommendation Systems:** Dijkstra's algorithm can be applied to suggest the most relevant connections or items in recommendation systems, improving user experiences.

Conclusion

In conclusion, graph algorithms, particularly Dijkstra's algorithm, provide powerful solutions to diverse problems by efficiently analyzing relationships between data points. Whether it's finding the shortest path in navigation, optimizing network routing, or making personalized recommendations, graph algorithms help us navigate complex networks and make informed decisions. Aspiring computer scientists and programmers should explore the significance of graph algorithms and understand their applications in solving real-world challenges.

In this chapter, we explore advanced data structures that cater to specific needs in various domains. Hash tables offer fast data retrieval, heaps and priority queues handle priority-based tasks, and graph algorithms enable efficient analysis of interconnected data.

These structures are fundamental to solving complex problems across computer science and beyond.

Part V: Additional Topics

Chapter 14: Error Handling and Debugging

In the realm of software development, encountering errors is inevitable. To create robust and reliable programs, it's essential to understand error handling and debugging techniques. This chapter delves into the strategies and tools that help identify, manage, and rectify errors in your code.

14.1 Common Programming Errors and Debugging Strategies

Mistakes in programming are commonplace, and recognizing and addressing them is a crucial skill. This section explores common types of errors and provides effective debugging strategies.

14.1.1 Types of Programming Errors

Programming errors are common issues that developers encounter while writing code. Understanding the different types of errors helps programmers identify and fix them effectively:

1. **Syntax Errors:**
    - Syntax errors are mistakes in the code structure that violate the rules of the programming language.
    - These errors occur when the code is not written in a way that the language's compiler or interpreter can understand.
    - Examples of syntax errors include:
        - Missing semicolon at the end of a

statement:

```
print("Hello, World!") # Correct
print("Hello, World!") # Syntax error: missing semicolon
```

- Mismatched parentheses:

```
x = (5 + 3) * 2 # Correct
x = (5 + 3 * 2 # Syntax error: mismatched parentheses
```

- Using an invalid keyword:

```
for i in range(5): # Correct
for i in rang(5): # Syntax error: invalid keyword
```

1. **Logic Errors:**
    - Logic errors, also known as semantic errors, are flaws in the program's design or algorithm.
    - These errors lead to incorrect outputs or unexpected behavior, even if the code is syntactically correct.
    - Examples of logic errors include:
        - Incorrect calculation:

```
# Calculate the average of two numbers
num1 = 10
num2 = 20
average = (num1 + num2) / 2 # Correct
average = num1 + num2 / 2 # Logic error: incorrect calculation
```

- Incorrect loop condition:

```
# Print numbers from 1 to 5
```

```
for i in range(1, 6): # Correct
print(i)
# Incorrect loop condition
for i in range(6, 0): # Logic error: incorrect loop condition
print(i)
```

1. **Runtime Errors:**
    - Runtime errors, also called exceptions, occur during program execution.
    - These errors typically result from unforeseen conditions that disrupt the normal flow of the program.
    - Examples of runtime errors include:
        - Division by zero:

```
x = 10
y = 0
result = x / y # Runtime error: division by zero
```

- Accessing invalid memory:

```
int arr[5] = {1, 2, 3, 4, 5};
int value = arr[10]; // Runtime error: accessing invalid memory
```

- Opening a non-existent file:

```
file = open("myfile.txt", "r") # Runtime error: file not found
```

Identifying and addressing these types of programming errors is crucial for producing robust and reliable software. Debugging tools and techniques are essential for locating and fixing errors, ensuring the code functions correctly and meets its intended purpose.

14.1.2 Debugging Strategies

Debugging is the process of identifying and fixing errors in software code. Effective debugging strategies are essential for resolving issues and producing reliable software. Here are some commonly used debugging strategies:

1. **Print Debugging:**
   - Print debugging involves inserting print statements in the code to monitor variable values and program flow during execution.
   - Developers strategically place print statements to track the values of variables at specific points in the code.
   - Example (Python):

```
def add_numbers(a, b):
print("Entering add_numbers function")
result = a + b
print("Value of a:", a)
print("Value of b:", b)
print("Result:", result)
return result
```

1. **Code Reviews:**
   - Code reviews involve collaborative examination of code by peers or team members to identify potential issues and provide feedback.
   - During code reviews, developers can spot errors, suggest improvements, and ensure that the code adheres to coding standards.
   - Code reviews promote code quality and knowledge sharing within the team.

2. **Rubber Duck Debugging:**
    - Rubber duck debugging is a technique where a developer explains the code to an inanimate object (like a rubber duck) or a colleague.
    - The act of verbalizing the code often helps the developer gain new insights and identify errors in their thinking.
    - This method encourages developers to approach problems from different perspectives.
3. **Debugger Tools:**
    - Integrated Development Environment (IDE) tools provide built-in debuggers that assist developers in inspecting code and variables during program execution.
    - Debuggers allow developers to set breakpoints, step through code line by line, examine variable values, and understand the program's flow.

Combining these debugging strategies can significantly improve the efficiency and effectiveness of the debugging process. Debugging is an integral part of the software development lifecycle, enabling developers to create stable and reliable software products.

14.2 Exception Handling and Error Messages

Exception handling provides a structured way to manage errors and unexpected events in code. Properly handling exceptions enhances program reliability and user experience.

14.2.1 Exception Handling

Exception handling is a crucial aspect of programming that allows developers to gracefully handle errors and unexpected situations in their code. It ensures that the program can recover from errors and continue executing without crashing. Here are two commonly used techniques for exception handling:

1. **Try-Catch Blocks:**
    - Try-catch blocks, also known as exception blocks, are used to handle exceptions that may occur during the execution of a specific section of code.
    - The risky code that might throw an exception is enclosed within the try block, and the corresponding error-handling procedures are specified in the catch block.
    - If an exception occurs within the try block, the program immediately jumps to the corresponding catch block to handle the exception.
    - Example (Java):

```
try {
// Risky code that might throw an exception
int result = divide(10, 0);
System.out.println("Result: " + result);
} catch (ArithmeticException e) {
// Handling the exception
System.out.println("Error: Division by zero");
}
```

Throwing Exceptions:

- Throwing exceptions allows developers to explicitly generate exceptions to indicate errors or unusual situations in their code.
- When an exceptional condition arises, the program can

generate an exception using the **throw** keyword, and the control will be transferred to the nearest catch block.

- Developers can define custom exception classes to provide more context-specific error messages and information.
- Example (Python):

```
def check_age(age):
    if age < 0:

      raise ValueError("Age cannot be negative")
      elif age < 18:
      raise ValueError("Must be at least 18 years old")
      else:
      print("Age is valid")

    try:
    user_age = int(input("Enter your age: "))
    check_age(user_age) except ValueError as ve: print("Error:", ve)
```

By utilizing try-catch blocks and throwing exceptions, developers can effectively manage and handle exceptional conditions in their code. Proper exception handling enhances the robustness and reliability of the program by ensuring it can gracefully recover from errors and continue its execution.

14.2.2 Error Messages

Error messages play a crucial role in communicating issues within software to both developers and end users. Well-crafted error messages can significantly improve the debugging process and enhance user experience. This section focuses on the attributes that contribute to effective error messages.

14.2.2.1 Clear and Informative

Error messages should provide a clear and concise description of the problem at hand. Ambiguous or vague error messages can lead to confusion and frustration. A clear error message should:

- **Identify the Problem**: Clearly state what went wrong or what condition triggered the error.
- **Provide Context**: Offer information about the specific operation or action that led to the error.
- **Offer Diagnostic Details**: Include relevant details such as variable values, file names, or line numbers to aid in pinpointing the issue.
- **Suggest a Solution**: If possible, provide a hint or suggestion on how to rectify the error. This can guide developers toward the right direction.

Example:

Error: Division by zero

Location: File: calculator.py, Line: 36

Description: The division operation attempted to divide a number by zero, which is undefined. Please check the values you are using for the division and ensure the denominator is not zero.

Possible Solution: Make sure the denominator is a non-zero value before performing the division.

14.2.2.2 User-Friendly

Tailoring error messages to the target audience is essential. End users may not possess the technical knowledge that developers do, so error messages should be designed with their perspective in mind. A user-friendly error message should:

- **Avoid Technical Jargon**: Steer clear of using complex technical terms that might confuse non-technical users.
- **Use Plain Language**: Express the error in simple and plain language that is easily understandable.
- **Provide Actionable Steps**: Offer clear instructions on what the user can do next to resolve the issue.
- **Minimize Blame**: Frame the error message in a way that doesn't make the user feel at fault for the error.

Example:

Error: Unable to connect to the server

Description: We encountered a problem while trying to establish a connection to the server. This might be due to a network issue or server unavailability.

Possible Solution:

- Check your internet connection and ensure you're connected to a stable network.

- Verify if the server address is correct.

- If the problem persists, please contact our support team for assistance.

By adhering to the principles of clarity, informativeness, user-friendliness, and context, error messages can become valuable tools for guiding users and developers through the debugging and troubleshooting process. Well-designed error messages contribute to a smoother user experience and more efficient software development.

14.3 Testing and Troubleshooting Techniques

Thorough testing and systematic troubleshooting are integral to producing high-quality software. This section outlines effective testing strategies and techniques to identify and resolve issues.

14.3.1 Testing Strategies

Testing is an integral part of the software development process, aimed at identifying and rectifying defects and ensuring the reliability and quality of the software. This section explores various testing strategies that contribute to building robust and error-free software.

14.3.1.1 Unit Testing

Unit testing involves the isolation and testing of individual components or units of a software application. The goal is to validate that each unit functions as expected in isolation. Unit testing helps in early detection of bugs and facilitates easier debugging. Key aspects of unit testing include:

- **Isolation**: Each unit is tested independently of the others, ensuring that its behavior is predictable and consistent.
- **Automation**: Unit tests are typically automated, allowing for frequent and efficient testing during development.
- **Test Cases**: Test cases are designed to cover various scenarios, including normal inputs, edge cases, and error conditions.
- **Assertion and Validation**: Unit tests use assertions to compare the actual outcome with the expected outcome.

Example:

```
# Unit Test for a Calculator's Addition Function
def test_addition():
result = add(3, 5)
assert result == 8, "Addition test failed"
# Run the unit test
test_addition()
```

14.3.1.2 Integration Testing

Integration testing focuses on verifying the interactions and connections between different components or modules of a system. It ensures that integrated components work together as intended. Integration testing can be performed at various levels, including module-to-module and system-to-system interactions. Key aspects of integration testing include:

- **Component Interaction**: Testing the communication and data exchange between interconnected components.
- **Stubs and Drivers**: Placeholder components (stubs) or programs (drivers) are used to simulate the behavior of untested components.
- **Top-Down or Bottom-Up Approach**: Integration testing can follow a top-down or bottom-up approach, where components are integrated incrementally.

Example:

```
# Integration Test for a Payment System
def test_payment_integration():
customer = create_customer("John")

  product = create_product("Smartphone", 500)
  order = create_order(customer, product)
  result = process_payment(order)
  assert result == "Payment successful", "Payment
  integration test failed"

# Run the integration test
test_payment_integration()
```

14.3.1.3 Regression Testing

Regression testing ensures that new code changes or updates do not introduce new defects or break existing functionality. It involves re-running previously passed test cases to confirm that the software still performs as expected. Key aspects of regression testing include:

- **Test Suite Maintenance**: Maintaining a comprehensive suite of test cases to cover different aspects of the software.
- **Continuous Integration**: Integrating regression testing into the development process to catch regressions early.
- **Automated Testing**: Automating the execution of regression tests to ensure consistent and frequent testing.

Example:

```
# Regression Test for a Text Editor's Save Function
def test_save_function():
document = create_document("sample.txt")
write_text(document, "Hello, World!")
save_result = save_document(document)
assert save_result == "Document saved", "Save function regression test failed"
# Run the regression test
test_save_function()
```

By employing a combination of these testing strategies, software developers can identify and address issues at different levels of the application's architecture. This helps create software that is more reliable, maintainable, and less prone to errors.

14.3.2 Troubleshooting Techniques

- **Divide and Conquer**: Narrowing down problem sources

by systematically isolating sections of code.

- **Binary Search**: Efficiently identifying faulty segments by successively narrowing the search space.
- **Testing Environments**: Replicating production environments to recreate and fix bugs.

In conclusion, error handling and debugging are vital skills for developers. Understanding and addressing common programming errors, mastering exception handling, and employing effective testing and troubleshooting techniques are essential for delivering reliable and robust software products. By honing these skills, programmers can enhance the quality of their code and provide better user experiences.

Chapter 15: Introduction to Web Development

Web development is the process of creating dynamic and interactive websites that are accessible through web browsers. This chapter provides an overview of the fundamental technologies and concepts involved in web development, including HTML, CSS, and JavaScript.

15.1 HTML Fundamentals and Structure

HTML (Hypertext Markup Language) serves as the backbone of web development, providing the framework to structure and present content on the internet. This section serves as a foundational guide to the essential concepts of HTML and how it constructs the fundamental structure of a web page.

15.1.1 HTML Basics

HTML (Hypertext Markup Language) forms the foundation of web content creation and communication. This section serves as an introduction to the fundamental principles of HTML, encompassing key concepts such as tags, elements, attributes, and the overall architecture of HTML documents.

15.1.1.1 HTML Tags and Elements

HTML tags play a pivotal role in structuring and delineating the content of a webpage. This subsection delves into the significance of HTML tags and their function as markers that define the structure and composition of web content.

- **Tag Syntax**: Understanding the syntax of HTML tags, which consists of an opening tag, content, and a closing tag.
- **Semantic Markup**: Exploring how HTML tags carry semantic meaning, aiding in the organization and interpretation of content.
- **Block-level and Inline Elements**: Differentiating between block-level and inline elements and their impact on content layout.

15.1.1.2 Attributes

Attributes augment the capabilities of HTML elements by providing supplementary information and altering their behavior. This portion delves into the concept of attributes and their role in shaping the presentation and functionality of web content.

- **Attribute Syntax**: Understanding the syntax of HTML attributes within the context of HTML elements.
- **Common Attributes**: Exploring frequently used attributes like **class, id**, **src**, **href**, and their impact on element behavior.
- **Custom Attributes**: Introducing the concept of custom attributes for specific user-defined purposes.

15.1.1.3 HTML Document Anatomy

A comprehensive comprehension of the basic anatomy of an HTML document is essential for effective web development. This segment acquaints learners with the foundational elements that constitute the structure of an HTML document.

- **<!DOCTYPE> Declaration**: Explaining the role and significance of the **<!DOCTYPE>** declaration in specifying the document type and version of HTML.
- **<html> Element**: Understanding the function of the **<html>** element as the root container of the entire HTML document.
- **<head> Element**: Exploring the purpose of the **<head>** element for housing meta-information and external resources.
- **<body> Element**: Familiarizing with the role of the **<body>** element as the container for visible content.

Mastery of these HTML basics serves as a cornerstone for constructing coherent and well-structured web content. Subsequent sections expand upon this foundation, introducing additional facets of web development, styling, and interactivity.

15.1.2 Document Structure

Creating a coherent and logically organized structure is of paramount importance when developing web content. In this section, we will delve into the fundamental elements that comprise the structure of an HTML document, ensuring that your web pages are well-organized and user-friendly.

15.1.2.1 <!DOCTYPE> Declaration

The **<!DOCTYPE>** declaration holds a critical role in establishing the type and version of HTML being utilized in a document. This subsection elucidates the purpose and significance of the **<!DOCTYPE>** declaration in ensuring proper rendering and interpretation of your HTML content.

- **Defining Document Type**: Understanding how the **<!DOCTYPE>** declaration defines the version and standard of HTML, aiding browsers in rendering the content accurately.
- **Browser Compatibility**: Exploring the influence of the **<!DOCTYPE>** declaration on browser compatibility and ensuring consistent display across different platforms.

15.1.2.2 <html> Element

At the core of every HTML document resides the **<html>** element, serving as the root container. This portion sheds light on the pivotal role played by the **<html>** element in organizing and structuring the entire document.

- **Structural Foundation**: Understanding how the **<html>** element encapsulates the entire document and serves as the foundational structure for all content.
- **Language Specification**: Exploring the **lang** attribute within the **<html>** element for specifying the primary language of the document.

15.1.2.3 <head> Element

The **<head>** element houses essential meta-information and external resources that contribute to the overall functionality and presentation of the web page. This section delves into the diverse elements encompassed by the **<head>** element.

- **Meta Tags**: Exploring the utilization of meta tags within the **<head>** element to provide metadata about the document, such as character encoding and authorship.

- **External Resources**: Understanding how the **<head>** element facilitates the inclusion of external resources like stylesheets and scripts.

15.1.2.4 <body> Element

The **<body>** element encapsulates the visible content of the web page, encompassing text, images, links, and other elements that users interact with. This subsection illuminates the pivotal role played by the **<body>** element in presenting content to users.

- **Content Container**: Exploring how the **<body>** element acts as a container for all visible content displayed to users.
- **Text and Multimedia**: Understanding the versatility of the **<body>** element in accommodating text, images, videos, and other multimedia elements.

By mastering the intricacies of document structure, you establish a solid foundation for crafting web pages that are both aesthetically pleasing and logically organized. These elements collectively contribute to an enhanced user experience and effective communication of your web content.

15.1.3 Text and Headings

Textual content serves as the backbone of web communication. This section delves into the art of effectively presenting and formatting textual information on web pages, enhancing both readability and visual appeal.

15.1.3.1 Headings (<h1> - <h6>)

Headings play a crucial role in conveying the hierarchical structure of content. This subsection delves into the utilization of heading tags to impart clarity and organization to your web page.

- **Hierarchical Importance**: Understanding the significance of heading tags in denoting the importance and hierarchy of different sections.
- **Semantic Meaning**: Exploring how heading tags contribute to the semantic meaning of your content, aiding both users and search engines.
- **Styling and Formatting**: Integrating CSS styles to customize the appearance of headings and harmonize them with the overall design.

15.1.3.2 Paragraphs (<p>)

The **<p>** tag is the cornerstone of structuring and formatting paragraphs of text. This portion emphasizes the role of the **<p>** tag in maintaining coherence and readability.

- **Text Division**: Understanding how the **<p>** tag demarcates distinct paragraphs, preventing content from appearing as an indistinguishable block.
- **Whitespace Handling**: Exploring how browsers interpret whitespace within **<p>** tags and strategies for managing spacing.

15.1.3.3 Text Emphasis (<strong> and <em>)

Infusing text with emphasis can significantly impact user comprehension. This section delves into the use of **<strong>** and **<em>** tags to apply emphasis and convey importance.

- **Strong Emphasis (<strong>)**: Understanding the significance of the **<strong>** tag in denoting text with strong importance or significance.
- **Emphasized Text (<em>)**: Exploring the utilization of the **<em>** tag to emphasize text for readers, conveying subtle nuances in meaning.
- **Styling Emphasized Text**: Applying CSS styles to **<strong>** and **<em>** tags to modify their appearance and align with design aesthetics.

By effectively mastering the art of text and heading manipulation, you empower yourself to craft web pages that are not only information-rich but also visually appealing. The proper application of heading tags, paragraphs, and text emphasis contributes to a seamless reading experience and conveys the intended message with precision.

15.1.4 Lists and Links

Lists and hyperlinks are integral components of web content, offering a structured navigation experience and interconnectivity between different pages and resources. This section explores the art of crafting both lists and hyperlinks, enhancing the usability and accessibility of your web pages.

15.1.4.1 Ordered Lists (<ol>)

Ordered lists provide a systematic and organized way to enumerate items. This subsection delves into the utilization of the **<ol>** tag to create lists with automatic numbering.

- **Sequential Presentation**: Understanding how the **<ol>** tag introduces a sense of sequence and order to listed items.
- **List Item Numbers**: Exploring how ordered lists automatically assign numbers to each list item for a coherent presentation.
- **Nesting and Hierarchy**: Implementing nested ordered lists to convey hierarchical relationships and sub-categories.

15.1.4.2 Unordered Lists (<ul>)

Unordered lists offer a versatile approach to presenting items without enforcing a specific sequence. This portion emphasizes the use of the **<ul>** tag to generate visually distinct lists.

- **Visual Differentiation**: Understanding how unordered lists use bullet points to visually separate items, aiding clarity and readability.
- **Choice without Sequence**: Exploring scenarios where unordered lists are preferred, such as when listing options or features without prioritizing their order.
- **Nesting Unordered Lists**: Creating nested unordered lists to establish sub-groups and related concepts.

15.1.4.3 List Items (<li>)

List items are the building blocks of both ordered and unordered lists. This section delves into the use of the **<li>** tag to encapsulate individual list elements.

- **Structuring Content**: Understanding how the **<li>** tag wraps around each list item to define its boundaries and association with a list.
- **Formatting List Items**: Applying CSS styles to list items for customized visual representation, aligning with the overall design theme.

15.1.4.4 Hyperlinks (<a>)

Hyperlinks empower seamless navigation across web pages and external resources. This subsection explores the **<a>** tag's role in integrating hyperlinks.

- **Linking Web Pages**: Understanding how the **<a>** tag establishes connections between different web pages, enhancing user exploration.
- **Hyperlink Text**: Exploring the incorporation of descriptive and meaningful hyperlink text to guide users to relevant content.
- **URL Specification**: Learning how to specify the target URL using the **href** attribute within the **<a>** tag.

By mastering the creation of lists and hyperlinks, you equip yourself with essential tools for structuring content and providing efficient navigation pathways. Whether it's organizing content hierarchically or guiding users to related resources, the proper utilization of ordered lists, unordered lists, and hyperlinks contributes to a cohesive and user-friendly web experience.

Mastering these HTML fundamentals and structure principles lays the groundwork for constructing well-organized and visually appealing web pages. The ensuing sections build upon this foundation, introducing additional components and techniques to create dynamic and interactive web content.

15.2 CSS Styling and Layout

- Cascading Style Sheets (CSS) serve as the artistic palette of web development, enabling the transformation of raw HTML content into visually appealing and organized web pages. This section immerses you in the world of CSS, from its fundamental concepts to the creation of sophisticated layouts that elevate your web design.

15.2.1 CSS Basics

CSS is the artistic heartbeat of the web, and understanding its syntax and mechanics is your entryway to a world of captivating visual experiences.

Rule Structure

CSS rules are the magic spells that transform plain HTML into a visually enchanting spectacle. Dive into the core structure that wields this sorcery:

- **Selectors**: These are your spell chants. They determine which HTML elements will be subjected to your styling whims.
- **Properties and Values**: Consider these your magical ingredients. Properties like 'color' and 'font-size', combined with their values, conjure the appearance you desire.

Example:

```
/* Selectors: Targeting a specific class */
.button {
color: #ffffff; /* Property: Text color */
background-color: #007bff; /* Property: Background color */
```

```
padding: 10px 20px; /* Property: Padding */
}
```

Selectors

Imagine selectors as your magnifying glasses, zooming in on the precise elements you wish to transform. They range from broad strokes to surgical precision:

- **Tag Selectors**: Applying styles to all elements of a certain type, like every **<p>** for paragraphs.
- **Class Selectors**: Crafting styles for elements with a particular class attribute, allowing you to target specific groups.
- **ID Selectors**: Exclusively styling elements with a unique ID attribute, ensuring a one-of-a-kind look.

Example:

```
/* Tag Selector: Styling all paragraphs */
p {
font-size: 16px;
}
/* Class Selector: Styling buttons */
.button {
background-color: #ff9900;
}
/* ID Selector: Styling a unique element */
#header {
color: #333333;
}
```

Properties and Values

Properties are your painter's palette, and values are the shades you mix to craft your masterpiece. There's an array of properties and a universe of values to explore:

- **Font Styling**: Tweak 'font-family', 'font-size', 'font-weight', and more to create your desired text style.
- **Colors**: Experiment with 'color', 'background-color', and 'border-color' to infuse vibrancy.
- **Spacing**: Manipulate 'margin' and 'padding' to orchestrate the spatial rhythm of your design.

Example:

```
/* Font Styling */
h1 {
font-family: 'Helvetica', sans-serif;
font-size: 28px;
font-weight: bold;
}
/* Colors */
.button {
color: #ffffff;
background-color: #007bff;
border: 2px solid #007bff;
}
/* Spacing */
.container {
margin: 20px;
padding: 15px;
}
```

Dive into the symphony of CSS, where your imagination fuses with code to produce awe-inspiring visuals. The dance of selectors and the orchestration of properties await your creative direction.

15.2.2 Styling Text and Fonts

Text is the voice of your website, and in this section, we'll immerse ourselves in the art of textual metamorphosis and typographical brilliance.

Color and Font Color

Just as a painter selects their palette, you can breathe life into your words by applying colors that evoke emotions and convey meaning:

- **Color**: The 'color' property empowers you to change the hue of your text, allowing it to resonate with your website's theme or mood.

Example:

```
/* Applying Color to Text */
p {
color: #333333; /* Dark gray color */
}
.link {
color: #007bff; /* Bold blue for links */
}
```

Font Properties

Typography is your font's personality, and CSS lets you customize it to exude elegance, playfulness, or seriousness:

- **Font Family**: Choose a typeface that speaks to your website's character, like 'Arial', 'Times New Roman', or custom web fonts.
- **Font Size**: Adjust the 'font-size' property to dictate the size of your text.

- **Font Style and Weight**: Experiment with 'font-style' to make text italic or 'font-weight' to achieve varying degrees of thickness.

Example:

```
/* Applying Font Properties */
h1 {
font-family: 'Helvetica', sans-serif; /* Modern, sans-serif font */
font-size: 36px; /* Large font size */
font-weight: bold; /* Bold text */
}
.emphasis {
font-style: italic; /* Italicized text */
font-weight: 600; /* Semi-bold text */
}
```

Text Alignment and Spacing

Like a conductor orchestrating harmonious symphonies, you can control the arrangement and spacing of your text:

- **Text Alignment**: Align your text to the left, right, center, or justify it for a clean and polished look.
- **Letter and Word Spacing**: Adjust 'letter-spacing' and 'word-spacing' to sculpt the spaces between characters and words.

Example:

```
/* Text Alignment and Spacing */
h2 {
text-align: center; /* Center-aligned heading */
}
.paragraph {
text-align: justify; /* Justify-aligned text */
```

```
letter-spacing: 1px; /* Slight letter spacing */
word-spacing: 2px; /* Spaced-out words */
}
```

Through the magic of CSS, you wield the power to transform mundane text into captivating narratives. Experiment with color, font, and alignment to craft a symphony of words that resonates with your audience.

15.2.3 Box Model

In the realm of web design, the box model stands as the architect's blueprint, defining the spatial arrangement and dimensions of every element on your canvas.

Content, Padding, Border, Margin

The box model is a concept that segments an element into layers, each contributing to its overall size and spacing:

- **Content**: This is the innermost layer, housing the actual content of the element, be it text, images, or other media.
- **Padding**: Surrounding the content is the padding, creating a buffer between the content and the element's border.
- **Border**: The border delineates the boundary of the element, providing a visible edge that can be styled using CSS properties.
- **Margin**: Finally, the margin is the outermost layer, creating space around the element, influencing its position in relation to other elements.

Example:

```
/* Box Model Components */
.box {
```

```
width: 200px;
height: 150px;
padding: 10px;
border: 1px solid #ccc;
margin: 20px;
}
```

Box Sizing

The 'box-sizing' property acts as the maestro, determining how an element's total width and height are calculated:

- **Content-Box (Default)**: The element's width and height include only the content, excluding padding, border, and margin.
- **Border-Box**: The element's width and height include content, padding, and border, but exclude the margin.

This property is pivotal in ensuring consistent layouts and managing spacing intricacies.

Example:

```
/* Controlling Box Sizing */
.content-box {
box-sizing: content-box;
width: 200px;
padding: 20px;
border: 2px solid #f44336;
}
.border-box {
box-sizing: border-box;
width: 200px;
padding: 20px;
border: 2px solid #4caf50;
}
```

Understanding the box model empowers you to craft pixel-perfect layouts, ensuring your design translates seamlessly across different devices and screens. Embrace the interplay between content, padding, border, and margin, and harness the box-sizing property to maintain your design's integrity.

15.2.4 Layout and Positioning

Creating a visually captivating and organized web page involves more than just aesthetics. It's about orchestrating elements in a dance of visual harmony and functional cohesion. This section unveils the tools that give you mastery over the positioning and layout of your web elements.

Display and Position

The **display** and **position** properties are your conduits to element arrangement.

- **Display**: This property dictates how elements behave in relation to one another. It influences whether an element is treated as an inline or block-level element, or even as a flexible container for other elements (flex and grid displays).
- **Position**: The position property is your portal to absolute control. It allows you to precisely place elements relative to their containing element or the viewport. Options include static, relative, absolute, fixed, and sticky positioning.

Example:

```
/* Display and Position */
.inline-block {
display: inline-block;
```

```
}
.positioned {
position: relative;
top: 20px;
left: 30px;
}
```

Float and Clear

The **float** property introduces an element into the flow of the document, causing it to align to either the left or right of its container. It's commonly used for images and text wrapping. However, when elements are floated, you might encounter unintended overlaps. Here's where the **clear** property comes to your rescue, ensuring elements steer clear of floated elements.

Example:

```
/* Float and Clear */
.float-left {
float: left;
width: 200px;
margin: 10px;
}
.clear {
clear: both;
}
```

Flexbox

Flexbox is the conductor of layout symphonies. It offers unparalleled control over element positioning, alignment, and distribution within a container, both horizontally and vertically. With its intuitive syntax and powerful capabilities, it's your ticket to crafting responsive designs with elegance.

Example:

```
/* Flexbox Magic */
.flex-container {
```

```
display: flex;
justify-content: space-between;
align-items: center;
}
```

Embrace these properties to transform your design visions into living, breathing layouts. Whether you're seeking pixel-perfect precision or fluid responsiveness, mastering display, position, float, clear, and flexbox will set your web designs apart.

15.2.5 Responsive Design

In a world where the web is accessed through an array of devices, responsive design isn't just a luxury – it's a necessity. This section equips you with the art of crafting designs that seamlessly adapt to various screen sizes and orientations.

Media Queries

Media queries are your responsive design Swiss Army knife. They allow you to apply different styles based on the characteristics of the device viewing your page. Want larger text for mobile users? A different color scheme for tablets? Media queries make it happen.

Example:

```
/* Media Query Magic */
@media screen and (max-width: 600px) {
body {

 font-size: 16px;

}
}
```

Flexible Layouts

Embrace the dynamic. Flexible layouts, driven by the power of relative units like percentages and the flexible flexbox model, ensure that your content gracefully adapts to diverse screen sizes. Whether it's fluid grids, images that scale with the screen, or text that wraps intelligently, flexible layouts are your ticket to responsive nirvana.

Example:

```
/* Flexbox at Play */
@media screen and (max-width: 768px) {
.flex-container {

  flex-direction: column;
  align-items: center;

}
}
```

With responsive design, you're not just designing for the screen in front of you – you're designing for the world. Media queries and flexible layouts aren't just tools; they're the essence of empathy for your users, ensuring your designs look and work beautifully, no matter where they're viewed.

And with this, you've not just navigated the seas of CSS styling and layout; you've equipped yourself to transform digital landscapes into inviting, engaging, and universally accessible web experiences.

15.3 Introduction to JavaScript and DOM Manipulation

- JavaScript, the dynamic powerhouse of web development, empowers you to infuse life and interactivity into your web pages. This section serves as your gateway into the world of JavaScript and its mastery in manipulating the Document Object Model (DOM), turning static content into engaging user experiences.

15.3.1 JavaScript Basics

JavaScript, the heartbeat of web interactivity, is your passport to dynamic web experiences. In this sub-section, we embark on a journey to unravel the essence of JavaScript and lay the groundwork for mastering its transformative capabilities.

Introduction to JavaScript

JavaScript, born in the mid-90s, emerged as a scripting language that revolutionized web pages from static to dynamic. It's the driving force behind animations, forms that adapt to user input, and the magic that happens when you click a button.

Variables and Data Types

Enter the world of variables. They're like containers that hold information – numbers, text, and even more complex things like lists of data (arrays) and descriptions of objects (objects). And don't forget the data types. Think of them as JavaScript's toolkit – numbers (for math), strings (for text), and more.

Example:

```
// Variables and Data Types
let name = "Alice";
let age = 30;
let hobbies = ["coding", "reading", "gaming"];
```

Operators

Operators, the gears of JavaScript, bring your code to life. They're like the + and - signs in math, but they're also the === sign (for checking if things are equal), and the && sign (for checking if multiple things are true at once).

Example:

```
// Operators
let x = 10;
let y = 5;
```

```
let sum = x + y; // sum is now 15
let isSame = x === y; // false
let areBothTrue = x > 0 && y > 0; // true
```

Basic Control Structures

Get ready to steer your code's flow. Loops let you repeat things, like showing a list of items, while conditionals let your code make choices, like showing a message if a user is logged in.

Example:

```
// Basic Control Structures
for (let i = 0; i < 5; i++) {
console.log("Loop iteration: " + i);
}
if (age >= 18) {
console.log("You're an adult!");
}
else {
console.log("You're still a minor.");
}
```

JavaScript's heart beats with these core concepts – variables, data types, operators, loops, and conditionals. It's the gateway to logic and magic in web development.

With these JavaScript basics under your belt, you're primed to venture deeper into the realm of web interaction and create engaging, responsive, and user-friendly web experiences.

15.3.2 DOM Manipulation

JavaScript is more than just a scripting language – it's a wizard's wand that transforms web content on the fly. In this sub-section, we dive into the enchanting realm of DOM manipulation, where JavaScript wields its magic to reshape web pages dynamically.

Document Object Model (DOM)

Imagine the DOM as a virtual representation of your web page. It's like a tree where each branch is an element (like headings, paragraphs, images), and each leaf is a piece of content. JavaScript can traverse this tree, change leaf values, and even rearrange branches.

Selecting DOM Elements

With JavaScript, you don't need a magic spell to choose elements on your page. The DOM has a toolkit of commands – like getElementById, getElementsByTagName, and querySelector – that let you pick any element you want to enchant.

Example:

```
// Selecting DOM Elements
let heading = document.getElementById("main-heading");
let allParagraphs = document.getElementsByTagName("p");
let specialElement = document.querySelector(".special");
```

Manipulating HTML and CSS

Prepare to be amazed as JavaScript tinkers with your web page's very essence. It can change an element's content, attributes, or even its structure. And don't forget about styles – JavaScript can modify CSS properties on the fly, from colors to positions.

Example:

```
// Manipulating HTML and CSS
heading.textContent = "Welcome to My Website";
specialElement.classList.add("highlight");
```

With JavaScript's wand (or rather, code), the DOM transforms into your playground. You can add interactivity, update content in real-time, and even make your web page respond to user actions.

Dive into DOM manipulation, and you'll wield the power to create engaging web experiences that leave users spellbound.

15.3.3 Event Handling

Welcome to the heart of web interactivity – event handling. Think of it as your web page's way of saying, "I'm listening!" In this sub-section, we'll unravel the mysteries of events and how JavaScript choreographs the dance of user interactions.

User Interactions and Events

Every click, tap, or keystroke on your web page is like a cue for JavaScript. These cues are called events. When a user clicks a button, submits a form, or scrolls the page, an event is born. JavaScript then leaps into action, responding to these cues like a seasoned performer.

Attaching Event Listeners

Meet the conductor of this interactivity orchestra: the event listener. This magical entity waits for a specific event, like a click, and responds with a symphony of code. It's like saying, "Hey, when that button is clicked, here's what I want you to do."

Example:

```
// Attaching Event Listeners
const button = document.getElementById("my-button");
button.addEventListener("click", function() {
// Code to run when the button is clicked
alert("Button Clicked!");
});
```

With an event listener, JavaScript doesn't just listen – it's ready to act. And the best part? You can attach listeners to almost any element, making your web page a responsive and engaging experience.

So, dive into event handling, and let JavaScript be your dance partner. With its guidance, your web page will respond to user cues with grace and precision, delivering an unforgettable performance.

15.3.4 Form Validation

Welcome to the realm of form validation – where JavaScript steps in to ensure data accuracy and elevate user experiences. Imagine a world where users receive real-time feedback as they input data into your web forms. With JavaScript by your side, that world becomes a reality.

Form Basics

Forms are the gateways to user input. They allow users to submit information, from simple text to complex selections. But what good is the data if it's inaccurate? That's where form validation comes in.

Real-time Feedback

JavaScript takes form validation to the next level by providing real-time feedback. As users type, JavaScript can instantly analyze their input and offer helpful hints or warnings. It's like having a friendly assistant guiding users through the form-filling journey.

Example:

```
// Form Validation
const emailInput = document.getElementById("email");
emailInput.addEventListener("input", function() {
const emailValue = emailInput.value;
const isValid = validateEmail(emailValue);
if (isValid) {

 emailInput.classList.remove("invalid");
 emailInput.classList.add("valid");
 } else {
```

```
emailInput.classList.remove("valid");
emailInput.classList.add("invalid");

}
});
function validateEmail(email) {
// Validation logic here
}
```

With JavaScript, form validation becomes more than just error messages after submission – it becomes a fluid conversation between the user and your web page.

So, embrace the power of form validation with JavaScript. Guide your users, ensure data accuracy, and transform the form-filling experience into a seamless and interactive journey.

15.3.5 Introduction to Libraries and Frameworks

Welcome to the world beyond JavaScript's core! As you've delved into JavaScript and DOM manipulation, you're now ready to explore the broader universe of JavaScript libraries and frameworks – tools that can turbocharge your development process and expand your capabilities.

jQuery: A Swift Touch

Meet jQuery – a swift and concise JavaScript library that wields the power of simplicity. jQuery is your ally in DOM manipulation and event handling. With its elegant syntax, you can traverse and manipulate the DOM with ease. Say goodbye to lengthy lines of code and welcome streamlined interactions.

Example:

```
// jQuery DOM Manipulation
$("#myButton").click(function() {
```

```
$(this).toggleClass("active");
});
```

React: The Dynamic Enchanter

Enter React, a JavaScript library that takes UI building to the next level. React empowers you to create dynamic user interfaces with reusable components. It's the magic wand for crafting interactive web applications that respond to user actions seamlessly.

Example:

jsxCopy code

```
// React Component
function Counter() {
const [count, setCount] = React.useState(0);
return (

  <div>
  <p>Count: {count}</p>
  <button onClick={() => setCount(count +
  1)}>Increment</button>
  </div>

);
}
```

A Fusion of Possibilities

As you traverse the realms of JavaScript, HTML, and CSS, the integration of libraries and frameworks enhances your prowess. With jQuery, DOM manipulation becomes intuitive, and React empowers you to craft user interfaces that breathe life into your web applications.

JavaScript's fusion with HTML and CSS opens the door to immersive web environments. From fluid user interactions to real-time data updates, you have the tools to orchestrate dynamic web experiences that respond with finesse and flair.

So, venture forth into the world of JavaScript libraries and frameworks. Your journey to create captivating and interactive web environments is just beginning

By exploring these fundamental aspects of web development, you will gain a solid foundation for creating interactive and visually appealing websites. This chapter sets the stage for more advanced topics in web development, enabling you to build dynamic and engaging web experiences.

Chapter 16: Software Development Best Practices

In this chapter, we embark on a journey into the realm of software development best practices – the tried-and-true methodologies that elevate your code from functional to exceptional. By embracing these practices, you're not just writing code; you're crafting a masterpiece.

16.1 Code Documentation and Commenting

Code is more than just a collection of characters; it's a narrative of your logic and intentions. Effective code documentation and commenting are the ink that paints this narrative, making your codebase comprehensible, maintainable, and inviting to fellow developers.

16.1.1 The Art of Documentation

Documentation is the key to unlocking the secrets of your code. It transforms complex algorithms and logic into a comprehensible narrative that speaks to both present and future developers. In this section, we dive into the art of documentation, exploring how to craft descriptions that turn your codebase into a self-explanatory treasure trove.

Why Documentation Matters

1. **Clarity Amid Complexity**: Code can be intricate, but documentation shines a light on its purpose and functionality. It provides a roadmap for understanding complex functions and algorithms.
2. **Ease of Maintenance**: When you return to your code after

months or years, documentation acts as your guide, reducing the time and effort needed for updates or modifications.

3. **Collaborative Magic**: Documentation fosters collaboration. It enables other developers to seamlessly understand, contribute to, and build upon your work.

Levels of Documentation

1. **Function-Level Documentation**: Learn the art of crafting clear and concise descriptions for each function or method. Explain its purpose, parameters, return values, and potential exceptions.
2. **Class and Module Overviews**: Elevate your documentation to provide a high-level overview of classes or modules. Describe their roles, relationships, and how they fit into the grand scheme.
3. **Project-wide Documentation**: Discover the power of README files and project-level documentation. Create a welcoming entry point to your codebase, outlining its goals, installation instructions, and usage examples.

Mastering Documentation Style

1. **Consistency is King**: Establish a consistent documentation style throughout your codebase. Whether you prefer Javadoc, Google-style, or your own hybrid, coherence is key.
2. **Markdown Magic**: Dive into Markdown, a lightweight markup language, to format your documentation with headings, lists, code blocks, and hyperlinks.
3. **Balancing Detail and Brevity**: Strike the perfect balance

between depth and brevity. Provide enough detail to understand the function's purpose without overwhelming readers.

4. **Illustrate with Examples**: Enhance understanding by including usage examples and scenarios. Illustrate how each function works in practice.

Automated Documentation Tools

1. **JSDoc and Doxygen**: Discover tools like JSDoc for JavaScript and Doxygen for multiple languages. These tools generate documentation from specially formatted comments in your code.
2. **Documenting Frameworks**: Learn the nuances of documenting code that integrates with frameworks or libraries. Provide context to users unfamiliar with the underlying architecture.

In the realm of coding, documentation is the bridge between understanding and implementation. In this section, you'll unravel the art of transforming your codebase into a self-explanatory treasure trove, empowering fellow developers to seamlessly navigate and contribute to your creations.

16.1.2 Comments as Clarity

In the realm of coding, comments are your allies in the pursuit of clarity. They provide a voice within your codebase, narrating its intentions, unraveling complexities, and offering foresight. This section delves into the art of using comments to enhance code clarity, making your creations more understandable and maintainable.

Why Comments Matter

1. **Enhanced Understanding**: Comments provide context. They elucidate the reasoning behind decisions, helping both current and future developers grasp the logic.
2. **Navigating Complexity**: For intricate algorithms or convoluted logic, comments act as guiding beacons, helping programmers navigate the labyrinth of code.
3. **Future-Proofing**: Inject insights into your code's evolution. Explain why certain solutions were chosen, discuss potential improvements, or highlight considerations for future updates.

Strategies for Effective Commenting

1. **Code Anatomy**: Describe the purpose of each function, method, or class. Explain inputs, expected outputs, and any side effects.
2. **Algorithm Illumination**: Break down complex algorithms step by step. Comment on the rationale behind each decision and how it contributes to the bigger picture.
3. **Edge Cases and Assumptions**: Note assumptions made during coding. Comment on potential edge cases or scenarios that might not be immediately apparent.
4. **Caveats and Workarounds**: If you encounter quirky behaviors or unconventional workarounds, elucidate them with comments to save future developers from confusion.
5. **TODOs and FIXMEs**: Mark tasks for the future. Whether it's an unfinished feature (TODO) or a known issue (FIXME), these comments provide a to-do list for improvement.

Commenting Best Practices

1. **Clear and Concise**: Write comments that are succinct yet informative. Avoid verbosity and focus on delivering the most relevant information.
2. **Consistency**: Adopt a consistent commenting style across your codebase. Whether you use single-line comments (//) or block comments (/* */), uniformity fosters readability.
3. **Update Alongside Code**: As you modify code, remember to update comments accordingly. Outdated comments can be more misleading than no comments at all.
4. **Mindful Placement**: Place comments near the code they explain. This reduces the cognitive load of scrolling back and forth.

Balancing Comments and Self-Explanatory Code

1. **Strive for Self-Explanatory Code**: While comments elucidate, aim for code that's readable on its own. Meaningful variable names and structured logic can often negate the need for excessive comments.
2. **When in Doubt, Comment**: If a piece of code isn't immediately clear, add a comment. It's better to provide extra context than to leave fellow developers in the dark.

Unleash the power of comments to create a narrative within your codebase. By weaving insights, explanations, and clarifications into your code, you create a bridge between intent and implementation. In this section, you'll master the art of using comments to enhance clarity, making your code a masterpiece of comprehension and collaboration.

16.2 Version Control Systems (e.g., Git)

Welcome to the world of version control – the backbone of organized and collaborative coding. Dive into the realm of Git and other version control systems, where you'll learn to track changes, collaborate seamlessly, and travel through the history of your code.

16.2.1 Git Basics

Git, the cornerstone of version control, empowers developers to manage code evolution with finesse. This section takes you on a journey through Git's fundamental concepts, equipping you with the tools to traverse your code's history, collaborate seamlessly, and embrace the world of distributed development.

Repositories: The Code Haven

1. **Understanding Repositories**: Delve into the heart of version control – repositories. Grasp the concept of a repository as a centralized storehouse for your codebase.
2. **Initializing Repositories**: Learn the art of creating repositories, both locally and on remote platforms like GitHub or GitLab.

Commits: The Building Blocks

1. **Committing Changes**: Unlock the power of commits – snapshots that capture the state of your code at a specific moment. Understand how to craft meaningful commit messages.
2. **Branching Out**: Embrace the power of branching to experiment, develop features, or fix bugs without affecting the main codebase.

3. **Merging Brilliance**: Merge branches with elegance. Combine different code paths while resolving conflicts and preserving the sanctity of your codebase.

Navigating Through Time: Your Code's Timeline

1. **Time Travel with Git Log**: Traverse your code's history using the **git log** command. Uncover the who, what, and when of each commit.
2. **Reverting with Confidence**: Master the art of reverting to previous states when unforeseen hiccups occur.

Remote Collaboration and Beyond

1. **Remote Repositories**: Explore the realms of remote repositories. Push your code to shared platforms and pull down collaborators' changes.
2. **Collaborative Workflow**: Learn collaborative Git workflows like Pull Requests, Code Reviews, and Forks to foster efficient teamwork.

Git Best Practices

1. **Frequent Commits**: Make incremental commits to capture granular changes and facilitate easier debugging.
2. **Descriptive Commit Messages**: Craft informative commit messages that succinctly capture the essence of each change.
3. **Branch Management**: Use branches wisely. Create feature branches for new work and keep the main branch clean and deployable.
4. **Consistent Workflow**: Adopt consistent Git practices

across the team to minimize confusion and streamline collaboration.

The Power of Git Unleashed

Git is more than a version control system – it's a chronicle of your code's journey. In this section, you'll grasp the essence of repositories, commits, branches, and merges. Navigating your code's timeline with Git equips you with the confidence to explore new horizons, experiment boldly, and collaborate seamlessly. As you delve deeper into Git, you'll find it's not just a tool, but a way to weave a symphony of code contributions into a harmonious masterpiece.

16.2.2 Collaborative Coding with Git

In the realm of coding, collaboration is the symphony that produces harmonious software. This section unveils the art of collaborative coding using Git, where developers dance in synchronization, creating intricate software masterpieces. From branching to conflict resolution, you'll embark on a journey of seamless teamwork.

Branching for Brilliance

1. **Branches Reimagined**: Dive into collaborative coding through branching. Understand how branches isolate workstreams, fostering parallel development.
2. **Feature Branches**: Craft dedicated branches for each feature or bug fix, allowing developers to work on different aspects concurrently.
3. **Branching Strategies**: Explore different branching strategies like Gitflow or Feature Branching, tailoring your workflow to project needs.

Pull Requests: The Gateway to Collaboration

1. **Understanding Pull Requests**: Unearth the power of pull requests – gates through which code journeys from branches to the main codebase.
2. **Code Reviews**: Embrace the art of code review, where peers assess code quality, suggest improvements, and ensure alignment with project goals.
3. **Feedback Loop**: Discover the feedback loop of collaboration. Iterate on code, address comments, and refine the pull request until it's ready for integration.

Conflict Resolution: The Diplomacy of Code

1. **Conflict Dynamics**: Navigate the intricate terrain of code conflicts that arise when merging divergent branches.
2. **Resolving Conflicts**: Master the skill of conflict resolution. Understand tools like merge tools or manual editing to harmonize conflicting changes.

Collaboration Best Practices

1. **Clear Communication**: Foster open communication among team members to align on coding standards, objectives, and expectations.
2. **Atomic Commits**: Make small, focused commits to minimize conflicts and ease review processes.
3. **Branch Hygiene**: Keep branches up-to-date with the main codebase, reducing the risk of complex conflicts during integration.
4. **Continuous Integration**: Integrate changes frequently to ensure a continuous flow of code and early detection of

issues.

The Symphony of Collaboration

Collaboration amplifies creativity and propels coding to new heights. In this segment, you'll uncover the magic of collaborative coding with Git. From the intricacies of branching to the elegance of pull requests, you'll learn how to harmonize diverse code contributions into a unified, refined whole. Conflict resolution becomes an art of diplomacy, and feedback cycles nurture growth. As you delve into collaborative coding, you'll realize that the symphony of teamwork is the crescendo that elevates software craftsmanship.

16.3 Collaboration and Teamwork in Programming Projects

Coding is often a team effort, and effective collaboration can elevate your project to new heights. Delve into the dynamics of collaboration, from dividing tasks to effective communication, and learn how to harmonize your team's efforts.

16.3.1 Task Allocation and Coordination

In the realm of software development, orchestrating a symphony of code requires careful coordination and task allocation. This section unveils the strategies that transform individual developers into a harmonious team, each contributing their unique notes to the composition.

Dividing the Coding Canvas

1. **Task Identification**: Explore the art of breaking down complex projects into manageable tasks. Identify features,

bug fixes, or improvements to create a coding canvas.
2. **Task Granularity**: Strike a balance between fine-grained tasks and broad milestones, ensuring efficient progress tracking.
3. **Prioritization**: Dive into the world of task prioritization. Determine which tasks need immediate attention and which can wait in the wings.

Team Synchronization

1. **Task Assignment**: Discover how to assign tasks based on team members' strengths, expertise, and availability.
2. **Clear Deadlines**: Define deadlines for tasks to maintain focus and align efforts toward a common goal.
3. **Regular Updates**: Establish a rhythm of updates, where team members communicate progress, roadblocks, and dependencies.

Harmonizing the Workflow

1. **Daily Stand-ups**: Explore the practice of daily stand-up meetings, where team members share their accomplishments, plans, and any obstacles faced.
2. **Code Integration**: Understand the importance of frequent code integration to detect conflicts early and ensure a cohesive codebase.
3. **Dependency Management**: Learn the art of managing task dependencies, ensuring that tasks are completed in the right sequence.

Collaborative Tools

1. **Task Tracking Tools**: Explore tools like JIRA, Trello, or

Asana to manage and track tasks, fostering transparency and accountability.
2. **Version Control Systems**: Leverage version control systems like Git to orchestrate parallel development without chaos.

Effective Communication

1. **Open Channels**: Foster open communication channels where team members can discuss ideas, seek help, and provide updates.
2. **Active Listening**: Embrace active listening, ensuring that everyone's perspectives are valued and contributions acknowledged.

The Choreography of Success

Software development is akin to a choreographed dance, where each developer plays a unique role. Task allocation and coordination transform individual steps into a seamless routine. From identifying tasks to prioritizing and assigning them, the journey is marked by efficient communication and alignment. As you delve into task allocation, you'll realize that the choreography of success requires teamwork, communication, and a shared commitment to crafting exceptional code.

16.3.2 Communication and Code Reviews

In the intricate tapestry of software development, effective communication weaves the threads of understanding, cooperation, and excellence. This section illuminates the significance of communication, particularly through the lens of code reviews, feedback loops, and the tools that facilitate seamless collaboration.

The Communication Canvas

1. **Code Reviews: An Art and a Science**: Uncover the artistry behind code reviews – a practice that marries technical scrutiny with constructive critique.
2. **Peer Learning**: Embrace code reviews as an opportunity for peer learning, where developers share insights, techniques, and alternative approaches.
3. **Quality Assurance**: Recognize code reviews as a quality assurance checkpoint, preventing bugs, enhancing performance, and ensuring adherence to coding standards.

Constructive Feedback Loops

1. **Constructive Critique**: Master the art of delivering and receiving constructive feedback, fostering a culture of continuous improvement.
2. **Balancing Objectivity and Empathy**: Explore the delicate balance between objective analysis and empathetic communication in providing feedback.
3. **Incremental Improvement**: Understand how incremental changes, inspired by feedback, lead to the refinement of both code and skills.

Communication Tools

1. **Code Review Tools**: Delve into tools like GitHub, Bitbucket, or GitLab that streamline the code review process, facilitating seamless collaboration.
2. **Real-Time Chat**: Explore the power of real-time messaging platforms like Slack or Microsoft Teams to facilitate quick communication and problem-solving.
3. **Documentation Platforms**: Leverage documentation

platforms like Confluence or Google Docs to create a shared knowledge repository.

Feedback-Driven Iteration

1. **Iterative Refinement**: Embrace a culture of iterative refinement, where code undergoes multiple rounds of review and enhancement.
2. **Celebrating Feedback**: Celebrate the transformational impact of feedback on code quality and individual growth.

Fostering a Collaborative Spirit

1. **Open Discussions**: Create spaces for open discussions where developers can seek guidance, clarify doubts, and share insights.
2. **Transparency**: Foster transparency by sharing project updates, challenges, and successes through regular team meetings or newsletters.

The Symphony of Collaboration

Effective communication and code reviews compose the symphony of collaboration in software development. Through thoughtful feedback and open discussions, team members harmonize their efforts, fine-tuning code and elevating skills. In this communication-rich landscape, code reviews are not just about catching bugs – they're about nurturing a culture of growth, sharing, and excellence. As you immerse yourself in the realm of communication and code reviews, you'll discover that building exceptional software requires not only technical expertise but also the ability to engage in meaningful dialogue and continual refinement.

16.3.3 The Art of Conflict Resolution

In the vibrant tapestry of collaborative software development, conflicts are like colorful threads that, when woven thoughtfully, contribute to the richness of the final creation. This section delves into the art of conflict resolution, equipping you with the skills to navigate challenges and maintain the harmony of your project.

Navigating the Conflict Landscape

1. **Conflict Awareness**: Develop a keen sense of conflict awareness, recognizing signs of tension or discord within the team.
2. **Issue Identification**: Hone your ability to identify the root causes of conflicts, whether they stem from technical disagreements, miscommunication, or differing perspectives.
3. **Embracing Diverse Opinions**: Understand that conflicts often emerge from diverse viewpoints, and learn to embrace these differences as catalysts for innovation.

The Path to Resolution

1. **Open Dialogue**: Foster an environment where team members feel comfortable expressing concerns and engaging in open discussions.
2. **Active Listening**: Cultivate active listening skills to truly understand each party's perspective and concerns.
3. **Mediation**: Embrace the role of a mediator, facilitating conversations and guiding the team toward common ground.

Collaborative Solutions

1. **Brainstorming**: Encourage collaborative brainstorming

sessions where team members collectively explore potential solutions.

2. **Compromise**: Embrace the spirit of compromise, finding middle ground that addresses the concerns of all parties.
3. **Win-Win Outcomes**: Strive for win-win outcomes, where conflicts are resolved in a way that benefits both the project and the individuals involved.

Clear Communication

1. **Clarity in Communication**: Emphasize clear and concise communication as the cornerstone of conflict resolution.
2. **Seeking Context**: When conflicts arise, seek to understand the full context before drawing conclusions or making judgments.
3. **Respecting Boundaries**: Respect personal and professional boundaries when engaging in conflict resolution discussions.

Learning and Growth

1. **Reflect and Learn**: After conflicts are resolved, encourage the team to reflect on the experience, identifying lessons learned and opportunities for improvement.
2. **Feedback Loop**: Establish a feedback loop to continually refine conflict resolution processes based on real-world experiences.

Preserving Team Harmony

1. **Long-Term Vision**: Keep the long-term vision of the project in mind, ensuring that conflicts do not detract from the collective goal.

2. **Building Strong Relationships**: Recognize that effective conflict resolution strengthens team relationships and fosters a positive work environment.

Conflict as Catalyst

In the dynamic realm of collaborative software development, conflicts are not mere obstacles; they are catalysts for growth and innovation. By mastering the art of conflict resolution, you transform potential disruptions into opportunities to refine ideas, enhance communication, and strengthen team bonds. Just as skilled artists blend contrasting colors to create masterpieces, adept developers weave conflicts into the fabric of collaboration, creating projects that are not only technically exceptional but also harmoniously nurtured by the diverse voices that shape them. As you embark on the journey of conflict resolution, you lay the foundation for a cohesive and empowered team, ready to overcome challenges and create software that truly shines.

Did you love *Basics of Programming: A Comprehensive Guide for Beginners*? Then you should read *Where Can I Invest? Unlocking a World of Opportunities*[1] by DG. Junior!

2

"Where Can I Invest? Unlocking a World of Opportunities" is your ultimate guide to navigating the complex world of investments and discovering a myriad of opportunities to grow your wealth and secure your financial future.

Whether you're a seasoned investor or a complete novice, this comprehensive book empowers you with the knowledge and insights needed to make informed investment decisions. Explore a wide range of investment options, from traditional assets like stocks and bonds to innovative opportunities such as cryptocurrency and impact investing.

---

1. https://books2read.com/u/3RYVwG
2. https://books2read.com/u/3RYVwG

Learn the art of portfolio diversification and risk management, understanding how to balance potential returns with your risk tolerance. Discover the power of compounding and how it can significantly enhance the value of your investments over time.

Unravel the secrets of dividend investing, a proven strategy for generating passive income and building long-term wealth. Understand the significance of gold and precious metals as safe-haven assets during times of economic uncertainty.

Explore the world of blockchain and decentralized networks, unlocking the potential of cryptocurrencies and smart contracts as the future of financial transactions.

Delve into the realm of retirement accounts like IRAs and 401(k)s, discovering how to maximize tax advantages and choose the right investment options for your retirement savings.

"Where Can I Invest?" is more than just a book; it's a roadmap to financial independence and prosperity. Emphasizing the importance of ongoing education and staying informed, this guide empowers you to confidently navigate the ever-changing landscape of investments.

With expert insights, practical tips, and real-world examples, you'll gain the confidence to create a personalized investment approach that aligns with your goals and aspirations. From building passive income streams to securing your retirement, this book opens the door to a world of investment opportunities, helping you achieve financial freedom and peace of mind.

No matter your financial situation or investment experience, "Where Can I Invest? Unlocking a World of Opportunities" is your key to unlocking a world of financial possibilities. Get ready to embark on an exciting journey to wealth-building and financial success. Start investing in your future today!

Also by DG. Junior

Essential Coputer Skills
Basics of Programming: A Comprehensive Guide for Beginners

Get Your Finances In Order
Where Can I Invest? Unlocking a World of Opportunities
FROM IDEA TO PROFIT: A Guide for New Entrepreneurs on Building a Successful Business

Standalone
Financial Control Blueprint: Building a Path to Growth and Success

www.ingramcontent.com/pod-product-compliance
Lightning Source LLC
LaVergne TN
LVHW090306210926
848480LV00001B/152

* 9 7 9 8 2 2 3 2 2 9 9 8 8 *